Iron Brigade General

John Gibbon as Brigadier General, circa 1862.

IRON BRIGADE GENERAL

John Gibbon, A Rebel in Blue

Dennis S. Lavery & Mark H. Jordan

Foreword by ALAN T. NOLAN

CONTRIBUTIONS IN MILITARY STUDIES,
NUMBER 138

Greenwood Press
Westport, Connecticut • London

Library of Congress Cataloging-in-Publication Data

Lavery, Dennis S.
    Iron Brigade general : John Gibbon, a rebel in blue / Dennis S.
Lavery and Mark H. Jordan ; foreword by Alan T. Nolan.
        p.   cm.—(Contributions in military studies, ISSN 0883–6884
; no. 138)
    Includes bibliographical references and index.
    ISBN 0–313–28576–4 (alk. paper)
    1. Gibbon, John, 1827–1896.   2. Generals—United States—
Biography.   3. United States.   Army—Biography.   I. Jordan, Mark
H. II. Title. III. Series.
E467.1.G42L38   1993
973.7′092—dc20   92–36516
    [B]

British Library Cataloguing in Publication Data is available.

Library of Congress Catalog Card Number: 92–36516
ISBN: 0–313–28576–4
ISSN: 0883–6884

First published in 1993

Greenwood Press, 88 Post Road West, Westport, CT 06881
An imprint of Greenwood Publishing Group, Inc.

Printed in the United States of America

The paper used in this book complies with the
Permanent Paper Standard issued by the National
Information Standards Organization (Z39.48–1984).

10 9 8 7 6 5 4 3 2 1

Copyright Acknowledgments

The author and the publisher are grateful to the following for granting the
use of material:

John Gibbon letters held by USMA Library courtesy Special Collections, United
States Military Academy Library.

Gibbon papers, MS. 1284, courtesy Manuscripts Division, Maryland Historical Society.

To Alastair T. Crawford
and
To Louise

Contents

Illustrations

Foreword

At last we have a biography of General John Gibbon, and it is a fine one, filling a significant void in the literature of the Civil War. And, because of Gibbon's large involvement, the book also adds to our knowledge of the sad story of the Indian fighting after the war.

Gibbon initially attracts our attention as a North Carolina resident, a regular from West Point, who stayed with "the old Flag" while his three brothers enlisted with the Confederacy. He was a lifelong Democrat, a McClellan loyalist, and from a slaveholding family. It is always difficult to determine with certainty what caused such men to stand by the Union; perhaps they did not themselves know precisely why. In Gibbon's case, it seems ultimately that his oath of allegiance as a soldier tipped the balance in behalf of the North.

A brief reference to Gibbon's military career provides more substantial reasons for his entitlement to our interest. An excellent artillerist, he started the war as Captain of historic Battery B of the 4th United States Artillery. As an infantry officer, he proceeded during the war from a brigadier generalship of volunteers to a major generalship. He commanded the Iron Brigade, a division of the Army of the Potomac's First Corps, a division in that army's Second Corps, and temporarily commanded the Second Corps. Transferred then to the Army of the James, he temporarily commanded the XVIII Corps and finished the war as commander of the XXIV Corps in that army. Along the way he was wounded twice and participated in the battles at Brawner Farm, Second Bull Run, South Mountain, Antietam, Fredericksburg, Chancellorsville, and Gettysburg. He was then significantly involved in Grant's 1864–65 Overland Campaign. On hand at Appomattox, he was one of three Federal Commissioners appointed by Grant to carry out the terms of the surrender document. Inevitably, his personal experiences involve the story of the war in the Virginia theater.

His story after the war is that of the Indian Wars. His command buried Custer's dead at the Little Big Horn and fought Chief Joseph and the Nez Perce at Big Hole in 1877. He finished his career directing the army in essentially police activities, protecting the Chinese in the northwest at the time of riots against those immigrants.

What kind of a man was Gibbon? The authors are not writing a *Life of the Saints* biography and they present Gibbon, warts and all. The individual reader can make his own decision. To this reader, he appears as a family man of high personal character and habits, a brilliant combat leader, an effective commander, and an honest and courageous person. He was direct, "no nonsense," and followed the book in his leadership. As the authors note, he was not a "twentieth-century man in his attitudes" and this meant that he had a Victorian's touchiness about his "honor"—he was outspoken and contentious and participated actively in the well-established game of army politics. These characteristics led him into celebrated, unseemly, and virtually endless controversies with Generals Hancock, McDowell, and Pope, several of which were to his personal disadvantage. On the other hand, he presented an admirable modern side; he had keen psychological insights in pre-Freudian times and was humane, departures from the traditions and practices of the army of the time. Most noteworthy in this regard are his attitudes toward the Indians he was fighting after the war. The authors authenticate their statement that Gibbon was "a sensitive human being" when they set forth his statements about the war against the native American, "a people forced into war by the very agents of the government which makes war upon them." In addition he wrote:

The Indian, although a savage, is still a man with . . . quite as much instinctive sense of right and wrong as a white man. . . . He argues this way: the white man has come into my country and taken away everything which formerly belonged to me. He even drives off . . . and destroys the game which the Great Spirit gave me to subsist on. He owes me something for this, but refuses to pay.

If more white Americans had shared these perceptions, the Indian story might not haunt American history.

Biography is a useful form because it permits the telling of "the times" of its subject. The authors have done a fine job of informing the reader from the context of Gibbon's life: the impact of the Sumter news on officers from the North and South stationed at an isolated United States military base; the emotionally charged relationships between soldiers and their commanders at brigade level; the nature of Civil War tactics; Federal morale problems incident to the incessant combat and casualties of Grant's Virginia Campaign; how a family divided by conflicting loyalties carried on; and details of the Appomattox surrender.

Of particular interest to this reader is the book's description of the relationship between Gibbon and the Iron Brigade, the relationship that dictated the title of the book. Promoted from a captaincy in the artillery to Brigadier General of Volunteers on 2 May 1862, Gibbon took command of a brigade of Indiana and Wisconsin volunteers, the only all-Western brigade in the Eastern armies of the Union. As a result of Gibbon's training and under his leadership—he led the brigade at Brawner Farm, Second Bull Run, South Mountain, and Antietam—these soldiers earned the sobriquet "Iron Brigade." Fighting typically with Gibbon's old battery, B of the 4th U.S., the brigade was reinforced after Antietam by the 24th Michigan Volunteers, thus retaining its distinctive regional identity. The brigade carried forward its storied career after Gibbon's promotion to division command. The eminent T. Harry Williams has called these Western soldiers "probably the best fighting brigade in the army." Gibbon retained his relationship with the Iron Brigade all of his life. The veterans selected him as the permanent President of the Iron Brigade Association.

Following his final service in the Northwest, Gibbon retired in 1891 and settled in Baltimore. Dying there in 1896, he was buried in Arlington Cemetery, his monument marked by the Iron Brigade Association's badge and paid for by veterans of the brigade.

This book is marked by outstanding research. Official government records, obscure primary documents, family papers and correspondence, and appropriate secondary reports give the book authority. Having mined these sources, Messrs. Jordan and Lavery have given us a rich, detailed, and excellent account of the life and times of a significant and neglected soldier of the Union.

Alan T. Nolan

Preface

This book recounts the life and career of a nineteenth century U.S. Army combat officer, at a time when the United States underwent a sea change in its history, both in the areas of politics and economic expansion. Specifically, it tells the story of how its subject moved within and interacted with the events of that period, and his contributions to that time. John Gibbon began his career when the U.S. Army's main weapons were the smoothbore musket and muzzle-loading cannon, when men could only fire at other men in battle if they could see them. When he died, in 1896, the art of war had moved beyond his beginnings, and was approaching a new and terrible time. Yet, as the book shows, he remained fundamentally unchanged by the events around him.

Gibbon was the quintessential combat officer. His personal courage, acceptance of responsibility, and steady nerve in the face of personal danger made him invaluable on the battlefield. These same qualities were apparent away from the fighting. His courage found expression there in his desire to have the truth, as he saw it, on the record. Once Gibbon allied himself with a friend and his cause, or once he took a stand on his own part, he defended his position with a degree of tenacity that, at times, proved embarrassing to all. Yet, although warned that he placed his career in jeopardy, he persisted.

Gibbon's outstanding quality, one shared only with the cream of the Regular Army officers who fought for the Union, was his ability to understand the Civil War citizen-soldier and find the means to draw the best from him. Gibbon saw this man for what he was: a prize of great worth, a terrifying force on the battlefield, and an irrepressible individual in a situation that sought to suppress individuality. By quickly realizing that such men could always be led, but never driven, he found the qualities that created the Iron Brigade. The book shows how humane training on the part of a commander could create a cohesive, prideful unit and how exemplary leadership under fire would forge it into an unbreakable shock force.

Gibbon's Civil War years were the high point of his career, but his later service showed him to be an administrator, troop handler, and planner of ability, a man of good judgment with a sense of proportion and, in his last major command, a keen awareness of the division between civil and military authority in a republic. His qualities were those any army would look upon with approval and pride.

In the course of our pursuit of John Gibbon, we have incurred many debts. We now seek to discharge them in some measure.

First and foremost, we must mention Alan Nolan. Having initially contributed to bringing about our collaboration, he gave encouragement to our early efforts; then, after the work had been sidetracked in favor of other endeavors, he took the initiative in getting it restored to life. To him we are also grateful for permission to use maps from his *The Iron Brigade: A Military History.* We owe him more than we can possibly repay.

Second, we should name Dr. Warren Hassler, formerly of the Pennsylvania State University Department of History. It was his guidance that led to the successful completion of Lavery's dissertation, "John Gibbon and the Old Army: Portrait of an American Professional Soldier," the predecessor work to the present book.

No biography of John Gibbon would be possible without the generous support of the Gibbon family. Mrs. Winthrop H. Battles of Media, Pennsylvania, grandniece of John Gibbon, lent extensive letter collections and other family documents to each author in turn for extended periods. The late Mrs. Bancroft Hill of Baltimore, John Gibbon's granddaughter (and foster daughter), provided family oral history and directed the authors to various sources in which John Gibbon's letters could be found. The late Dr. James W. Gibbon of Charlotte generously lent a typescript copy of Nicholas Gibbon's journal. Mrs. John Morris of Bethesda, Maryland, great-granddaughter of John and Fannie Gibbon, kindly authorized extensive quotation from Gibbon's *Recollections.*

Dr. Robert M. Utley of Dripping Springs, Texas generously allowed the use of maps from *Frontier Regulars: The United States Army and the Indian, 1866–1891.*

The Gibbons' 1860 journey to Utah, Chapter 2, appeared in the September-October 1981 *Military Images* as "Across the Plains," and is reproduced with the permission of editor Harry Roach.

Many librarians, archivists, and custodians of source materials have cheerfully given us assistance. The Pennsylvania State University library gave unstinted support to Lavery's dissertation research. The staff of the National Archives in Washington provided an impressive volume of letters, reports, and returns from which the minutiae of Gibbon's forty-nine years in the Army were gleaned. Records of his cadet days, his years as an instructor at West Point, and his letters held there were made available through the courtesy of the library staff at the U.S. Military Academy. At the State Historical Society of Wisconsin we were able to mine its extensive files of correspondence by members of the Iron Brigade. The Maryland Historical Society provided access to John Gibbon's letters which it holds. The Montana Historical Society was an invaluable source of information on Montana in the 1870s not available elsewhere. The Historical Society of Pennsylvania provided ready access to the Gibbon family papers which it now holds. The Library of Congress book collection and its Congressional Reference Service were most helpful. The library of the Catholic University of America enabled us to find many of John Gibbon's published writings, not available elsewhere at the time of our search. The Bureau of Naval Personnel, Navy Department, furnished information on the naval career of Lardner Gibbon. At the Department of the Army library in the Pentagon we were able to study the Official Records. In the New York State Library at Albany we found an excellent collection of Civil War unit histories, by no means restricted to New York regiments.

Essential guidance in the final preparations for publication was provided by our editors at Greenwood Press—Mildred Vasan, Maureen Melino, and Sasha Kintzler. Adele Horwitz of Presidio Press was most helpful in suggesting improvements in an earlier version of the manuscript. The late K. Jack Bauer of Rensselaer Polytechnic Institute provided encouragement early on.

Anita Roby-Lavery and Joan Racicot performed invaluably in the typing of the various versions of the manuscript.

Jordan would like to express appreciation to his shipmates of the Sixth U.S. Naval Construction Battalion of World War II. He feels that his service as the only regular in this distinguished all-volunteer unit of Middle Westerners, many of them from the Iron Brigade states of Wisconsin, Indiana, and Michigan, gave him valuable insights into the viewpoints and attitudes which John Gibbon and his "Black Hats" brought to their service together.

Finally, and most important of all, the authors acknowledge the steadfast support of their respective wives, Anita Roby-Lavery and Louise Jordan, without which this work would not have been possible.

Abbreviations

ACQR American Catholic Quarterly Review
AGO Adjutant General's Office
BVM Blessed Virgin Mary
CB Commissions Branch
CLG Catharine Lardner Gibbons
FG Fannie Gibbon
FL Fannie Lardner
GP Gibbon Papers
HSP Historical Society of Pennsylvania
JG John Gibbon
MHS Maryland Historical Society
NA National Archives
OR Official Records
RG Record Group
RSCJ Religious of the Sacred Heart of Jesus
SHSW State Historical Society of Wisconsin
USMA United States Military Academy
USMAA United States Military Academy Archives
WD War Department

Iron Brigade General

1 Soldier From the Wars Returning

Mild winter weather enveloped Washington, D.C., on the morning of 10 February 1896, as a train steamed into the station of the Pennsylvania Railroad. John Gibbon—Brigadier General, United States Army; professional soldier; Civil and Indian War fighter—had made his final journey. Meeting the coffin were as distinguished a group as the Army's small headquarters staff could muster, headed by Secretary of War Daniel Lamont, Commanding General Nelson A. Miles, and Brigadier General David Stanley. Standing with them on the platform were two of the official pallbearers, General Henry Rucker and the man who had opened the great battle at Gettysburg, Confederate General Henry Heth.

Also among the mourners were nine members of the Iron Brigade Association—the 1st brigade of the 1st division, I Corps, the men whom Gibbon had trained, led, and converted into a legendary unit. The coffin was placed on a gun caisson of the 4th Artillery. Battery B of the Fourth, John Gibbon's first command, had fought beside the Iron Brigade through all its brief and violent history. With the casket and the horse-drawn caisson went an escort of infantry and two troops of cavalry from Fort Myer. The cortege wound through the streets of Washington, passed over the Aqueduct Bridge and up the hill to Arlington National Cemetery. There, about two hundred yards from the greenhouse of the Custis-Lee mansion, near where Gibbon had drilled his artillerymen in the chaotic days of 1861, the bearers placed the casket on its supports, above a grave dug on an abrupt slope. The site commanded a fine view of the city and the Potomac Valley, stripped bare by winter. For a moment, three volleys of rifle fire tore away the silence on the peaceful hillside. The flag was removed, the coffin lowered, the men departed. Quiet fell again. A career started a half-century before in North Carolina was over.[1]

John Gibbon was born on 20 April 1827 in the Philadelphia suburb of

Holmesburg. His parents, representatives of a solid group of middle-class professional people, had deep roots in eastern Pennsylvania and its history. Although information about his father, Dr. John Heysham Gibbons,[2] remains obscure, the family lineage of his mother, Catharine Lardner, was familiar to many prominent Philadelphians. The Lardners, well-to-do English physicians from Norfolk and Essex, established a branch in the New World along the Delaware when Lynford, Catharine's direct ancestor, crossed the Atlantic in 1740. Settling in Lancaster, he prospered and served both on the Governor's staff and as a provincial assemblyman. A supporter of American independence, Lynford saw one son serve in the Continental Army as a cavalry officer, and a second son follow him as a doctor. His daughter Catharine was born on 31 March 1800. She married Dr. John Gibbons on 11 November 1820.[3]

Although medicine remained the mainstay of the growing family's support, John Gibbons' chief interest centered in geology and mineralogy. His avocation, supported by certain ill-defined political connections, brought him to a new career that eventually opened a world far from Philadelphia for all his children and especially for his son. In 1837 Gibbons turned his back on medicine and became an employee of the federal government.

The occasion for this move came from the discovery of substantial gold deposits in North Carolina. Although the presence of the precious metal had been known since 1790, profitable mining operations did not begin until 1825, when the United States Treasury began extracting the ore and transporting it to Philadelphia for refining and conversion into coin. Congress appropriated $50,000 in March 1835 for a substantial mint and assay operation at Charlotte, and the cornerstone of the main building was laid in January of the next year. John Gibbons secured appointment as an assayer in 1835. His now substantial family had to leave their ancestral home in Pennsylvania and migrate southward, into an area where they would all be subjected to a new and strange environment, with slavery as the norm.[4]

Leaving Catharine in Holmesburg, John Gibbons departed for Charlotte in late 1837 to take up his new appointment, find a home for the family, and absorb the new surroundings. He turned over to his wife the management of the family's trip south. Catharine, now with a seven-month-old son, Nicholas, gathered seven children and their movable possessions to begin her journey. A steamer took them from Philadelphia to Wilmington, Delaware, whence a stage and the exciting novelty of the railroad brought them to Washington. From this point on she had to rely on the disjointed and uncertain transportation system of the antebellum South. Informed by a man at the train station office that she could find her way to Charlotte by simply traveling in a southerly direction and making inquiries along the way, Catharine obtained deck passage on another steamer to Aquia Creek and then to Fredericksburg, where confusion intervened.

First two trunks were sent by error to Richmond. Then the manager of the stage confused Charlotte, North Carolina, with Charlottesville, Virginia. Only a quick reaction from a waiting passenger brought a departing freight wagon to a halt and saved the loss of the luggage. After a journey of 600 miles in six days, sleeping on moving vehicles and in less than attractive inns, the stagecoach brought the migrants into Charlotte. Catharine wrote to her sister that she was amazed to have made the passage in so short a time.[5]

To a family used to the conveniences and attractions of Philadelphia, Charlotte seemed rustic, rude, and provincial. In 1840 the town had a population of 849, of whom 301 were slaves. The entire business community consisted of twelve stores, a bank agent, two taverns, a tannery, and the Mansion House, the community's closest claim to a hotel. For news of the outside world, there was a weekly paper. The stage and mail line passed through Charlotte from Richmond, terminating at Fayetteville and Lincolnton. Although the Northeast was in the midst of a railroad construction boom, the steam locomotive did not reach Charlotte until 1852, when the first train ran up from Columbia, South Carolina.[6]

Antebellum America presented a political scenario that featured bitter and divisive electoral contests. The Jacksonian spoils system, which probably brought Dr. John Gibbons his new position, exacerbated a climate of strong political feeling in Mecklenburg County, where the Whigs and Democrats extended their party politics to personal relationships. They "cut each other dead" on the street, and walled their families off from social and intermarital contacts with their partisan opposite numbers.[7]

Catharine Gibbons did not care for Charlotte. Dr. Gibbons had been unable to locate housing, so the family took rooms in one of the town's taverns, a situation Catharine described to her sisters as "comfortable and private." Little else about the community appealed to her. "An expensive, miserable place to live," she wrote, where the tavern keepers were compelled to scour the countryside for provisions. The cost of drygoods and shoes, because of heavy freight charges, was double that of Philadelphia. Staying at the tavern, she calculated, would keep expenses down, and all "false troubles" about a home she banished from her mind.[8]

If Catharine Gibbons did not care for Charlotte's economic realities, she disliked its society even more. After observing the parade outside the tavern on market day, she reported back to Pennsylvania that transplanted "Philadelphia women" had easily transformed themselves into "Southern ladies." "Dressed in silks, bird of paradise feathers, flowers, and jewels," and accompanied by black nurses, they thronged the streets on the most crowded days. Their personal habits were no better. A custom of taking snuff in large amounts turned their skins saffron and stunted growth, Catharine noted.[9]

She was anxious to move the family out of Charlotte, where all the people did was "gamble, get drunk, fight about politics, and attend sheriff's sales." Two months after their arrival, the tavern owner's wife evicted them, for reasons unknown. After living a short time at "White Oak," a rented home, Dr. Gibbons located "Claremont," a choice piece of rental property, and there the family set up housekeeping just before Christmas 1839.[10]

Claremont was indeed an attractive house. The property belonged to a man in the mining business. Included in the rent was a lot of thirty acres of cleared land. On it sat a house of thirteen rooms and a summerhouse. Here John Gibbon had his first contact with slavery, for his father leased two young women from a nearby planter to help Catharine with the household tasks.[11]

Once out of Charlotte the family discovered how pleasant life could be in North Carolina. Under Catharine's watchful eye, the expenditures consumed only one-half of Dr. Gibbons' salary, and the family raised much of their own vegetables in a large garden. John's father placed the plot under the supervision of John and his brother Robert, paid them respectively six and nine dollars per quarter, and largely left them to their own devices. A beautiful peacock, whose tail Catharine pulled every June, enlivened the yard with its calls. Cornshucking and possum hunting provided fall entertainment. The greatest gap they felt was the lack of intelligent companions and books.[12]

John's childhood was distinguished for its uneventfulness and normality. Few events of future significance seem to have occurred, and he was not one of those men whose future character could be read in his early life as a child. A member of a large and loving family, he had a comfortable youth, unencumbered by material wants, and with a few luxuries. The gift of a pony would not have been possible for many fathers. Although Dr. Gibbons was a careful provider and solicitous promoter of his son's future, his sturdy and realistic mother, with her ability to make the best of any situation, was doubtless the chief force in shaping John Gibbon's character.

A major problem for the family was an inadequate school system. Catharine attempted to teach her children, but they needed more than she could give them. For boys, Charlotte had the Charlotte Male Academy, run by the Rev. A. J. Leavenworth. A public school system remained underdeveloped because of lack of funding. John began attending the academy in 1838. Based on the idea of an English public school, its curriculum concentrated on classical literature, grammar, and rhetoric. His parents also enrolled John in the Latin class. Catharine did not place a great premium on what her son might learn there, for she discovered that "they graduate and give diplomas . . . without teaching them to write." But she firmly supported John's efforts to gain an education.[13]

Life at Claremont and the Mint continued with little from the outside world impinging on the family. The election of 1840, which turned the Democrats out of power, brought little alarm, for technical people such as Dr. Gibbons, once appointed, were usually exempt from the displacements brought about by the spoils system. Even should her husband lose his job, Catharine Gibbons expressed herself to her sister as unconcerned; "We all know how to work." As things developed, only the superintendent was replaced.

Meanwhile, John's exposure to slavery increased. He had seen his father at the Mint supervising hired slaves. Now Dr. Gibbons himself became a slaveholder. By 1847 he owned several, and that year bought an old man to prevent his being sold to Mississippi. Catharine had her own contacts with the "peculiar institution." A young slave girl hired by the family as a nurse gave birth, with her mistress acting as midwife.[14]

The years passed pleasantly enough, and John's parents began to discuss his future. For a family of limited means, the choices were somewhat circumscribed. John had not revealed any inclination or aptitude for medicine. Law was definitely out. The family had a tradition of entering the professions, and toward that direction the Gibbons turned. Catharine's brother, James Biddle Lardner, had served in the Navy as a midshipman until his death at an untimely early age. Cousin James Biddle had been a naval officer for many years, and the Gibbons' eldest son, Lardner, had become a midshipman early in 1838, just before the move to Charlotte. Very possibly these contacts with the military profession suggested West Point to them. The free tuition and technical education were undoubtedly attractive. John would have a career, at least for a period of time after graduation, and his father could probably exert some influence in obtaining an appointment. One thing is certain: although there were no prejudices against things military in the family, a "martial spirit" was not a reason for seeking admission to the Military Academy.

On the eve of his son's fifteenth birthday, Dr. Gibbons wrote to Charlotte's congressman, Green W. Caldwell, asking him to nominate John for admission to West Point. A Democrat and soon to become superintendent of the Mint, Caldwell wrote the standard letter to Colonel Joseph G. Totten, Chief of Engineers, United States Army, recommending John Gibbon "as a suitable person for admission to the Military Academy." Dr. Gibbons also sent a detailed letter to Secretary of War John C. Spencer, on 1 March 1842, supporting the admission. He described his son as "able to render any military service," and inclined toward mathematics, a necessary requirement for a technical education.[15]

On 19 April the first hurdle toward an army career was cleared when Spencer signed the admission form, accepting Gibbon only if he fulfilled certain conditions. The next step was an entrance examination, designed to eliminate insincere or undesirable candidates. John was to present himself at West Point between 1 and 20 June for the examination. On 28 April he returned the signed acceptance to Spencer, taking the initial step toward an association with the Army that did not end until 1896.[16]

The ease with which the appointment had been obtained surprised Catharine, since two North Carolinians had already been nominated that month. Neither she nor her husband were under any illusions about the adequacy of the candidate's past education, so they enrolled him in a school that they hoped would prepare the young man for the entrance examination. Although not happy at the prospect of parting with her son for eight years (four at the Academy and four of mandatory Army service), she came to "rejoice now everyday at his good fortune in getting away from here." As to his chances, she remarked to her sister that John, not as staid as Lardner, nor as quiet as Robert, would have had a hard time leaving such an isolated place as Charlotte, and would be "utterly bewildered." Catharine began gathering the family together in a letter-writing campaign to protect John from loneliness, but abandoned plans to go with him as far as Philadelphia. Baby Margaret, not yet weaned, was too young to be left behind.[17]

In late May, as the signs of summer appeared in North Carolina, the fifteen-year-old boy packed his belongings and took a steamer from New Bern to Philadelphia, making the trip north with more ease than his mother had coming south in 1838. After a brief vacation with his three maiden aunts in Philadelphia, he boarded the Hudson Valley steamer, the quickest transportation to West Point.[18]

Gibbon's first exposure to the West Point routine was a disagreeable one. Upon the arrival of the new candidates, instructors and upperclassmen took them in hand for a series of rigorous tutoring sessions to "prep" them for the forthcoming tests. Gibbon found this, the military routine, and the food distasteful. Most of the new men were tired and wanted to go home, and of the nine from North Carolina, only he and two others remained.[19]

The 119 members of the incoming class, in addition to meeting physical requirements, had to be able to read and write the English language with a satisfactory degree of proficiency, to perform basic arithmetical operations, and to comprehend vulgar and decimal fractions. While this may seem extremely lax as a set of entrance requirements, for a fifteen-year-old, far from home, and with an educational background generously described as slight, the exercise was as formidable as an operation in integral calculus. When the results were posted, John Gibbon stood among the twenty-five marked "inadequate." His deficiencies were in spelling. Although a hard blow to Gibbon and his parents, this did not mean complete rejection. In another two months an examination would be held for those who had failed, and if he could pass the spelling portion, he would be admitted.[20]

A return to Philadelphia ushered in a brief period of intense cramming. His parents made arrangements for him to stay with relatives, who could provide a quiet environment and add to the pressures that his parents, through forceful letters, now piled on the young man. His mother, seeing her reputation as well as that of her son's at stake, wrote a strong and encouraging letter, telling John "that you could do anything you were determined to." A dictionary, properly used, would do much to improve spelling, and use of a slate to correct writing mistakes was an absolute necessity. John need feel no shame about his failure, as only the immediate members of the family knew anything about it. "Think how happy," Catharine wrote, "we shall be to hear of you, your success, and not only we but our friends who have interested themselves for you. . . . I hope all will yet go well." As she remarked to her sister, "I know his industry and perseverance enough, but he needs someone to impress upon him the necessity of exerting himself."[21]

Dr. Gibbons was less subtle; writing on 21 July 1842 he told his son, "Your writing and spelling must be improved. *You must* [emphasis in original] go to Phila. to different Masters that you may be fully prepared—every hour is important—and I must *insist* [emphasis in original] that you pursue the means I have pointed out in my former letters to you. . . ." After this encouragement and prompting, and two months of tutoring and hard work, John Gibbon took passage up the Hudson once again. On 31 August he passed the spelling examination and the next day he joined the Corps of Cadets. Of the classmates with whose lives his would be associated at the Point and for many years thereafter, the ones whose names would be most familiar in history were George B. McClellan, Thomas J. Jackson, and George E. Pickett. Another, whose life would intersect with his in a very personal way, was John G. Foster.[22]

The Military Academy that John Gibbon now entered was the major source of officers for the small United States Army. It was an elite institution, the first engineering school in North America. Although Sylvanus Thayer had not been the Superintendent since 1833, his system still governed the conduct of affairs along the Hudson, even as it does today. A graduate of both Dartmouth College and the Military Academy, Thayer became the Point's chief executive officer in 1817, and his reforms in the areas of conduct, class standing, and curriculum were entrenched by 1842.[23]

In order to avoid any hint of partiality toward a particular cadet, Thayer devised the merit roll for class standing. This became the heart of his program. Its aim was to determine each cadet's place in the class, so that assignment to a particular branch of the Army would be simple. Thorough and impersonal, the merit roll reflected both classroom and field drill performance positively and general conduct and deportment negatively. All cadets had ample opportunity to compile demerits. The demerit standards reflected his belief that the cadets were wild youngsters who could not be left alone at any time. Thayer prohibited all activities he regarded as worthless, which included drinking wine or spirits, card or game playing, smoking, cooking in the rooms, reading light fiction, and playing musical instruments in the quarters. He feared that if instructors played cards it might tempt the cadets, so he forbade it for both groups.

To keep the cadets from wasting time, and to insure that everyone would be occupied at all times in meaningful activity, Thayer instituted a rigid schedule that began at 5:30 A.M. in winter, 6:00 A.M. in summer. Lights-out sounded at 9:30 P.M. The men had little free time between these two reference points. Classes, kept small for daily recitation, required thorough preparation. French and mathematics constituted a significant portion of the curriculum. French was necessary because so many of the technical books used were in that language; mathematics because of the heavy emphasis on civil and military engineering. There was little history taught and less English literature.

The curriculum did not focus on developing an understanding of broad theories of war or military strategy, but sought to make the graduate an expert in small-scale military tactics and turn him out after four years a Christian soldier and gentleman, who could control both his men and himself. As one of the officials wrote, the Academy ". . . expects of every individual rigid conformity to its standard. It stands in loco parentis not only over the moral, physical and so to speak, the official man. It determines every phase of his development. There is very little of his time over which it does not exercise a close scrutiny, and for which it does not demand a rigid accountability."[24]

Although the entrance examination—usually consisting of asking a candidate to define a basic mathematical operation or term, having him read a sentence or two, and write a dictated passage on a blackboard—was not very formidable, many cadets found the combination of rigorous discipline and the course of study, heavily focused on science and mathematics, a hard chore to master. As one historian has written, it was "a stiff enough exchange for boys from the South and West with sketchy grammar school training."[25] Only boys with a desire and determination to work could expect to receive commissions.

John Gibbon moved from a close-knit family based on love and friendship into this alien environment, impersonal, rigid, and disciplined. He would have to grow up fast, and for a boy of not yet sixteen years this would be a task. Although he started off well, reporting to his parents praise from one of the instructors, Gibbon ran afoul of the demerit list very soon. The instance was triggered by hazing on the part of an upperclassman. During the fall of 1842, he was asked to deliver a pair of gloves to a sentry and, since speaking to the guard was forbidden, laid them on a rack of muskets. Neatly framed, he was promptly reported to the Officer of the Guard for "tampering with the guns on the color line." With that the accumulation of demerits began.[26]

Two hundred demerits a year set the upper limit before dismissal or enforced resignation took place. By the end of September Gibbon's class-mate Williamson had accumulated 111; his name disappeared from the rolls in November 1842. Despite his youth and the hazing, John managed to survive the first half-year examinations, a formidable and fearsome ordeal. The Superintendent swore him and eighty-five other plebes into the Corps on 19 February 1843. By June only seventy-two of the eighty-five still remained.[27]

February was a good month for John, for he managed to avoid all demerits, while Cadet Ulysses S. Grant, whom Gibbon later remembered as having a "quiet, undemonstrative nature," underwent a seven-day ar-rest for maltreating his horse. In May the boyish character reasserted itself, and Gibbon was assigned to extra Saturday guard duty for throw-ing bread in the mess hall. By June his troubles were manifest. Besides three extra tours of guard duty, for allowing gunpowder to be burned in quarters, he ranked close to the bottom of the class in academic and deportment matters. He had 133 demerits.[28]

Summer brought no respite from work. The stern schedule of the Academy denied all furloughs until the end of the second year, so Gibbon enlivened the summer encampment and accumulated additional demerits by using A. P. Hill's cap and musket during a reveille call. In addition he managed to insinuate himself further into West Point's demerit books by sitting down while acting as sentry, not walking his post, and having a slovenly appearance at drill, with his pants dirty. He also received de-merits for inattention at drill. Gibbon was working himself into trouble, and his lax manner and inability to discipline himself soon seeped into his academic record, particularly in the general area of English gram-mar.[29]

When the cadets gathered to learn of their marks in the June 1844 examinations, seventeen discovered that they had failed. John Gibbon, sadly but not unexpectedly, was among that group. He stood a dismal sixty-fifth in a class of seventy-eight, and his discipline record reflected that standing. Fortunately, his career was not finished, for he was one of four of the seventeen who were allowed to repeat the year. Thirteen left the Corps of Cadets forever.[30]

This failure, rather than his appointment to the Academy, constituted the turning point of his life. He had shamed his parents and himself. After this episode, he never again came close to dismissal or disgrace. Al-though an innate sense of humor characterized him throughout his life, this sobering experience led Gibbon to true self-mastery; externally he became something of a martinet, cold and strictly Regular Army. Along with his personal adherence to regulations went a strict enforcement of them on his subordinates. He developed an insistence that his superiors likewise obey the letter of the law in their relations with him. His trait of standing immovably on what he perceived as his rights would bring him into repeated controversy with higher authority throughout his career, sometimes to his own disadvantage. When among intimates, or when his career demanded it, he could be merry, convivial, friendly, a loving husband and good father. But from this point on he never lost control over himself. He would never sink so low again.

Entitled to a furlough after the first two years of study, he returned to North Carolina in June 1844 to meet a new member of the family, baby Frances, born the previous winter. (Of the ten Gibbon children, Frances would be the only one not to live to maturity; not quite a year old, she died the following January.) The life of the Gibbons was enlivened that summer by the burning of the Mint on 27 July. After an otherwise quiet vacation, much taken up by talk and visiting, John returned to West Point via Philadelphia in August.[31]

When Gibbon rejoined the Corps of Cadets, he found among his new classmates at least four with whom his life would later intersect, Ambrose Burnside, James B. Fry, Charles Griffin, and Harry Heth. Chastened and perhaps scared by his academic setback, Gibbon began to work harder, keeping regular study hours, and while never managing to master the demerit system—few could do that—he never again allowed it to affect his classroom work. By June 1845 he stood nineteenth in a class of forty-four, his best ranking a six in drawing and his worst a thirty-one in English. He had also managed to accumulate 120 demerits, and to acquire a new nickname, "Yadkin." Catharine Gibbons had previously expressed her disapproval of "Jack" as an appellation for her son; her reaction to "Yadkin" is not on record.[32]

For the Corps of Cadets and the United States Army, 1846 was significant for the outbreak of war with Mexico. Friction between the two countries arose with the Texan revolt of 1836 and the prompt recognition by the United States of Texas's independence, which Mexico did not acknowledge. With the signing in April 1844 of a treaty annexing Texas to the United States, conflict was virtually assured. A boundary dispute provided the focal point; Texas, and the United States, asserted that the border followed the Rio Grande River, while Mexico claimed sovereignty to the Nueces, which empties into the Gulf of Mexico at Corpus Christi. In the summer of 1845, American forces under General and future President Zachary Taylor moved to occupy the contested territory. Efforts to negotiate a peaceful solution failed, and when hostilities commenced in the Spring of 1846, they grew from skirmishing over the disputed lands into a full-scale American invasion of Mexico.[33]

The year 1846 was also an eventful one for Gibbon family members; in

October Catharine found herself with a typhus outbreak on her hands. She was the only one to escape infection, and nursed the entire household, including two slaves, back to health. The only lingering remembrance was the loss of much of Dr. Gibbons' hair. In Mexico, Lardner, now an acting master in the Navy, was sent ashore from the naval forces at Veracruz to serve on the staff of Brigadier General William J. Worth. Subsequently he found for himself another role, evidenced by his sending his mother a newspaper clipping featuring "Acting Master Gibbon and his flying artillery."[34]

Gibbon held his own academically in 1846 and 1847, ranking nineteenth out of forty the first year and twentieth of thirty-eight the second. He was also a cadet lieutenant in his final year. Graduation saw him attain a standing of twenty in engineering, twenty-one in artillery tactics, and seventeen in infantry tactics; hardly a brilliant record, but that of a solid performer. He had become a man who could envision a goal and carry through until he reached it.[35]

Very little about the United States Army of 1847 resembled the massive forces of Europe, or even the limited ground strength of the world's chief colonial power, Great Britain. In the first place, the soldier in the United States had none of the privileges of status that he enjoyed in, for example, Prussia. One point upon which almost all Americans seemed to agree was that they might need a standing army, but they did not have to accord it respect. For a man to join as a private soldier was the firmest piece of evidence possible that he was a dissolute and improvident person, unable to function in a free society and take advantage of the myriad opportunities available to an enterprising individual. Public opinion of the professional officer stood little higher. As one of Gibbon's contemporaries exclaimed: "We see our officers now in almost every city strutting about the streets in indolence, sustained by the laboring people, fed from the public crib, but doing nothing whatever to support themselves or increase the wealth of the nation."[36]

This gentleman certainly exaggerated. New York City was hardly Berlin, and the vast bulk of the Army in 1847 was in Mexico. Upon its return it would be stationed on the frontier to garrison the vast new territories America's newest burst of imperialism had acquired. But the Army's main problem was not public opinion, it was manpower. By 1853 the Army's authorized strength was up to 13,821 officers and men; the actual strength was 10,417. The fifty-four western posts had garrisons that averaged 124 men. Because of terrible living conditions, wretched pay (before 1853, $7.00 for an infantryman, $8.00 for a cavalryman), brutal discipline, and boring, routine-ridden activity, the War Department was simply unable to keep its units up to strength. Disease, desertion, and failure to reenlist caused an annual manpower turnover of 28 percent, and often actual strength fell below authorized numbers by as much as 18 percent. This persistent failure to maintain regimental rolls at even the meager limits set by Congress guaranteed a stagnant army and a general inability to field more than a token force in the western territories. The advent of a major war, such as the Mexican conflict, quickly caused the denuding of garrisons and a heavy reliance upon militia and short-service volunteers.[37]

In addition to a pronounced weakness existing in the body of enlisted soldiers, the officer corps, because of the absence of a retirement system, was plagued with aged superiors, unable to lead men or provide much in the way of direction for the Regular Army. In 1850, the Adjutant General estimated that twenty-five officers should be retired. Of nineteen regimental colonels in 1860, eleven were veterans of the War of 1812. Two had entered service in 1801, and only eight had less than forty years of service. Promotion was painfully slow and strictly by seniority, first through the regiment to captain, then by corps to colonel. General officers were selected by the President. Longevity made for an accumulation of superannuated men at the top, which only death or extreme disability could alleviate. A man could spend forty years rising to colonel. In addition, infirmity limited the usefulness to the Army of some of its more able men. In 1861 both the general-in-chief and the chief engineer had to disqualify themselves from field service on account of age and illness. And the glut at the top, coupled with the fact that West Point turned out too many officers, meant that new graduates could count on spending perhaps several years as brevet second lieutenants before receiving regular commissions. Little wonder that George B. McClellan, the future Civil War Union leader and Gibbon's classmate, exclaimed in 1846, "War at last sure enough! Ain't it glorious! 15,000 regulars and 50,000 volunteers!" And, he might have added, battle, death, expansion of the officer corps, and promotions.[38]

When Gibbon graduated from West Point, the basic unit of the Army was the regiment, a fact that would remain true until the end of the century. In 1847 there were four artillery regiments, eight of infantry, and three of mounted troops. In 1855 Congress authorized the addition of two more regiments of foot and two of cavalry. Their average strength was 300 to 400 men. The regiment was seldom assembled to operate as an entity. The company was in fact the normal administrative and tactical unit, and generally was the largest aggregate with which officers in the field were familiar. Not until the Civil War did colonels have the opportunity to maneuver their men together under central control, and then normally as part of a brigade. Common soldier loyalty was to the company.[39]

Providing guidance, supplies, and administration was the prerogative of the War Department, its bureaus, and the general-in-chief. The bureaus remained all-powerful, their staffs diverted from possible service in the field and under the authority of the Secretary of War. The general-in-chief occupied an anomalous position, exercising very little actual control over the field forces. The whole officer corps was so jealous of its rights that the preferring of charges for minor offenses became a major pastime, and countless courts-martial were convened over ridiculous and trivial matters. So small was the officer corps that it could be likened to a disputatious family, quick to take offense and correspondingly slow to forget slights, real or imagined. The events of 1861–65 were to provide ample ammunition for controversies, as John Gibbon would discover. These would echo down the years until all the disputants had passed from the scene and the remaining interpretation existed only to supply material for the work of historians.

This "high command" of the Army did not exercise any of the functions that were beginning to be a part of general staff activities in Europe, especially in Prussia. No planning went forward; no real policy was adopted or even formulated; no strategy was developed. With post-1848 warfare tending to degenerate into mere police operations, the Army sought to preserve its existence, live within the strict confines of economy dictated by Congress, carry out the missions assigned, and live for today and possibly tomorrow. Such was the Regular Army of John Gibbon, and except for the Civil War years, this would be the world he would know all of his active life.

While John Gibbon was completing his studies at the Point, the war with Mexico proceeded. United States forces established control over present-day New Mexico, Arizona, and California. However, operations in northern Mexico did not lead to a satisfactory conclusion, and in August 1846 the administration of President James K. Polk decided to open a second front by seizing the Mexican Gulf port of Veracruz and proceeding thence toward the capital, Mexico City. This invasion, led in person by the General-in-Chief of the U.S. Army, Winfield Scott, was mounted in the late fall and winter of 1846–47; Veracruz surrendered at the end of March, and the move inland toward Mexico City commenced promptly on 2 April. By the time in August that John Gibbon was sworn in as a brevet second lieutenant, Scott's army had reached Ayotla, fifteen miles east of the capital.

In June 1847 John Gibbon walked for the last time down to Benny Havens' tavern, where he and numerous other cadets had received a warm welcome, decent food, friendship, and credit. The young man paid his outstanding bill of $15.59 and departed for an interlude in North Carolina with his family. This was a more pleasant visit than that of three years before, when the cloud of failure had hung over him and three more grim years at the Academy was the only future he faced. Days were spent hunting and fishing, passions Gibbon enjoyed all his life. Evenings he passed quietly, sitting with Maggie, his young sister, on his lap, pulling on his long pipe and ruminating with his parents about the future. When August came he began watching the mail.[40] His class standing enabled him to avoid the infantry and receive a brevet commission as second lieutenant of artillery on 5 August 1847. On 13 August he forwarded to the Adjutant General his acceptance and oath of allegiance, thus completing his transition to officer status.[41] On 14 August the stage brought orders from the War Department, directing him to report to his regiment, the 3rd Artillery, and he left for New Orleans, there to take passage on board the *James L. Day* to Veracruz.

Gibbon's service with the 3rd Artillery was short. When he joined his regiment on 8 December 1847, Scott's army had already fought its climactic battle and captured Mexico City on 13 September. The death on that day of Captain Simon Drum of the 4th Artillery in heavy fighting at the Garita (gate) of Belen, and the consequent promotions within the 4th, created a vacancy for a regular second lieutenant in that regiment. Gibbon, as the senior brevet second lieutenant of artillery, was entitled to the promotion. However, he continued to serve with the 3rd until the following June.[42]

With the fighting in Mexico ended, John's failure to graduate from West Point in four years had kept him from going to war, and duty in Mexico now meant only occupation responsibilities. The 3rd Artillery kept busy by responding to alarms about possible guerrilla forces in the area of Toluca, twenty miles west of Mexico City. At one point Gibbon acted as captain for his company, with a welcome $10.00 per month increase to his $25.00 lieutenant's pay.[43]

Upon the signing and ratification of the treaty ending hostilities, the American forces and John Gibbon left Mexico. He landed at Pascagoula, Florida, from which he went to Old Point Comfort, Virginia, and the Artillery School of Practice at nearby Fortress Monroe in September 1848. From there he obtained a two-month leave for a visit to Charlotte. During October he relaxed at home, talked over Mexican adventures with his brother Lardner, also at home on leave from the Navy, and agreed to act as groomsman for the wedding of his friend Daniel Harvey Hill, a fellow West Point graduate and artillery officer and a future Confederate general. Lardner and John also managed nearly to incinerate the family when they built up a fire in the summerhouse fireplace so that it charred and ignited the boards in the ceiling and floor. Luckily their mother awoke during the night and alerted the household. Nevertheless, delighting in the presence of her two sons, Catharine wrote to her sister: "I begin to dread the time which must soon arrive to part with them. . . ." John, who entertained the family with songs and tales from Mexico, did not want to go, but told his mother that he could not in good conscience apply for another leave extension. Lardner departed for duty at the Naval

Observatory in mid-November and ten days later John made his way south to a new assignment at Tampa, Florida.[44]

NOTES

1. *Washington Star*, 10 February 1896; Major General George D. Ruggles to Commanding Officer, Washington Barracks, 8 February 1896, AGO, NA, RG 94.

2. John Gibbon to Fannie Moale Gibbon, 20 April 1862, Gibbon Papers, Historical Society of Pennsylvania ("HSP"). Exactly when and why Dr. Gibbons dropped the extra letter from his name is uncertain. To differentiate him from his son, it has been retained when referring to him.

3. This, and all other family history, is contained in the Lardner-Gibbon Papers, HSP; Catharine L. Gibbon to Fannie Lardner, 2 February 1832, HSP (hereafter cited as CLG to FL).

4. D. A. Tompkins, *History of Mecklenburg County and the City of Charlotte* (Charlotte, 1903), I, 129.

5. CLG to FL, 2, 16 April 1838, HSP.

6. Tompkins, *Mecklenburg County*, 118, 126.

7. J. B. Alexander, *History of Mecklenburg County* (Charlotte, 1902), 178.

8. CLG to FL, 16 April, 13 July 1838, HSP.

9. CLG to FL, 19 March, 17 November 1839, HSP.

10. CLG to FL, 6 November 1840, 13 December 1839, HSP.

11. CLG to FL, 28 February 1840, HSP.

12. CLG to FL, 13 July, 6 August, 12 November 1838, 3 July 1840, 9 May 1842, HSP.

13. Tompkins, *Mecklenburg County*, I, 111; CLG to FL, 1 December 1838, HSP.

14. CLG to FL, 28 November 1840, 21 October 1841; CLG to Hannah Lardner, 11 April 1847, 12 October 1838, HSP.

15. John Heysham Gibbons to Green W. Caldwell, 14 February; Caldwell to Joseph G. Totten, 23 February; Gibbons to John C. Spencer, 1 March 1842, AGO, NA, RG 94; memoranda from Office of Naval History.

16. John C. Spencer to John Gibbon, 19 April; Gibbon to Spencer, 28 April 1842, AGO, NA, RG 94.

17. CLG to FL, 5, 9 May, 25 June 1842, HSP.

18. CLG to Margaret Lardner, 1 June 1842, HSP.

19. CLG to FL, 25 June 1842, HSP; Kenneth W. Rapp, Assistant Archivist, USMA, to Mark H. Jordan, 23 October 1978.

20. Stephen Ambrose, *Duty, Honor, Country: A History of West Point* (Baltimore, 1966), 128–129; CLG to FL, 2 July 1842, HSP.

21. CLG to JG, 21 July 1842; to FL, 2 July 1842, HSP.

22. John Heysham Gibbons to JG, 21 July 1842, GP, HSP; Register of the Officers and Cadets, United States Military Academy, 1842, USMAA.

23. This picture of West Point in the Thayer era is drawn largely from Ambrose, *Duty, Honor, Country*, 147–166.

24. Quoted in Ambrose, *Duty, Honor, Country*, 150.

25. Theodore Ropp, *War in the Modern World* (New York, 1962), 178.

26. John Gibbon, *Address to the Graduating Class at West Point*, 12 June 1886 (Vancouver Barracks, Department of the Columbia, 1886), 3, 7.

27. Records of the U.S. Military Academy, National Archives; Register of the U.S. Military Academy, 1843.

28. John Gibbon conduct record, USMAA; Register, 1843.

29. Gibbon conduct record, USMAA.

30. Register, USMA, 1844.

31. CLG to FL, 20 August 1844, HSP; Tompkins, *Mecklenburg County*, II, 68.

32. Register, 1845; CLG to FL, 12 February 1845, HSP.

33. For general material on the Mexican War, the authors have drawn on K. Jack Bauer, *The Mexican War, 1846–1848* (New York, 1974).

34. CLG to Lardner Gibbon, 6 October 1846; CLG to FL, 14 February, 3 October 1847, HSP.

35. Register, 1846, 1847; Post Order No. 87, USMA, 20 October 1846, USMAA.

36. Quoted in Robert Utley, *Frontiersmen in Blue: The United States Army and the Indian, 1848–1866* (New York, 1966), 29.

37. Utley, *Frontiersmen in Blue*, 18–19, 36.

38. Utley, *Frontiersmen in Blue*, 32; McClellan's remark is in Ambrose, *Duty, Honor, Country*, 140.

39. Utley, *Frontiersmen in Blue*, 20–21.

40. Receipt in John Gibbon scrapbook, Gibbon Papers, HSP; CLG to FL, 10 August 1847, HSP.

41. General Orders No. 27, 5 August 1847; John Gibbon to Adjutant General, 13 August 1847, AGO, NA, RG 94.

42. Returns of the 3rd Artillery and 4th Artillery, 1847–48, NA, RG 94.

43. CLG to FL, 25, 28 January, 3 October 1848, HSP; General Orders No. 36, 4 December 1847, AGO, NA, RG 94.

44. CLG to FL, 26 October, 24 December 1848, HSP.

2 Toward Civil War

Fort Brooke, with its access to the broad waters of Tampa Bay and the beautiful Gulf of Mexico, had two characteristics widely shared by ante-bellum Army posts: quiet and loneliness. Situated on the fringes of a sparsely populated state, the garrison had little to do but watch the Indians and get on one another's nerves. Gibbon found it a pleasant enough place. When his commander had to leave, he often found himself acting as post commander. With a good deal of free time left to him, he could hunt and fish as he chose, and even begin a garden. This uneventful duty came to an end when uncertain relations with the Seminole Indians threatened to start an Indian War.[1]

The Seminoles, the 4th Artillery's principal reason for maintaining a detachment at Fort Brooke, caused continual anxiety for the settlers. Dealings between the United States government and the tribe traced back to a treaty in 1790 with the Creeks that included reference to the "Samanolies." During the War of 1812 the Seminoles became involved in hostilities with the United States, in consequence of which General Andrew Jackson invaded Florida, then Spanish territory, with 3,000 men in 1817–18, a conflict known as the first Seminole War. This invasion led to the cession of Florida to the United States by Spain in 1819. Treaties between the United States and the Seminoles followed in 1823 and 1832; in the first the Indians ceded much of their land to the federal government, and in the second they agreed to move to present-day Oklahoma. A large part of the tribe repudiated the second treaty, and under the leadership of the famous Osceola, commenced the second Seminole War in 1835. It lasted until 1842, and ended with the exile of most of the tribe to Oklahoma. An estimated 300 remained in Florida; they faded back into the interior of the Everglades, where they grew to be a source of irritation to the settlers, and the settlers to them. The Army did its best to keep the two groups apart.[2]

In mid-July 1849 a group of settlers and some Seminoles fought a skirmish along Indian River that ended with the death of a man known as Barker or Baker and the wounding of a deputy tax collector, a Major Russell. No one knew exactly what had triggered the violence. The trouble then spread toward Pease Creek, and Gibbon's commanding officer, Major W. W. Morris, led a scouting party into the area. There he found the bodies of two more settlers. At once Morris took steps to aid the settlers, for his small command could not protect everyone.[3]

Morris detached John Gibbon with a small patrol to the town of Manatee with guns and ammunition for the settlers. Toward dusk Gibbon somehow managed to get himself separated from his small command and spent the hot and humid Florida night wandering in the woods on his mule. Perhaps used to inept first performances, Major Morris omitted this incident from his report and described Gibbon to the Adjutant General as "equally prompt and energetic." While local units struggled to bring the potentially explosive situation under control, the Army reinforced its frontier forces. Brigadier General David Twiggs, commander of the Western Division, transferred his headquarters to Tampa from New Orleans and tried to arrange negotiations before a war the Army did not want or need forced deployment of troops into Indian country.[4]

Gibbon's first exposure to American Indians proved him both a sympathetic observer of their plight and a stern advocate of honest negotiation. With the no-nonsense rectitude that characterized his life, he was able to see clearly that the Seminole situation had more than its share of unexpected twists and turns. Gibbon's outlook may have been influenced by a rather remarkable man, Captain John C. Casey, Fort Brooke's subsistence officer. In addition to his normal duties, Casey had often served as an intermediary with the Seminoles, and Gibbon attributed the trust that Casey had gained to his habit of never lying to them and never making promises he could not fulfill. If something was unpleasant or impossible, he told them before they found it out for themselves.[5]

After Gibbon obtained permission to accompany Casey on a peace mission, the two men waited for the Indians to send an indication that they wanted to talk. A Spaniard named Felipe brought Casey word that a Seminole leader whom the soldiers called Billy Bowlegs desired an end to the dispute. Casey, a black interpreter named Samuel, Gibbon, and two soldiers went back to Felipe's cabin with him. Having arrived a day ahead of the scheduled conference, the two officers went on a deer hunt to amuse themselves, and Gibbon, riding to what he thought was a sandy peninsula, found himself isolated on a tidal island at the mouth of Charlotte Harbor. A boat from a coasting sloop brought him back to the mainland.[6]

On 31 August Gibbon and Casey met with the Indians, who expressed apologies for the trouble. After being told that they must meet with Twiggs, they replied that Casey was their choice as intermediary. Gibbon and Casey took a subchief back to Fort Brooke as an earnest of the Seminoles' peaceful intentions. Then Twiggs followed them back to Charlotte for the conference with Billy Bowlegs.[7]

Gibbon's involvement with the negotiations almost entangled him in a disciplinary affair. To augment his pay, he had been writing articles on the Indian trouble for the *New Orleans Picayune*, and in one piece he remarked that "perhaps General Twiggs will go with him [Casey] to Charlotte." Twiggs, nicknamed "The Bengal Tiger" by contemporaries, was a cold, ill-tempered man who could be vindictive. Instantly furious at being placed in status below Casey, he searched for the offender. His suspicion fell on a captain as author of the article. The accused but innocent officer and his company were sent to build a bridge on the desolate Alafia River, and Twiggs remarked to an aide that "It will give him something to write about." Gibbon, who kept an extremely low profile, escaped detection.[8]

By 19 November the small crisis burned itself out. After the Army negotiators yielded to the demand of the Seminoles to bring a chief from the Arkansas reservation to the negotiations, the Indians agreed to surrender the three men involved in the Pease Creek and Indian River killings. But now the War Department intervened and ordered Twiggs to dispossess the Seminoles in that area, buy their land, and transport them to Arkansas. During the fifty-day period allowed for negotiations, Twiggs began to construct a series of armed posts to control the threatened areas, and brought up another company of the 4th Artillery from Key West. He dispatched it to Fort Chokonikla, in the heart of Billy Bowlegs' country, where Casey and Gibbon were conducting negotiations with the Indians.[9]

One blustery and rainy night at the lonely post of Chokonikla, while John Gibbon fought off loneliness and tried to keep warm, a tall army lieutenant and his orderly splashed their horses through the mud and into the parade area. This man, whom Gibbon described as thin, even gaunt, "with a hatchet face and a prominent aquiline nose," was Lieutenant George Gordon Meade, of the Corps of Topographical Engineers, engaged in a survey ordered by Twiggs to find favorable sites for the military posts he wanted to build. Meade was tired, hungry, and, if the future was any indication, ill-tempered. But he gladly accepted hot food, a dry uniform, and a warm bed for the night.[10]

After life on the damp Florida peninsula, Gibbon's next assignment was a welcome change. On Christmas Day 1849 orders arrived from the Adjutant General sending him to Company B, 4th Artillery, stationed at Ringgold Barracks, Texas. The uncertain transportation of the Southwest delayed his passage, but on 21 January 1850 he reported to the company commander, First Lieutenant John P. McCown.[11]

McCown had an elite unit with a proud past, unusual for such a young army. As the "Washington Battery," it had greatly distinguished itself at Buena Vista, where Zachary Taylor's light artillery almost won the battle alone. Although the company had an exciting history, its present life was dull and monotonous, and Gibbon began to slip into the duties of an antebellum military post, training his men (and himself), drilling the battery on the hot, dusty practice ground, and attending to the mass of paperwork without which no western army seemed to manage. The entire regiment's disposition remained typical of the Old Army. A transfer of Company B in early 1850 brought it and Company K to Fort Brown, Brownsville, but I Company was at Baton Rouge, the regimental headquarters at Pensacola, and the remaining components were strung out along the Florida peninsula.[12]

Gibbon kept rotating between two companies, serving as replacement for junior officers sick or on leave. While acting commander of Company K, he received his promotion to first lieutenant on 12 September 1850. In February 1851 and again in April he attempted to obtain leave to see his parents, but was quickly turned down by the departmental commander because of the unsettled conditions along the frontier. Late in the year Company K left Fort Brown for an expedition up the Rio Grande to prevent the passage of arms and ammunition across the border to the rebel Mexican general Carvajal. A month passed; the threatened gun-running failed to materialize, and in April 1852 Gibbon departed on six months' leave.[13]

Once back in North Carolina, the far-traveled first lieutenant was passed from relative to relative on a steady stream of family visits. Still on detached service, he spent some time in Washington, sitting on various courts-martial. In early March 1853, he received orders to join Company H, 4th Artillery, at Fort Niagara, New York.[14] Before this transfer had been carried out, he encountered General Twiggs by chance in the War Department and learned that the touchy situation in Florida had been further strained by the actions of a civilian Indian agent. Twiggs told Gibbon that the agent had been removed and Casey appointed to his place in order to persuade the remaining Seminoles to emigrate. Twiggs then arranged to have Gibbon assigned to detached service in the Indian Department, and ordered him to accompany Casey to the reservation in Arkansas; their mission, to gather a delegation of Seminoles and bring it to Florida. After returning to Fort Brooke, Casey, Gibbon, and the delegation prevailed upon the older Indians to move to Arkansas, but the younger members of the tribe simply retreated further into the interior for another two years.[15]

By the summer of 1854 Gibbon was once again available for assignment. To add to the qualities of promptness and energy that he had displayed as a second lieutenant, he had now shown initiative, a lively professional curiosity, and skill in negotiation. Still a junior officer, he had headed an artillery battery—a captain's command—in garrison and in the field. He had come favorably to the notice of one of the Army's senior generals. Clearly, here was a coming officer, one who could serve as a model for others. So he must have appeared to the Adjutant General, and in the last week of September, in compliance with new orders, Lieutenant Gibbon, now an instructor of artillery tactics, reported at West Point to the Superintendent of the Academy, Brevet Colonel Robert E. Lee.[16]

Gibbon found the Academy much as he had left it in 1847, ruled by the traditions of Sylvanus Thayer and guided by his successors in the Corps of Engineers. Lee, the Superintendent, was a man widely respected and pointed out by some as likely to follow Winfield Scott as the Army's ranking officer. Dennis Hart Mahan, one of the forty-four member faculty, still taught his rigorous and demanding course of military engineering and the art of war. One of his faculty associates was Fitz John Porter, a cadet contemporary of Gibbon (class of 1845), a fellow officer of the 4th Artillery, and a future Union general; his later career would involve John Gibbon over much of Gibbon's life.

Academy service signaled another milestone in Gibbon's life: his decision to marry. Although he had not shown any great interest in the subject in his early years of officer service, by 1853 he had begun an uphill courtship of a Baltimore woman, Frances (Fannie) Moale. Gibbon had made her acquaintance while on temporary duty in Washington following his years in Texas, probably through the agency of a West Point classmate, John Foster. Foster, an officer of the Corps of Engineers, had served at Fort Carroll, near Baltimore, and while there had met and married Fannie's sister Mary. During Gibbon's stay in the capital in the winter of 1852–53 he renewed his friendship with Foster and through this association was introduced to Fannie.[17] For the next two years the relationship between the two developed. The arrival of the Fosters at West Point, where Lieutenant Foster joined the faculty in January 1855, provided additional stimulus to the growing attachment.[18]

In addition to the opportunity for family life offered by the new assignment, his brother Lardner's wedding may have prompted Gibbon to marry. Lardner, recently returned from a secret exploratory mission to the Amazon basin, asked and received his parents' permission to marry his cousin, Alice Shepard. At the same time he obtained their approval of his resigning his Navy commission. On 28 January 1855 Lardner and Alice married and settled down to a new life ashore.

Gibbon broached the subject of his hopes to his parents in July 1855, telling them that he had been attached to Fannie for more than two years. The main obstacle was her parents. First, they did not view with pleasure the prospect of another daughter marrying an officer. The father had been obstinate over John Foster's proposals, and did not look forward to having a second daughter living on distant military posts. Second, Fannie was a Roman Catholic. Gibbon's parents harbored no prejudices on this subject, but this was a time when anti-Catholic prejudice stood at a high pitch in America. Fannie's parents doubtless desired to have her marry within the family's faith. Gibbon belonged to no church. His mother was an Episcopalian and regularly entertained high church officials. Dr. Gibbons was a nominal Quaker. How strongly either parent felt toward religion, beyond mere convention, is uncertain.

Gibbon, however, refused to be deterred. Fannie, he reported, loved him, but would not marry without parental consent. She urged John not to write to her ill and angry father, fearing that it would merely complicate matters. Through him she sent Catharine "love and a kind message," in return for the encouragement that John Gibbon's mother had sent to her son; Catharine Gibbons had told him that he was old enough to trust in his own judgment. On the religious question the senior Gibbons kept an open mind.[19]

John finally decided that a direct frontal assault would resolve the impasse, either in his favor or against it. He obtained seventy days' leave from the Academy to go to Baltimore.[20] Doubtless the Fosters contrived to apply pressure, and Gibbon apparently settled the matter by obtaining an interview with Fannie's parish priest. The Reverend H. B. Coskery's advice to Fannie was terse: "Marry him." On 16 October 1855, John Gibbon and Frances Moale, with Colonel J. P. Taylor and Mary Helen Scott acting as witnesses, were married at the bride's home. Father Coskery performed the ceremony.[21]

Although Catharine expressed surprise at this rapid change in her son's marital fortunes, she responded at once in a typical gesture by writing her daughter-in-law and "welcoming her to my heart and home." As she wanted to meet Fannie and see her son at his work, a trip to West Point was planned, tentatively for June 1856. As she wrote to her sister, "I want to see her very much, and can see no reason *now* why I should not be gratified" [original emphasis].

Even before his entry into married life Gibbon obtained separate quarters at West Point, and, with the aid of two ladies who volunteered to put up his curtains and arrange his furniture, had made a start at housekeeping. It was to this home that he brought his wife after their honeymoon at Niagara Falls.[22] If all went well, John and Fannie Gibbon would be at West Point to complete a five-year tour of duty.

By this time Lee had relinquished the superintendent's post; on 31 March 1855, Major Richard Delafield had replaced him. Soon after John Gibbon settled in with his wife, he found Delafield assigning him additional responsibilities. Made Post Treasurer in 1855, he had his tasks further expanded when Delafield appointed him Assistant Instructor of Artillery and Cavalry Tactics, although Gibbon had no operational experience in the latter subject. By August 1856, he had succeeded Fitz John Porter as the artillery instructor. Although now relieved of responsibility for cavalry tactics, he was commanding the enlisted artillery and dragoon detachments.[23]

John Gibbon's interest in artillery reflected the Army's attraction to that military branch. Manuals for use by cadets existed, but they did not incorporate the new advances in ordnance, such as rifling, long-range fire, improved shell fuses, and guns of increasing size and power, previously impossible to cast. The work of Thomas Rodman and John Dahlgren, officer ordnance experts of the Army and Navy respectively, had made it possible to produce a gun of fifteen-inch caliber. Experiments with light artillery in the 1830s and 1840s culminated in the Mexican War in an arm of exceptional mobility and firepower. The influence of French military thinking also bore heavily upon this development, for Napoleon had been one of the great proponents of powerful field guns and their massed use.

Using notes he prepared for his class lectures, and revising extensively the outdated manuals then in use, Gibbon produced a text, *The Artillerist's Manual*, which was published in 1859 by D. Van Nostrand in New York City; its slow but steady sale brought a welcome supplement to his pay. Trubner and Company of London also issued an edition. In its fourteen chapters the text dealt with advances in both gunnery and metallurgy, and improvements in tactics learned from the Mexican and Crimean Wars. Gibbon stated in its preface that he had started to write a textbook for the cadets, but found himself expanding it with a view to spreading information not generally obtainable.[24]

The manual was distinguished chiefly for its clarity and thoroughness, and was adopted at the Academy. By 1861 the original edition had sold out. Gibbon's work as both instructor and author brought Delafield's praise as "a zealous officer and a keen student."[25]

The Gibbons' life in the Army could hardly have been luxurious, given the pay of a first lieutenant. Catharine had no illusions on this subject and told her sister of discouraging stories she had heard. But, she wrote, "Everything depends upon the wife, if she is willing to cut her coat according to her cloth, I *know* it can be done." [original emphasis]

Dr. and Mrs. Gibbons became grandparents on 28 July 1856, when a daughter, Fannie Moale Gibbon, was born. Family ties with North Carolina remained strong, and correspondence between there and West Point was heavy. Gibbon even found himself urged to "pay some attention" to the son of one of his mother's friends, now a cadet.[26]

Gibbon's duties continued to press upon any free time he may have had. Besides his classes, which were still conducted under the daily recitation plan, he was made post quartermaster in September 1856, and also officer of police. His chief responsibility in the latter capacity was to enforce a new regulation against grazing cows on the Academy's lawns.

By 1857 he had been relieved of his duties as artillery instructor to devote full time to administration. And several times he traveled to Washington on detached service.[27]

This continual work and unexpected travel led his mother to defer her plans for a visit to the Academy, but she continued, at long range, to express approval of and happiness over the marriage. Impressed by Fannie's lack of pretense and love of home, her mother-in-law declared that such characteristics "promise fair for her husband's happiness."[28] Finally, in June 1858, Catharine Gibbons was able to make the trip to West Point, in company with her daughter Jennie, now in her early twenties. After almost missing each other at the Jersey City pier, John Gibbon, his mother and sister were reunited and boarded the Hudson River steamer. (Fannie, now with two small children—a second daughter, Katie, had been born in February—had been kept at home by her maternal responsibilities.) A heavy rain during the river passage soaked Catharine's clothes, but did not dampen her happiness at seeing her son, daughter-in-law, and grandchildren. John, changed in appearance, now sported a red beard and a pipe of which he was very fond.[29]

Time passed too swiftly for Catharine's comfort, and her son made certain that she saw as much as possible. After viewing the graduation ceremony, fireworks, and evening ball, she confessed herself to be quite overwhelmed by the task of remembering the names of all the people she had met. But she found the officers to be "kind and cordial," and their manners and friendliness excellent. Catharine and Jennie left in August after a stay of some two months, the mother pleased with her new granddaughters and the life that her son and daughter-in-law had made for themselves.[30]

In the Fall Fannie Gibbon returned from a six-week visit in Baltimore. Her stay with her parents had been less than pleasant, and she vowed to her husband that she would accompany him to Fort Kearny or wherever the War Department might send him. Within the year she had an opportunity to make good on her promise. In August 1859 Gibbon and many other officers at the Academy were ordered to return to their regiments. Two officers—Lieutenant John T. Greble and Lieutenant Alexander S. Webb—took over his duties, and on 31 August 1859 he and his family left the Point. Their eventual destination was Fort Randall, the Army's frontier bastion on the upper Missouri, where Company H of the 4th Artillery was now stationed.[31]

Gibbon's career to 1859 showed what steady application to duty could achieve for an Old Army officer. By this time he had an assured future in the Army if he chose to stay. His wife was a firm ally, even though she had not yet been exposed to the hardships of life on a frontier post. He was rising in rank and in professional achievement. Army interests and his growing family now began to draw him away from the North Carolina home and its ties. By 1861 these connections would go into suspension indefinitely.

Before his departure for the West Gibbon was able to secure leave "for the benefit of his health," to extend until 1 June 1860. In March 1859 he had been incapacitated by pleurisy, and he was still recovering. On 3 December the Gibbons arrived in Charlotte, and Dr. Gibbons had the first sight of his daughter-in-law and grandchildren.[32] Christmas was especially joyful that year, but over it hung the prospect of a long separation and an even grimmer specter—the rising threat of a national rift. By this time the news of John Brown's raid on Harper's Ferry had reached North Carolina. Catharine wrote to her sister that "the people are very suspicious of strangers, and on slight ground take up, examine, tar, feather, and shave. Nobody professes a fear of the slaves, or if they do say nothing about it. It aggravates the Southerners that the Northern people make such a fuss about Brown."[33]

John Gibbon refused to allow himself to be disturbed by this news, and spent his furlough hunting, visiting friends, and taking Fannie on a visit to Charleston, South Carolina. There they were the guests of his cousin, Johnston Pettigrew, a prominent young lawyer and future Confederate general whom he would face at Gettysburg.[34]

During his leave promotion to a captaincy reached him, carrying with it the assignment to command Company B of the Fourth, the famous Washington Battery with which he had already served; it was now stationed at Camp Floyd in remote Utah. Early in June the entire family— John, Fannie, nursemaid Mary Monagan, and the girls—detrained at the end of the rail line, Fort Leavenworth, Kansas, to join an army convoy for the seventy-day westward trek to Utah. It was a sizable party with which they were to travel. Half of the 150 recruits were destined for the cavalry and therefore mounted. Sixteen officers and a civilian contract surgeon; six officers' wives; miscellaneous females such as Miss Kitty Heth, bound for Fort Kearny to visit an officer brother; Miss Howard, governess for the children of Mrs. Colonel Edmund B. Alexander; Mary Monagan, and other nurses; and assorted children made up the balance of the party.[35]

Once the column had settled into its march routine, the journey, despite its inconveniences, took on for the families many aspects of a prolonged picnic. Even though in its later stages their trek would take them through country that in recent years had witnessed heavy fighting, with their large escort little was to be feared from Indians. In many cases the assembly of the convoy represented a reunion of old friends and acquaintances. Captains Barnard Bee and John C. Tidball of the infantry, Captain John Buford and First Lieutenant Beverley Robertson of the dragoons all had been contemporaries of John Gibbon as cadets, and Second Lieutenant Francis Beach of the artillery had recently served as a fellow instructor at the Point. Miss Heth was a sister of Gibbon's classmate Harry Heth, now an infantry captain at Camp Floyd. In the closely knit family that was the Regular Army of 1860, any such gathering would find much in common—mutual friends, former posts of duty, shared traditions and memories—to break the ice of new acquaintanceship.

To be sure, there were mishaps now and then to mar the holiday note. In the first mile out of Fort Leavenworth, the mules drawing the ambulance of Mrs. Lieutenant C. H. Morgan (who, brave soul, was traveling manless with a nurse and baby to join the husband who had preceded her to Utah) got out of control on a steep downgrade. They wound up on their backs in the ditch, while the wagon, fortunately intercepted by a tree, hung half upright, two wheels in the air. The enlisted drivers, having sprung to safety during the wild ride, hauled a lustily squalling baby out of the window while John Gibbon, hastily dismounting, handed the mother and nurse out the door, badly frightened but unhurt. A valuable lesson had been learned; thereafter the brakes were locked on every grade.

Although soldiers were available to drive the ambulances in which the women and children rode, Gibbon soon decided to take the reins himself and thus spend the entire day with his family. His temporary duty as commanding officer of the four-man ordnance detachment demanded but little of his time or attention. Soon he was giving his wife lessons in managing a mule team four-in-hand, lounging on the front seat reading popular novels aloud while she handled the reins. The little girls were delighted when their father gave the mules new names. The wheel pair, two steady, sober old fellows, became "Bob" and "Nick" after two of his brothers. The more lively lead mules he christened "Gus" and "Cam" after Aunt Gussie Moale and one of her West Point beaus.

The daily routine was leisurely. Pitched to the capacity of the foot soldiers, an average march covered fifteen to eighteen miles. The families took the road at about half past six, by which time the troops and baggage wagons were already well on their way. After trotting briskly to the head of the column, the ambulances slowed their pace and rode along more sedately until the new camping site was reached around noon.

The process of establishing camp is best described in Gibbon's own words:

The ambulances being lighter than the wagons and travelling faster, the families reach camp in front of the baggage. As we are not yet in the Indian country, each officer with his family as he drives onto the ground previously selected by the Quartermaster selects his own camping place, and halts his ambulance on it. The mules are at once unhitched and either turned loose or picketed in the grass. The ladies and children remain in their seats until the tents are pitched, or if the weather is fine and they feel so inclined descend and walk about. As the wagons come in they are directed to the different positions convenient to the camping places. When they halt the drivers unhitch the mules and turn them loose with long ropes attached to their necks by means of which they are afterwards caught. They are then all taken charge of by two or three men, mounted, and driven to water and good grass, where they feed till near night when they are driven up, caught and fastened to the wagons or to picket pins for the night. As soon as the men reach camp, they are assigned their positions, and the mounted men, after unsaddling their horses and picketing them, are detailed in parties of 4 or 5 to pitch the officers' tents, unload the wagons, fetch wood and water, carry in the bedding &c. In this way an hour after the arrival in camp the ladies and children have a comfortable place to retreat to, to wash, dress and rest themselves. As we usually take a lunch about 9 or 10 o'clock there is no hurry about dinner which we usually take about 5. After the tents are pitched and every thing in order, I take my gun and dog and jumping on a pony sally out to see the country and shoot for our table.

The fruits of hunting and, when opportunity offered, fishing served to eke out a diet that was nourishing but must have become monotonous. A supply of fresh meat was provided in the traditional military form of beef on the hoof. Milk was deemed a great luxury, and a few milking cows with their calves were brought along for the benefit of the officers. Privately owned cattle could be driven with the government herd, and John Gibbon bought a cow and calf to take to Utah. The investment did not prove a sound one. The calf died a few days later after a hot march of twelve miles, and the cow became so weak that it could not continue the trek and was sold at a loss two days west of Fort Kearney.

For variety from the conventional recipes, John taught Fannie the soldier's way of roasting a beef head in the ground. To prepare it, the horns were knocked off, and the skin, left on, was tied around the neck to exclude dirt. A hole large enough to receive the head was dug, and a hot fire built therein. When the earth had been thoroughly heated, the fire was shoveled out; the cook then threw the head into the hole, covered it with three or four inches of earth, and built over it the camp fire, which was kept going all night. In mild weather, or when wood was scarce, two nights' roasting might be necessary. In any event, when done, "the meat is very soft and tender and the tongue like marrow."

With desiccated vegetables they had less success. Gibbon became too ill from indigestion to take his turn as Officer of the Day and attributed his trouble to "eating soup made of dessicated [sic] vegetables and bad water." When he learned that Fannie also credited a previous bout of stomach upset to the vegetables, they were banished from the Gibbon diet.

After two and one half weeks of travel, a brief stop at Fort Kearney, Nebraska Territory, offered a welcome interlude from the rigors of the road. Except for its name, the post offered little resemblance to a stronghold. Lying a few hundred yards from the south bank of the Platte, it consisted of an open square on the prairie surrounded by the barracks, quarters, and other buildings of the garrison. Apart from the flagstaff, the only martial air was provided by a dozen 24-pounder cannon, incongruously mounted on gun carriages designed for service in the casemates of a stone masonry fortress. The buildings—mostly frame, although there were some mud huts dating from the original establishment of the post— were fast falling into decay; the $60,000 that Congress had recently appropriated for erecting suitable buildings was evidenced only by the substantial quarters of the post commander.

Despite the dilapidation, the Gibbons were only too happy to accept the offer of Lieutenant Thomas J. Berry of the 2nd Dragoons, who rode out ten miles to meet the column, deliver the latest news, and tender the use of his two-room house for the three days of their stay. Taken all in all, however, even allowing for a good water supply and adequate provision for storing up ice in the winter, John Gibbon concluded that Fort Kearney was not the place he would choose for a summer residence. His disposition was not improved by receiving the intelligence that in Utah the department commander had temporarily reorganized Battery B and sent it into the field to operate as cavalry against the Indians—a measure that, in Gibbon's view, obtained the services of an indifferent troop of dragoons at the cost of the only artillery in the territory.

From Kearney the road led westward up the south bank of the Platte. The party was now in buffalo country, and its first view of the beasts was enlivened by the sight of a would-be huntsman, First Lieutenant John B. Villepigue of the 2nd Dragoons, mounted on a mule, giving vain chase to the herd. The Fourth of July came and was duly observed with a feast to which John and Fannie Gibbon invited two of the bachelor lieutenants, Beach and 1st Lieutenant Nathan A. N. Dudley—"broiled birds, venesen [sic] cooked in a chafing dish with quince jelly, a bottle of which I got at a store close by for $1.75, canned tomattoes [sic], peach pies, and a bottle of champagne obtained from the store for $3." The occasional Pike's Peak wagoner whom they encountered during the day provided fireworks with his six-shooter.

The fording of the South Platte, accomplished a couple of days later, proved eventful. It was completed without casualty, despite the temporary stalling of the Gibbon ambulance in three feet of water when Bob, Nick, Cam, and Gus all balked in midstream. Next came the longest day's march of the trip, a stretch of twenty-five miles in waterless country from Lodge Pole Creek to the North Platte.

As the caravan progressed into western Nebraska the scenery grew more spectacular by the day and inspired the artist in Captain Gibbon. In place of the sketches of camp scenes and Indian tepees that had adorned his earlier letters home, there now appeared views of Court House Rock (which he felt should be rather "Capitol Rock" for its resemblance to the Capitol in Washington), Chimney Rock, and Scott's Bluff.

Three weeks out from Kearney the caravan reached Fort Laramie, Wyoming Territory, where a four-day pause for shoeing horses gave the travelers another respite from the road. The dainties offered by their hosts of the garrison—oyster soup, roast chicken, boiled mutton, and iced champagne—were a welcome change from the simple camp fare, and the brief stay was enlivened by an evening parade during which the troops passed in review at double time to "Pop Goes the Weasel," played by the 10th Infantry band. Captain Bee, who was to remain at Laramie, found that the quarters assigned him contained a cook stove, and John Gibbon promptly struck a bargain to buy the one that Bee had brought with him, an article that was reported to sell in Utah for $150.

On the next leg of the journey Fannie Gibbon fell victim to a prank perpetrated by her husband. On returning from one of his hunting excursions, he handed over three wild fowl that he identified as a kind of large black bird native to Wyoming. After they had been eaten ("declared by all hands as rather insipid"), the huntsman revealed to his wife and their guests that they had just dined on young crows. Colonel Philip St. George Cooke, the senior officer of the party, had been let in on the secret by his prudent host, and "stuck industriously to the rabbit" which was also on the menu.

Up Sweetwater Creek and through South Pass the road led over the Continental divide. This was familiar territory to Colonel Cooke, who had made a difficult march with his 2nd Dragoons over this same route in 1857, en route to join General Albert Sidney Johnston in Utah. He had lost nearly half his animals in the trek, and on the stretch between Little Sandy and Big Sandy Creeks in southwestern Wyoming, pointed out to his companions the place where seven men had been frozen to death and his starving mules had eaten up the wagon tongues. At several points a circle of black ashes marked the traces of an Army wagon train that had been burned by the Mormons while corralled for the night—grim reminders of the reasons for the Army's presence in Utah: to watch the Indians and to ensure the supremacy of the federal government in this Mormon-dominated area.

The final pause in the trip was at Fort Bridger, in what is now the southwestern corner of Wyoming. The green sod of the parade ground and the whitewashed cottages that served as family quarters offered a pleasing contrast to the desolate country just behind. Several well-stocked trout streams flowed through the post, and Gibbon found ample opportunity to display his prowess as a fisherman during a three-day halt devoted to the usual routine of shoeing horses and repairing wagons. One more week on the trail completed the journey. On 18 August they arrived at Camp Floyd, forty-five miles south of Salt Lake City.

Gibbon formed a poor opinion of Mormon society. He later wrote: "Is it any wonder that in a community so governed, where all instruction is given by the church, that all true education is at fault, and that ignorance should prevail?"[36] But he enjoyed the contact with Mormons, if for nothing else than the opportunity of dangling theological bait in front of them. And the post offered ample opportunity for him to engage in his favorite pastimes, hunting and fishing.

His wife, on her part, now set about making a home for her family of four. Mary Monagan soon left them to marry a sergeant and Fannie was forced to act as her own chambermaid, nurse, and "chief of all work." Gibbon, however, managed to secure an orderly to help her in the kitchen and they were able to give a supper party for their fifth wedding anniversary. Her husband told her that she never was so contented in her whole life.[37]

Camp Floyd lay at the end of a tenuous communication line to the East. The telegraph reached only to Fort Kearney, and Pony Express riders carried mail and official correspondence to the post. Stationed there when Gibbon arrived were the headquarters of the 2nd Dragoons, with three companies of cavalry and two of the 10th Infantry. The remainder of the garrison consisted of Companies A, B, and C, 4th Artillery.[38]

Commanding these units were officers whose names would later become familiar in the Civil War. The Department of Utah chief was Colonel Cooke, who also commanded the 2nd Dragoons. Gibbon's classmate Captain Henry Heth, who would later face him as a Confederate general, had been post commander, but Lieutenant Colonel Charles F. Smith, the future hero of Fort Donelson, replaced him in the shuffle of officer assignments that resulted from Colonel Cooke's arrival. Other officers who would distinguish themselves in the near future were Stephen Weed, Alfred Pleasonton, and the efficient leader of a company of the 2nd Dragoons, Captain John Buford, with whom Gibbon formed a strong rapprochement.

Gibbon's activities were largely confined to his artillery duties. He took command of B Company upon its return to the post on 5 October, and served in addition as post ordnance officer. Soon he led out detachments on Indian patrol, using his artillerymen as mounted infantry.[39]

By December, with North-South antagonisms further exacerbated by the election of Abraham Lincoln to the presidency, the threat of internal disruption, deriving from the national political situation, began to pervade the Army. Nor were Gibbon's parents immune to trouble and apprehension. "An indefinable dread of something" had taken hold in the South. Catharine reported to her sister that secession was the chief topic of conversation; that "the people were perfectly rabid." The citizens of Mecklenburg County resolved to follow South Carolina out of the Union.[40]

John Gibbon's position as an officer and a Southerner, the son of a minor slaveholder, placed him between the competing forces of loyalty to his country and the Army on the one hand and to his state on the other. He later made it very clear that he knew what the 1860 election meant, for both him and the nation. And there were few to whom he could turn for advice. The Camp Floyd garrison continued to contain a high proportion of Northern officers, and few with Gibbon's background. As national tensions began to rise, the Buchanan administration fumbled for a policy, events soon outran any control, and more ominous news came from Gibbon's home state. At the end of November a refugee from South Carolina passed through Charlotte on his way to New York City. The vigilantes in Charleston had shaved half his head and put him on a stage, express "to Horace Greeley." He had also been horsewhipped.[41]

At Camp Floyd, each Pony Express rider was greeted by the garrison with a mixture of curiosity and apprehension. When the rider brought the news of the fall of Fort Sumter, officers of Southern background or sympathies found themselves facing a painful choice. As Gibbon later wrote, "All were quiet, serious and thoughtful as we wound our way back to our quarters to tell our wives and children that all our hopes of peace were blasted, and that our once happy and prosperous country was plunged into the horrors of civil war, the end of which no man could foretell."[42]

The complications engendered by the onset of actual hostilities soon swept over the post, now renamed Fort Crittenden in honor of Senator John J. Crittenden, a staunch Unionist from Kentucky. (Secretary of War John B. Floyd, the Virginian from whom its original name derived, had resigned from the Cabinet in January and Virginia had seceded in April.) These complications involved several officers, including John Gibbon. Despite his Pennsylvania birth, Gibbon felt state ties to North Carolina. His parents were Democrats, and at one time his father had held or leased twelve slaves or more. Although they held moderate opinions on the subjects of slavery and politics, the family had no patience with abolitionists or even for talk of ending the institution on a gradual basis.[43]

Not only did Gibbon's background raise problems, but so did the actions of his brother officers. Henry Heth, who was on leave, resigned after Virginia seceded, as did John Esten Cooke, the son of Colonel Cooke. Soon the post adjutant, Captain Beverley Robertson, also resigned, and now Gibbon, his loyalty suspect, became embroiled in controversy with fellow officers.[44]

Gibbon had never opposed the idea of officers' resigning from the Army. As witnesses later reported, he defended the right of every officer to follow his state, and pointed out to the men from the North that they did not have this problem. He did not, however, reveal what his own course would be. The choice would have to come soon; North Carolina left the Union on 21 May 1861.[45] By now, Gibbon later wrote, the officers from the South were ". . . looked upon with a certain amount of suspicion not calculated to add to the social feeling among us."[46]

Curiously enough, a song brought the awkward situation to a head. On

Friday, 14 June, the small figure of Fannie Gibbon, his five-year-old daughter, was seen during evening band concert to walk from her father's house to the bandmaster. She whispered to him, and soon the strains of "Dixie" sounded over the post. The episode raised a storm. Gibbon obviously had sent his daughter to request the tune. Complicating the situation was the fact that the new post adjutant, Lieutenant John Green, a Unionist, had forbidden the playing of the song unless ordered by Colonel Cooke; a further complication was that at the moment Gibbon was the ranking officer present on the post, hence temporarily in command.

What motivated Gibbon in this astounding act of political naivete remains a matter of conjecture. Although the song was not yet firmly established as the anthem of the Confederacy, its associations were clear to any intelligent person. Cooke had wisely refrained from waving any sort of red rag. Logically, Gibbon should have known better. It may have been a considered maneuver. It is quite possible that John Gibbon had taken enough interrogation about his loyalty and desired to throw something back at his inquisitors. The resulting blast came close to driving him from the Army.

On 15 June, Major Franklin E. Hunt, Captain Robert E. Clary, and Surgeon J. B. Porter wrote a joint letter to the Secretary of War, reporting that they had uncovered a secessionist conspiracy at Fort Crittenden that threatened to spread to the Department of Utah. This letter, a remarkable combination of Unionist ultra-patriotism, charges of guilt by association, and third-hand testimony, began with a fervent protestation of rectitude: "We the undersigned, believing that forebearance may cease to be a virtue and may under present circumstances become a crime, or in other words that duty to our country . . . requires every good citizen to expose treason and rebellion and the aiders and abettors of traitors and rebels. . . ."[47] It continued with accusations directed at members of the territorial government; the territorial governor, one A. Cummings, was a secessionist, as were the treasurer and the only judge remaining in Utah. The three watchdogs of loyalty then turned to the Army. Colonel Cooke, with his son and son-in-law (Lieutenant J. E. B. Stuart) out of the Army, was contemplating refusing to fight against Virginia. Moreover, Cooke had shown partiality to officers who had deserted, or tried to, before resigning. A member of his command had proposed a toast, "The assassination of Lincoln and Hamlin before the 4th of March," and others had openly displayed secessionist tendencies. Among these were Lieutenant Wesley Merritt, Lieutenant William P. Sanders, and John Gibbon; his crime was the playing of "Dixie." Having covered all possible instances of treason, the three men signed the letter and sent it directly to the War Department, without having it endorsed by Cooke and forwarded through channels.[48]

By 17 June news of the communication found its way around the post, and Gibbon, furious at the backhanded assertions, confronted Hunt in his quarters and demanded to see the letter. Colonel Cooke likewise was not amused, and, calling the three men to his office, ordered them to turn over copies of the correspondence and then explain why they had broken Army regulations themselves in going over his head to the Secretary of War.[49]

Gibbon also mounted a counterattack. He immediately wrote to the Adjutant General, Lorenzo Thomas, refuting all the charges against him. Declaring the entire matter "too childish and absurd to notice," he asked Thomas to contact General Winfield Scott if he required a character reference. He also emphasized the clandestine nature of the whole affair. Specifically, Gibbon made four main points: (1) that he would not resign if North Carolina seceded; (2) that he had repeatedly said that his duty lay with the federal government and had urged this course on others; (3) that he had always regarded his oath of loyalty as permanently binding; and (4) that he did ask the band to play "Dixie," but was unaware of its forbidden nature or its political implications. For someone who had once had trouble with the English language, it was a forceful letter. He concluded: ". . . I remain true to my allegiance, and ready to abide by the terms of my oath, to defend the U. States against all her enemies or opposers whatever."[50]

Cooke added further ammunition to this countermove, denying the impugning of his loyalty and assuring his superiors of Gibbon's. On 19 June Gibbon confronted Clary, who promptly expressed his "deep regret for doing such an act."[51] Clary then reversed himself, and he and the two others wrote again to the Secretary, saying that they would send affidavits and a list of witnesses by the next pony express rider. Cooke managed to intercept this correspondence, so the conspirators had to send duplicates, which Clary refused to sign. Cooke then forwarded the entire packet, announcing that he planned to prefer charges and cogently remarking that the treason charges were being made just as "many promotions by selection are to be made in the increased Army."[52]

By early July the entire affair had clearly grown out of hand, and all the participants were perhaps eager to resolve the matter. Gibbon demanded a formal court of inquiry, which convened on 5 July to determine if a court-martial should be ordered. Cooke's accusers tried to question his loyalty by asking if he had lately taken the oath [of allegiance to the United States.] The court's president dismissed this as not germane to the issue. Quartermaster Clerk Putz testified that Gibbon had said to him, "We had 'Dixie' played down here last night—sorry you were not here."[53]

Cooke and Gibbon jointly charged the three "patriots" with violation of the Articles of War and disrespect to a commanding officer. However, the court ended the affair on the day that it met. It found that "there is nothing in the evidence before it which can impeach the past or present loyalty of Captain John Gibbon, Fourth Artillery. . . ." Gibbon, the court decided, had made the statements attributed to him, but no criminality was attached. He had also ordered the playing of "Dixie." Quite clearly, the Army wanted nothing more to do with the business, and promptly consigned all the papers to the files.

For the rest of his life Gibbon regarded the entire episode as distasteful. References in later letters to his wife and in his reminiscences, written twenty years after the war, reflect an undercurrent of bitterness and anger. He had avoided controversy up to this point, and had no desire to become a controversialist. During the episode he acted wisely in saving his career, even if he and some other officers had been a bit free with their opinions in a confused time.

This may have been the final influence that kept Gibbon from joining the Confederacy. While the available evidence seems to indicate that by June 1861 he was fairly well decided on staying with the Union, the accusations pushed him into making that decision definite. However, Gibbon was a remarkably uncomplicated person; basically unsubtle, he never really saw his oath as other than binding. His ties were to the Army and his family, not to his state or to a political abstraction. Unlike Robert E. Lee, John Gibbon left no record of real anguish over his choice. His refusal to follow his state was a case in which the path of least resistance coincided with his preferred course of action.

The day of 5 July 1861 was eventful to John Gibbon for quite another reason than the findings of the court that cleared him. John Gibbon junior was born.

NOTES

1. Catharine L. Gibbon to Fannie Lardner, 29 January 1849, Gibbon Papers, Historical Society of Pennsylvania ("HSP") (hereafter cited as CLG to FL.)

2. The authors are indebted to former Representative Peter Frelinghuysen, Jr., and Dr. Ernest S. Griffith, Director of the Legislative Reference Service, Library of Congress, for much background information on a number of Native American tribes, including the Seminoles. Letter of Dr. Griffith to Representative Frelinghuysen, 5 March 1958; letter of Representative Frelinghuysen to Mark H. Jordan, 6 March 1958.

3. *Charleston Courier,* "Another Indian War,—Outbreak of the Indians," 23 July 1849.

4. CLG to FL, 19 August 1849, HSP; Major W. W. Morris to Major General R. Jones, 25 July 1849, quoted in *Charleston Courier,* 8 August 1849; John Gibbon, "Reading Signs," *Journal of the Military Services Institution,* December 1884, 22.

5. Gibbon, "Reading Signs," 22.

6. Gibbon told this story on himself in "Reading Signs," 24.

7. Gibbon, ibid.

8. Gibbon, ibid.

9. Orders, No. 32, 19 October 1849, Western Division, United States Army, AGO, NA, RG 94; Robert Utley, *Frontiersmen in Blue: The United States Army and the Indian, 1848–1866* (New York, 1967), 128.

10. John Gibbon, *An Address on the Unveiling of the Statue of Major-General George Gordon Meade,* in Philadelphia, 18 October 1887 (Philadelphia, 1887), 3.

11. Orders, No. 51, 25 December 1849, Western Division, United States Army, AGO, NA, RG 94; Monthly Returns, Company B, 4th Artillery, January 1850, AGO, NA, RG 94; CLG to FL, 3 March 1850.

12. CLG to FL, 29 April 1850; Monthly Returns, 4th Artillery, various months, 1850, AGO, NA, RG 94.

13. General Orders, No. 29, Adjutant General's Office, 1 October 1850, AGO, NA, RG 94; CLG to FL, 8 October 1850, 1 February 1852, HSP; Monthly Returns, 4th Artillery, September 1850; Special Orders, Adjutant General's Office, No. 155, 26 December 1851, AGO, NA, RG 94.

14. CLG to FL, 18 July, 4 August, 13 August, 1852, HSP; Special Orders No. 52, 21 March 1853, AGO, NA, RG 94.

15. Charles H. Coe, *Red Patriots* (Cincinnati, 1898), 209; CLG to FL, August 5, 25 September 1853, 16 April 1854, fSP; Special Orders, No. 29, Headquarters of the Army, New York City, 20 May 1853.

16. Special Orders, No. 135, 9 August 1854, AGO, NA, RG 94.

17. Catharine's letter to her sister of 5 August 1855, establishes the initial meeting during Gibbon's Washington tour of 1852–1853.

18. Except for specifically cited material, the story of Gibbon's courtship and marriage is family history, related to Mark H. Jordan by the late Mrs. Bancroft Hill, Baltimore, Maryland (John Gibbon's granddaughter.)

19. CLG to FL, 5 August 1855, HSP.

20. Monthly Returns, U.S. Military Academy, September 1855, NA; Special Orders, No. 143, 14 September 1855, USMA Archives.

21. Copy, Certificate of Marriage, 16 October 1855, Cathedral of the Assumption, B.V.M., Baltimore, Maryland.

22. CLG to FL, 3 October 1854, 4 November 1855, 26 February 1856, HSP.

23. Special Orders, No. 62, 16 April 1855, USMA; Special Orders, USMA, No. 117, 6 August 1856; Special Orders, No. 118, 7 August 1856, USMA Archives.

24. John Gibbon, *The Artillerist's Manual* (New York, 1859), xi.

25. U.S. Congress, commission appointed under Act of 21 June 1860, to examine the organization of the United States Military Academy, Report (Washington, D.C., 1860), no page.

26. CLG to FL, 9 November 1855, 26 July 1858, 26 February 1856, HSP.

27. As assistant instructor in artillery tactics, Gibbon was responsible for teaching the following topics: nomenclature and design of all artillery types and their employment; the science of gunnery, both theoretical and practical; and practical ordnance and manufacture of firearms, both cannon and small arms. (U.S. Military Academy, Regulations, 1853.) When police officer, his first task was to forbid the free ranging of cattle on the post, and particularly on the parade ground. (Special Orders, No. 80, 23 May 1859, USMAA.) For his detached service, see Special Orders, No. 88, 20 June 1857, and Special Orders, No. 93, 17 June 1859, USMAA.

28. CLG to FL, 22 March 1857, HSP.

29. The details of the visit may be found in CLG to FL, 13, 17 June, 26 July 1858, HSP.

30. CLG to FL, 5 December 1858, HSP; Special Orders, No. 77, 2 August 1859, Headquarters, U.S. Army; Special Orders, No. 157, 31 August 1859, USMAA.

31. Special Orders, No. 175, 23 September 1859, AGO, NA, RG 94; CLG to FL, 6 March and 11 December 1859, HSP.

32. CLG to FL, 11 December 1859, HSP.

33. CLG to FL, 11 December 1859, HSP.

34. CLG to FL, 12 February 1860, HSP.

35. The journey across the plains is described in a number of letters in the Gibbon papers, HSP.

36. John Gibbon, "Life Among the Mormons," *American Catholic Quarterly Review*, October 1879, 664.

37. CLG to FL, 2 December 1860, HSP.

38. John Gibbon, *Personal Recollections of the Civil War* (New York, 1928), 3; Monthly Returns, Camp Floyd, Utah Territory, August 1860, AGO, NA, RG 94.

39. Monthly Returns, 4th Artillery, October 1860, AGO, NA, RG 94.

40. CLG to FL, 2 December 1860, HSP.

41. CLG to FL, 2 December 1860, HSP.

42. Gibbon, Recollections, 5.

43. CLG to FL, 1 February 1852, HSP.

44. Monthly Returns, Camp Floyd, Utah Territory, October 1860, May 1861, AGO, NA, RG 94.

45. E. B. Long, *The Civil War Day By Day* (New York, 1971), 76.

46. Gibbon, *Recollections*, 5.

47. John Gibbon to Lorenzo Thomas, 18 June 1861; J. Porter, Franklin E. Hunt, and Robert E. Clary to Secretary of War, 15 June 1861, File 21 U 61, Letters Received, AGO, NA, RG 94.

48. Porter, Hunt, and Clary, File 21 U 61, Letters Received, AGO.

49. Philip St. George Cooke to Lorenzo Thomas, 17 June 1861, File 21 U 61, Letters Received, AGO.

50. Gibbon to Thomas, File 21 U 61, Letters Received, AGO; Cooke, in a telling phrase, described them as "hearsay informers of the Titus Oates class." Cooke to Thomas, File 21 U 61, Letters Received, AGO.

51. Clary to Gibbon, 19 June 1861, File 21 U 61, Letters Received, AGO.

52. This statement and the following details of the affair may be found in the record of the court of inquiry, File 21 U 61, Letters Received, AGO.

53. Court of Inquiry, File 21 U 61, Letters Received, AGO.

3 New Command, New Responsibilities

While John Gibbon made his choice between loyalties, events in the East both unraveled the ties of Union and complicated his family relationships. When Lincoln called for 75,000 volunteers on 15 April, John's brother Nicholas left the Jefferson Medical School in Philadelphia and made his way back to North Carolina. There he enrolled as a cadet in the North Carolina Military Institute. At Raleigh he drilled volunteer troops. Robert accompanied him as surgeon to the cadets, who would be incorporated into the 1st North Carolina Volunteers. Daniel Harvey Hill, John's friend, became its first colonel. Lardner, the eldest brother, also accepted a commission in the Confederate forces and joined the Ordnance Bureau at Richmond.[1]

The paucity of regular troops in the East dictated the War Department's policy of concentrating all available formations there as soon as possible, and Fort Crittenden soon became expendable. Colonel Cooke made preparations to march his command to the East, destroying what government property could not be moved. Usually surplus supplies were sold to the public at auction, but to allow munitions to fall into the hands of unfriendly Mormons would be pure folly. So Cooke told Gibbon to destroy all excess arms and ammunition. For days Gibbon and his men smashed the stocks of muskets and consigned thousands of cartridges to bonfires. A shortage of wagons and teams even forced the men of Gibbon's battery to abandon some personal possessions.[2]

None of the eager curiosity that marked the Gibbons' trip to Utah accompanied the grim march east. Rumors that Mormons would attempt to run off the horses and cattle put the command on a nervous alert. Cooke decided against approaching Salt Lake City, and detoured the column east through Timpanogas Canyon. On 1 August, in Echo Canyon, an express rider overtook the party, and told them that First Bull Run had been fought eleven days earlier. "Good God," said one of the dragoons, "there will be no government when we get there."[3]

Marching at a steady twenty miles per day, the Crittenden garrison, its ranks swelled by troops from Fort Bridger, arrived at Fort Leavenworth on 6 October. Here Gibbon found an old letter from brother Robert, predicting that North Carolina would secede. At first Gibbon thought he would be joining John Fremont in St. Louis, but on 10 October, Battery B left for Washington. Travel through sharply divided Missouri presented problems and raised anxieties about personal safety. At Ironton, where the men and equipment were loaded on a train, a company of Confederates could be seen. The railroad bridge at St. Joseph, burned by saboteurs, had to be repaired; here Gibbon mounted two six-pounders on flatcars to discourage possible attacks. At least once the command was obliged to detrain and go around destroyed bridges. Once over the Mississippi at Quincy, Illinois, the journey through Chicago, Pittsburgh, and Baltimore was uneventful. On 19 October, the battery went into camp in the vicinity of the Capitol.[4]

Gibbon immediately became caught up in Major General George B. McClellan's reorganization of the Army of the Potomac. As an experienced gunner and a West Point graduate his talents were invaluable and brought him larger responsibilities. Meanwhile he started to put his own command in order. A battery of field guns was equivalent to a company, and that meant a lot of men to supervise (148 officers and men), and a mass of equipment to maintain. The standard ordnance was the twelve-pounder Napoleon cannon, a brass smoothbore. This was a sturdy, dependable weapon, most effective at short range, when the use of canister converted it into a giant shotgun. Horses provided motive power; six were needed for each gun-caisson combination. In addition there were six spare caissons, a battery wagon (eight more horses to pull this), a portable forge, twelve spare horses, and sixteen saddle horses for the officers, sergeants, corporals, bugler, and guidon bearer. When the battery arrived in Washington, Gibbon found himself eighty-three men short of his required strength, and asked the Adjutant General to supply him with recruits.[5]

Soon Gibbon's battery received its permanent assignment to the 1st Division of Brigadier General Irwin McDowell. In the course of the change Gibbon brought the battery over to Virginia and camped on Munson's Hill. This reassignment was part of McClellan's plan to strengthen the artillery arm. Unlike the regular infantry, which was unfortunately kept together instead of being distributed as training cadres, McClellan made it policy to brigade one regular battery and three volunteer batteries together. This provided the volunteers with experienced trainers and exemplars, and leavened the stolidness of the regulars with the enthusiasm and inventiveness of the citizen-soldier. The three new units that joined

Gibbon were Battery D, 1st Rhode Island Artillery, Durrell's independent Pennsylvania battery, and Gerrish's New Hampshire Battery A. The Rhode Island and Pennsylvania batteries were equipped with the powerful rifled ten-pounder Parrott gun, which had a longer range than the Napoleon. The New Hampshire battery retained the smoothbore gun.[6]

As the only regular battery commander in the division, Gibbon was made chief of artillery. He now commanded the equivalent of a regiment and, thanks to McDowell, he obtained the manpower that Battery B required—from the volunteer infantry. His superior authorized him to recruit the requisite number of men from the various regiments of the division. The bulk of the division were New Yorkers, but some were Westerners of Rufus King's brigade. Gibbon made a special appeal to these soldiers, reminding them that at Buena Vista the battery had supported men from the west. He had small national flags prepared, inscribed with the names of the states represented by the volunteers. Fastening these to the cannons, he told the men that their guns belonged to their states, and it was their duty to defend them. In a sentimental era, when local ties meant much, this was a display of sensitive and effective leadership. He also applied for and received permission to inscribe "Buena Vista" on the battery's guidon, in recognition of its service in the Mexican War.[7]

This reorganization gave Gibbon his first close look at the volunteer soldiers, who were now inundating the tiny ranks of the Regular Army. Although a long-term professional in his outlook, Gibbon remained a marked exception in his opinions about these men. Prejudice against the volunteers was common among West Point graduates, and this new command constituted a challenge to them. Some adjusted and some were abject failures, while others muddled along almost indifferent to the presence of the volunteers. Most of these recruits had spent all of their lives in a free society, whose outstanding characteristic was an absence of regimentation. Most regular officers were unable to understand this and heaped scorn upon their "unmilitary attitudes." George G. Meade, writing after the most terrible battle fought up to that year in North America (Gettysburg), said to his wife, "The men behaved splendidly; I think they are really becoming soldiers." This statement was made a full year after Antietam. General C. F. Smith, a typical product of the Army, referred to the volunteers in equally patronizing terms during the assault on Fort Donelson.[8]

John Gibbon recognized the differences in the new men, but set out to make them work for him. The first fact he noted was "their quick intelligence." Once his men had been told how to do something, the directions needed no repeating. It was always best, if possible, to provide reasons for actions. These men were not regulars, and did not accept orders blindly. He also recognized their drive, initiative, and ingenuity. Part of this was because of the lack of distance between the private soldier and his immediate superior. The power of the volunteer soldier lay in the marked confidence he possessed. Such men could always be led, but seldom driven. One fact about the volunteer was obvious; despite his almost animal courage, if he did not want to do something, no punishment could force him to it.[9]

An acute observer of war has written that "Inside every army is a crowd struggling to get out. . . ."[10] While John Gibbon would never have said this, he would have understood it. Training the volunteer meant guiding an immense amount of energy and free-flowing patriotism, enthusiasm, and illusion into disciplined channels. Through training techniques, rote drill, and personal example, a commander had to shape this magnificent raw material into a unit. He had to create "an element compounded of affection for the soldiers he knows, a perception of the hostilities as well as the loyalties which animate a society founded on comradeship, some appreciation of the limits of leadership and obedience, a glimpse of the far shores of courage. . . ."[11]

The Army of the Potomac would always remember the winter of 1861–62 for two things: drilling and mud. In February, *Harper's Weekly* devoted an entire page to pictures of the mud and its effect: a guard detail, calf deep; horsemen whose mounts became sunk to the stirrups; a camp street where men, immersed to the ankles, stood in casual conversation. John Gibbon described conditions to Fannie in succinct phrases: "Not over knee deep in the dry places . . . the whole country is one vast mud hole . . . all the camps are over shoetops in mud."[12] In some of the stables, he reported, ". . . the horses stand knee deep. . . . Fortunately, I have mine in good sheds, where they are comparatively comfortable."[13]

Although Fannie had been staying in Baltimore, in January she brought the three children to Washington, taking rooms in a boarding house at 187 K Street, where her husband could visit them. During the week of her arrival McDowell reported to his superiors on the status of the artillery. Battery B was in good shape, but needed caissons; Monroe's Rhode Islanders were good "for volunteers." So were Gerrish's, but the New Hampshiremen needed much more training. The Pennsylvania battery, Gibbon reported, was "not in a fit condition to take the field"—training again being the drawback. Given the miserable weather, this evaluation is hardly surprising. On 13 February Gibbon was able to find a place "where the mud was only tolerable," and put his battery through the drill manual. But then a thaw started, and the mud became worse. Any attempt to maneuver the heavy guns under such conditions was bound to end in exhausted horses, filthy men, and mired weapons.[14]

Early in the new year Gibbon received one of his saddest communications of the war. He had written to his mother, and about a month later her reply, relayed through Fort Monroe and the picket boat there, reached him. It had not been mailed in Charlotte, for "I have nothing to fear from the intelligent and well-informed, but would not excite the curiosity of the ignorant and prejudiced." She had entrusted the communication to a messenger who could carry it into Union lines. Facing up to the reality of the situation, she advised her son: "Let us be content to know both families are in good health, and wait patiently for more settled times to renew our correspondence." To Fannie and the children she sent her love, and to the son who had made a painful choice, she signed herself "your affectionate Mother." [15]

Besides the separation, Gibbon's inability to attain more than a captain's rank was a source of irritation. Bad enough that Gibbon's classmate McClellan was now general-in-chief; his brother-in-law John Foster was already a brigadier, as was an old friend from West Point, William F. Smith. Gibbon could not hope for the colonelcy of a volunteer regiment from his home state, as could his fellow officers from the North. All of this bothered him. Writing of a dinner he attended at General C. C. Augur's, he remarked that the place was filled "with more Brig-a-Digs, Cols., etc., than you could shake a stick at." But he told Fannie to wait; promotion would come to her "old worthless poor miserable Captain." [16]

March 1862 brought an end to inaction. On 8 March, despite considerable resistance on the part of McClellan, Lincoln established a corps organization for the Army of the Potomac, and named five corps commanders. McDowell now took over I Corps; Rufus King moved up from brigade command to head McDowell's division. Gibbon looked on Lincoln's action, which he regarded as pure politics, with a jaundiced eye. As did many other professional soldiers, he saw war as an affair from which civilians should be excluded. And he had a low opinion of his superiors, later observing that "of the five commanders designated by the President, not one remained at the head of a corps in the army, at the expiration of a year." Few traits marked Gibbon as a regular more than this failure to recognize that the extremely political nature of the Civil War was bound to seep into the conduct of military operations. All wars have political aspects; in a democracy, the two worlds, political and military, could hardly exist apart. [17]

Immediately after the organizational shake-up, McClellan ordered his army to carry out its first field operation. News of a Confederate withdrawal from the Centerville positions arrived on 9 March, and that night McDowell ordered Gibbon to start his four batteries toward Centerville at first light. The rain poured down as the column made its way west. Putting his command into camp four miles west of Fairfax, Gibbon rode over to examine the deserted Confederate camps. As were most of his fellow officers, he was startled by the false "Quaker" guns: logs painted

to resemble cannon. The march back—for no Confederates were found—
led over the battlefield of Bull Run, and others pointed out to Gibbon
where the artillery had been overrun.[18]

With the Confederates gone, McClellan proceeded to put together an
operational plan that would utilize Federal seapower to move his army
within striking distance of Richmond. On 17 March the advance elements
of the Army of the Potomac began embarking for Fort Monroe. While
McDowell waited for orders, Gibbon and his battery lay in camp. He was
in no great anxiety to depart. His new duties as corps artillery chief took
up much time. His daughter Fannie was recovering from a sickly winter,
and John wanted to see her well before he departed.[19]

Gibbon and McDowell's corps remained around Alexandria because
Lincoln feared for the safety of the capital. Originally, McClellan had intended to take the powerful I Corps with him, but on 1 April the War
Department detached McDowell's command from the Army of the Potomac. Nothing could have pleased Gibbon more. He wrote to Fannie, after
the camp had been moved to Bristoe Station, that "the politicians had
better let McClellan alone and attend to their own business—we are of
no use here, but would be of great use to McClellan."[20]

Family matters occupied his thoughts. Since McDowell had been ordered to Fredericksburg, Fannie decided to leave the boarding house and
return to her Baltimore home. Gibbon cautioned her not to allow young
John to "forget his papa, and keep him out in the open air as much as
possible." As for Fannie's living in secessionist Baltimore, he told her that
"If anything is said in B. distasteful to you, take no other notice than to
quietly remark you don't think such remarks are in good taste considering how you are situated."[21]

McDowell spent most of his time marching and countermarching. A
tremendous rain, ice, and sleet storm thoroughly bogged down the column. Major General William B. Franklin's division of the corps was ordered back to Alexandria, and Gibbon, exasperated, remarked that
"Everyone is puzzled to know what this marching and countermarching
means."[22]

On 18 April a brigade of King's division, along with Battery B, occupied
Falmouth and watched the Rappahannock railroad bridge burn and fall
into the river. With a party of Confederate cavalry on the opposite bank,
Gibbon succumbed to temptation, and unlimbering two of his guns, fired
into their ranks. The horsemen scattered and disappeared.

As newly appointed provost marshal, Gibbon busied himself with paperwork and protecting property. By posting sentries at private homes,
and vigorously enforcing rules against foraging, he hoped to allay the
fears of the Southerners in the area. And on the 21st, McDowell brought
him word of his nomination to brigadier general of volunteers. Writing
happily to his wife, he bragged, "Did I not tell you so? I knew it would

be along after awhile. You need not be in a hurry and write to me as Genl. Gibbon . . . as you know I am such a great traitor that they may not see fit to put me through the Senate."[23]

Gibbon was quite right to be apprehensive; when the new list of confirmed promotions appeared on the 28th, his name was missing. None of the senators knew anything about him. McDowell ordered him to Washington, and Gibbon sought out General James Wadsworth, a powerful New York politician. A word from him to Senator Henry Wilson of Massachusetts was enough, and on 2 May 1862, the promotion was confirmed. Although resenting political influence in military matters, Gibbon was not averse to bringing politics into the picture when his own interests were involved.[24]

Gibbon's return from Washington took him by steamboat to Aquia Creek, with a stop at Alexandria, where he had an experience both embarrassing and personally gratifying. During a visit with a friend at the Army hospital, he was introduced to a Dr. Porter as Brigadier General Gibbon. While Surgeon Porter, Gibbon's accuser in the Fort Crittenden episode, stared in astonishment, Gibbon snapped, "Sir, I have met that man before." Porter soon departed, and Gibbon and the other man erupted in laughter. He later wrote to Fannie, "Was it malicious of me to feel so much satisfaction at his discomfiture?"[25]

In addition to the promotion, Gibbon received a choice assignment from McDowell, command of an infantry brigade. Delighted with this advancement, he was also apprehensive, for "I do not know how I should feel in the infantry." On 7 May he took formal command of the Third Brigade, Rufus King's division. When he put together his staff, he chose familiar faces. Captain J. P. Wood, 19th Indiana, became the assistant adjutant general—"the best volunteer officer I have yet met with." For his two aides he selected 1st Lieutenant Ned Moale, 19th U.S. Infantry, his brother-in-law, and 1st Lieutenant Frank A. Haskell, 6th Wisconsin. West Pointer Joseph Campbell followed him as Battery B's commander.[26]

In seeking the services of Fannie's brother, Gibbon ran counter to the policy of the Adjutant General's office, which opposed the assignment of regular officers to the staffs of generals commissioned in the volunteer service. His request for the appointment of 1st Lieutenant James S. Drum of the Indiana 19th as brigade quartermaster likewise was contrary to the established practice. John Gibbon was a determined man; when Colonel Townsend, the acting Adjutant General of the Army, turned him down, the North Carolinian went over his head to Secretary Stanton. Presently Ned Moale and James Drum were on Gibbon's staff, and thus were sown the seeds of a lifelong feud with the Adjutant General's Department.[27]

Although in service for almost a year, the four regiments of the brigade had never been fully disciplined—certainly not in the Regular Army manner—or even shaken down. Brigadier General King, the first commander, was best described as "bland and genial," universally liked by his men. After King's elevation to lead the division, and until Gibbon assumed command, Colonel Lysander Cutler, 6th Wisconsin, had been temporarily in charge. Cutler, one of whose significant characteristics seemed to be his capacity to irritate, was fifty-six, a grain and lumber merchant and man of means from Wisconsin. When he returned to regimental command, his subordinates rejoiced.[28]

The brigade, of considerable size and excellent raw material, had been formed exclusively from the West. The regiments were the 2nd, 6th, and 7th Wisconsin, and the 19th Indiana. With a total muster strength of 2,888 men, the four units were well officered.[29]

Upon assuming command Gibbon found himself with an unusual collateral responsibility. In withdrawing from the area the Confederates had destroyed much of the railroad connecting Fredericksburg to the Potomac River port of Aquia Creek; reconstruction of this road became a priority task for the army. The skilled lumberjacks of the Western brigade were ideally qualified for the key assignment as bridgebuilders at the two bottlenecks, the crossings of Potomac Creek and the Rappahannock. Erection of spidery timber trestles (Abraham Lincoln was to refer to them as built of "beanpoles and cornstalks") was well under way when the Tarheel general took over the brigade and received a surprise order from McDowell placing him in charge of the Rappahannock bridge construction. The mission stimulated an outrageous pun. In a letter to Fannie her husband assumed a new title: "I now call myself a Bridgeadier General."

Although Gibbon was under no illusions as to the amount of work ahead, he began his training program without reservations. Guilty at the outset of uttering the usual Regular's strictures on the lack of steadiness among certain volunteer units, he soon changed his mind and reported that "I have an excellent brigade." For an initial step, he decided upon regular discipline and adherence to appearances. First came the uniform. Considering the forage cap too casual, he ordered the full-dress hat to be worn daily. This was a formidable affair of black felt, slightly conical in shape, with one side pinned up and with a broad black plume. Along with it went a dark blue frock coat, light-blue collar trim, white leggings and, for dress occasions, white gloves. But what lasted was that hat.[30]

Besides the uniform, Gibbon spent much time on drill and discipline. He thought King had been too lax. His professional soldier's soul could not stand such offenses as destruction of private property. When news reached him of the ripping down of rail fences for firewood, he ordered that the regiment nearest to the dismantled fence rebuild it. When a sentry refused to walk his post, or salute officers, he had to sit on a barrel all day and night. Gibbon recognized that the volunteer soldier dreaded nothing more than the loss of his pride. The threat of shame in view of his peers was a far greater deterrent than physical punishment.[31]

No one escaped the brigade commander's scrutiny. Under King, officers had been excused from reveille. Now all had to attend. Gibbon also began a program of quick daily inspections of each unit, conducted in person from horseback. Once the men saw that not even the officers were exempt from regulations the atmosphere improved, and a spirit of unity began to emerge.[32]

Drill proficiency required attention to detail, and time. This was a subject of great importance; if the unit was to function in battle, it had to develop an inner cohesiveness and strict attention to orally delivered commands received when the regiment might be in the midst of heavy fighting. There was simply no substitute for continual practice. As a veteran later wrote, "There were early morning drills, afternoon drills, evening and night drills, besides guard mounting and dress parades."[33]

Gibbon, who had been acting as an observer at these exercises, was stung when he overheard a remark that he was an artillery officer and did not know anything about infantry. He purchased a copy of Coppee's brigade drill manual and did some intensive study. Soon he was instructing his subordinates and drilling the entire brigade as a unit.

The brigade contained at least one prankster. One morning at reveille, Gibbon walked out of his tent to find his horse outfitted with white leggings. Nonetheless, both officers and men came to respect the new commander. After a poor performance on the drill field, the 2nd Wisconsin's lieutenant colonel wrote, " I was chagrined to see it, because I know that we can drill first rate." He then went on to describe his new superior: "We have a splendid Brig. Genl. He is regular old fire on strict discipline—no officer or man can leave the ranks of the march—or the camp—without his permission. He attends to his troops very closely, knows all that is going on, in fact he is a model Genl." And a private soldier praised the way the new uniform improved the regiment's appearance. The command was starting to take on a new shape and character.[34]

Despite all the new activity, Gibbon was lonely. Separated from his wife and children and never sure when he could see them, he depended on Fannie for news. This she constantly failed to provide, perhaps because the amount of correspondence that Gibbon expected her to produce was an unreasonable one. He wrote to his wife about every three days, and sometimes every day, but she was simply unable to match that pace. As a result, his letters are full of half-jovial, half-angry recriminations. At one time he threatened to stop writing if she did not send him more letters.[35]

But soon summer approached and better weather promised more distraction. On 23 May Gibbon, along with other brigade and division commanders, was summoned to McDowell's headquarters to meet President Lincoln. The chief executive made a bad joke at Gibbon's expense, asking him if he had written *The Decline and Fall of the Roman Empire.* Nevertheless, Lincoln made a favorable impression on Gibbon as an "excellent and honest man."[36]

Although the lingering bivouac opposite Fredericksburg made the war seem distant and unreal, Confederate General Thomas J. Jackson's lightning campaign in the Shenandoah Valley soon brought McDowell back into the war. On 23 May, as Lincoln talked to the I Corps officers, Jackson overwhelmingly defeated the Union garrison at Front Royal, Virginia, and pushed Major General Nathaniel P. Banks' command back across the Potomac into Maryland. Lincoln, taking personal charge, ordered McDowell "to lay aside for the present the movement on Richmond, and put 20,000 men in motion at once for the Shenandoah." By nightfall King's division was six miles north of Fredericksburg, having marched fourteen miles during a day of tremendous heat. On 30 May, Gibbon's brigade pushed on through a Virginia summer's temperatures and rain that turned the miserable roads into clinging mud. One hundred fifty men of the 6th Wisconsin collapsed from heat prostration.[37]

When Gibbon got his men up to Catlett's Station on the railroad, he found that there were not enough railroad cars for all the troops to be transported to Front Royal. So part of the division went on, while he and Brigadier General Marsena Patrick, a fellow brigade commander, put their regiments into camp and waited. They never went any further than Haymarket. Jackson repulsed the encircling Union columns on 8 and 9 June and King reconcentrated, marching his command back to Falmouth by the 11th.

All of this plunging about did little to raise the morale of the Western men. While it seasoned them and got the brigade into better physical condition, the troops thought it stupid. Lucius Fairchild of the 2nd Wisconsin wrote that "this marching and carrying knapsacks is using up the men very fast." Gibbon concurred. Still wishing that he was down on the Peninsula with McClellan, he chided Fannie that she would "be too glad to know I am up here out of danger," and his exposure to the people of northern Virginia brought home the harsh realities of the time. "This horrible war," as he termed it, made him "feel like having the blues thinking what it [the nation] was and what it had become." Family friends had once greeted him warmly. "Now the same people look on me as an enemy and many of them . . . would as soon think of inviting a wolf into their houses." And he missed his family. "I want to see them so much." Looking at the wedding picture he kept, he wrote that it reminded him "of old times when we were young and gay." He was too much of a realist to see any glory in war; by 1862 the tragedy had become almost too self-evident.[38]

At least the brigade had returned to Falmouth with its march discipline in good shape. Gibbon did not have, and never developed, any patience toward stragglers. Once in camp, slackers were arrested and put to work for a week afterward on any disagreeable tasks available. This kept the column together and it was an unthinking man who left his unit to sleep or boil coffee.

But not all was work. Gibbon instituted a program of twenty-four hour passes for the smartest man at guard mounting, and on the fourth of July came a day of chasing a greased pig, horse racing, foot racing, and even a mule race with the winner the one who came in last. When night fell there were speeches, fireworks, and a thirty-four gun salute to the flag.[39]

The return to Falmouth led the brigade to expect an early departure to join McClellan before Richmond. Although Brigadier General George A. McCall's Pennsylvania Reserve division of the same corps left for the Peninsula on 10 June, and his own troops were placed on an hour's notice, Gibbon was lonely enough to gamble against a sudden move. When Fannie suggested that she visit him, an instant acceptance was wired to Baltimore. The Dr. Rose whose house he had occupied as Provost Marshal was to visit Washington and would escort her back to Fredericksburg; another new friend, a Mrs. Ficklen, would put her up. Warned to come prepared for at least a two- or three-day stay, she remained for ten.

The ten-day idyll at Falmouth seems to have been another honeymoon, despite the presence of little John. (His nourishment may well have been the reason for his accompanying his mother; in any event, the girls remained in Baltimore.) The couple found little occasion to go visiting. Shortly after Fannie's departure, her husband went to call on an old family friend living in the vicinity. Miss Scott "abused me very much," he wrote his wife, "for not letting her know you were here . . . I told her I was so busy when you were here, I did not have time to go round much, and so I was, and wish I could be busy in the same way again."[40]

Because of the fiasco in the Shenandoah Valley and increasing dissatisfaction with McClellan, Lincoln and Stanton decided to incorporate all Union forces in Virginia into a new field army under Major General John Pope. Brought east in an attempt to introduce bold, aggressive leadership into the war effort (something which he had demonstrated in the West and which McClellan was not providing), Pope began by reorganizing his "Army of Virginia." McDowell's, the largest formation, became III Corps. Increasing activity around Richmond made the gathering of intelligence vital, and Pope had King patrol the roads with his cavalry in an effort to discover Confederate intentions.[41]

By the end of July, Pope became very anxious over Confederate concentrations in the Gordonsville area, and ordered King to send out a reconnaissance in force to discover what was going on. Gibbon was assigned to command this group. Assembling a column of infantry, cavalry, and artillery, with two days' rations, he took the troops down the Orange Plank Road, and after a hot and dusty day made contact with Confederate cavalry pickets half a dozen miles south of Orange. Further probes established the presence of at least 30–35,000 Confederates within an hour's march of each other. Since he had been instructed to take no unnecessary risks, Gibbon then withdrew.[42]

A week later he went back out to cut the Virginia Central Railroad, one of Lee's main lines of communication. This time he took the entire brigade, plus two regiments of cavalry and eight guns. Leaving camp at 2 A.M. on 5 August, the column divided, with Colonel Cutler marching the 6th Wisconsin, a cavalry regiment, and two guns out the Orange Plank Road and then south on the Spotsylvania Court House Road, while Gibbon took the remainder on a parallel course down the Telegraph Road.

As the day grew increasingly warmer, Gibbon pushed his men along until they had covered fifteen miles. Then numerous cases of heat stroke forced a halt. Cutler had arrived at Spotsylvania Court House by 11 A.M., and continued another eight miles, halting after dark. Here a warning from Gibbon reached him. The cavalry had discovered that a large Confederate force was trying to insinuate itself between Cutler and his base on the Rappahannock.

Cutler, backed up by his subordinates, decided to push forward, and he got the column up to the railroad at Frederick's Hall Station late in the afternoon of the 6th. There the men destroyed two miles of track, all the railroad buildings, a turntable, and a large amount of corn and whiskey. By nightfall they were back across the North Anna River, a burned bridge covering their withdrawal.

Gibbon's column had no such success. With surprise lost, Confederate horsemen began to dog his every movement. The enemy captured the wagons of a supporting Union force (Brigadier General John P. Hatch's brigade of King's division) and some stragglers from Gibbon's column. Gibbon was still seventeen miles from the railroad, facing increasing opposition and the oppressive heat. On the morning of the 7th he moved to the Spotsylvania Road to cover Cutler's withdrawal, and on the 8th the two columns reunited and returned to Fredericksburg. Total casualties were fifty-nine men captured by the Southern cavalry.[43]

In his report Gibbon praised Cutler, giving him the entire credit for any success. It was an encouraging foray. The men had marched well, and had been exposed to enemy fire. Such an expedition was worth months of drill. Although a small affair, the Frederick's Hall raid was a useful shakedown for both Gibbon and his troops.

By this time McClellan's campaign on the Virginia Peninsula had ground to a complete halt. After its defeat in the Seven Days' Battles before Richmond, the Army of the Potomac found itself pinned into a defensive position around Harrison's Landing on the James River. Major General

Henry W. Halleck had assumed command in Washington as General-in-Chief on 23 July; he promptly decided to shift two bodies of troops northward to reinforce Pope—the Army of the Potomac and Major General Ambrose E. Burnside's force from North Carolina. The transfer had to be made by water as far as Alexandria or Aquia Creek; the operation of assembling the necessary transports, making other preparations, and executing the move lasted well into August.[44]

Robert E. Lee had no intention of permitting his antagonists to regroup their forces at leisure. Having achieved the repulse of McClellan's thrust, he began in July to move his Army of Northern Virginia northward from the Richmond area; his objective, to destroy Pope's Army of Virginia before it could be joined by McClellan's veterans.[45]

Events in Virginia were now moving toward a climax. Pope began to concentrate all his available forces, and when Burnside reached Aquia Creek King received orders to take his division to Culpeper Court House. Marching in weather that oscillated between heat and rain, and traveling over the usual wretched roads, King had his command up to Stevensville, six miles south of Culpeper, on the 11th. In a letter to his wife, Gibbon remarked on the number of troops in the area: "Everything around us shows the presence of a large army; the fences are all down, and wagons, men, and horses are spread all over the face of the country." From his camp he could see Confederate pickets. Not two miles away was the littered battlefield of Cedar Mountain, marking the site where Banks had been defeated a few days previously. The campsite was not very attractive. Although the dead had been buried, abandoned equipment, dead horses, and bodies that had been washed out of shallow graves by the rain made the atmosphere very unwholesome. The dead horses had to be burned, producing a smell "not exactly like roast beef."[46]

At Cedar Mountain Gibbon met an old friend from Fort Crittenden, John Buford, now a brigadier of cavalry. Also present was the Fort Crittenden accuser, Robert Clary, a quartermaster colonel on Pope's staff. When the commanding general complained about failures in that area, Gibbon and Buford warned him to expect little else from Clary. Resentment over the year-old incident still galled Gibbon.[47]

Because of Lee's rapid buildup on his front, Pope began to withdraw behind the Rappahannock and ordered King to fall back on 18 August. Ordered to start at 10 P.M., Gibbon was unable to do so because of road traffic. The staff managed to clog the roads thoroughly with supply wagons, and forced the brigade to stand by for twelve hours, without sleep. At 10 A.M. on the 19th the exhausted men were finally able to move out. But the march toward the river was not much better. Somehow the wagon train became lost, and the men had to sleep on the south bank without having anything to eat. Finally the brigade crossed, and found its missing commissary wagons. The retreat even involved a clash with Confederate cavalry. Three men of the Wisconsin regiments went into Confederate prisons.[48]

The next five days saw skirmishing with increasing frequency. At midnight on the 22nd Stuart raided Catlett's Station. Pope's headquarters wagons were captured, but Gibbon's brigade train, parked nearby, was saved in a spirited defense put up by sick men rallied by a sick officer. Lee now resolved upon a desperate move, and ordered Jackson to march his corps around Pope's flank and cut his supply lines. This precipitated the Union disaster at Second Manassas.[49]

Jackson smashed Pope's supply base at Manassas Junction and Bristoe Station on the 26th, burning everything his men could not carry and demolishing the railroad tracks and equipment. Having done so, he retired into hiding in a position east of Gainesville and slightly north of the Warrenton-Alexandria turnpike. Not until midnight did Pope realize his danger, and not until the following morning did he order a concentration at Gainesville. McDowell, who had moved to between Waterloo and Sulphur Springs, was put on a moment's notice to march, and at 10 A.M. the entire corps set out, via the Warrenton turnpike. King's division marched in the center.[50]

By the 28th the division was heading eastward on the Warrenton-Alexandria turnpike, making for Manassas. Suffering from a summer such as only Virginia can provide, and from which night brought little relief, the men were doubtless thankful that August, with its futile marches, and the summer, with its relentless drills under the new commander, would soon be over. When the troops reached Gainesville, they changed formation. Pope ordered McDowell and General Franz Sigel (I Corps) to march so as to sweep the area in their search for Jackson, still in hiding. Sigel was to bear south from the turnpike and keep his right on the railroad. General John Reynolds' independent division would echelon left and rear of Sigel, and King would follow to the left and rear of Reynolds, with his left flank on the turnpike.[51]

The march went slowly over a turnpike filled with traffic. At Gainesville Gibbon saw Buford and his cavalry pass, heading in the opposite direction. East of Gainesville Reynolds' men skirmished with and drove off some Confederate scouts. After noon McDowell called a halt, and Gibbon managed to use this time to feed his troops. Having been on short rations, they welcomed a distribution of fresh beef, although just newly butchered from cattle accompanying the column. Late in the afternoon the march resumed. Pope, now believing that Jackson was near Centerville, ordered McDowell there at once. This meant a return to the pike.[52]

About 5 P.M. King and the division went back to the turnpike, just as the shadows of the setting sun began to streak across the fields. No one knew where Jackson really was, but Hatch's men, of the brigade that led the column, flushed a group of pickets from a suspicious patch of woodland along the highway. Hatch soon marched on. The country through which Gibbon, following Hatch, now moved was gently rolling and covered with alternating fields and woods. To the left of the highway ran a smooth, high ridge, cleared for several hundred yards; on its crest stood the farmhouse of the Brawner family and an orchard. The wooded area that had bothered Hatch was shaped like a slope-sided M and bordered on the north by the cleared ridge. As Hatch's men drew off, they saw a single Confederate horseman studying the column. This man was Stonewall Jackson.[53]

King's division had become dangerously strung out; none of the four brigades was within supporting distance of the others, and all were marching directly under the Confederate guns. Gibbon, at the head of his troops, had his units in this order: 6th, 2nd, and 7th Wisconsin, then the 19th Indiana, and finally the six guns of Battery B. As he and his staff emerged from the shelter of the wood and topped a rise of ground, they swung off the road and started to scan the terrain. From a belt of timber came a troop of horsemen at a gallop. As the mounted column turned and wheeled, John Gibbon realized that this was a battery about to go into action—he had performed that maneuver often enough himself. Jackson had returned to his commanders and given the order: "Gentlemen, bring out your men."[54]

Gibbon immediately sent a staff aide off to summon the battery forward, just as the first salvo screamed over the heads of the 6th Wisconsin, which promptly loaded and lay down in the road. The action became hotter; a shell killed a staff officer's horse, sure sign that the Confederates had the range. Now Campbell brought the guns up, wheeled left of the pike, unlimbered, and opened counterbattery fire.

As Gibbon watched the exchange another section of Confederate guns opened fire to the left beyond the wood, driving the brigade of Abner Doubleday to cover and inaction. Gibbon now rode to the 2nd Wisconsin and ordered its colonel, Edgar O'Connor, to form line of battle and take the battery on the left.[55]

O'Connor was to advance quietly and quickly, Gibbon told him; with speed they might capture the guns. Gibbon went with O'Connor as he led his 500 men in two lines, colors in the center as a guide, up the rise toward the battery. Gibbon then went back and started closing up the rest of the brigade. As the 2nd Wisconsin swept up the rise, the guns fell silent, but at the crest "a perfect flame of musketry" raked O'Connor's ranks. Starke's brigade, 1200 men of Major General William B. Taliaferro's division, took the Union infantry in flank. O'Connor coolly wheeled his battleline to the right—now all that drill paid off—and opened volley fire. Gibbon immediately brought forward the Indiana regiment, leading them to O'Connor's left. There they engaged the five regiments of the Stonewall Brigade. As the Stonewalls approached, the 19th Indiana opened "a most terrible and deadly fire" upon them.[56]

Gibbon now realized that his combative instinct had him overmatched. His line on the left was too short, and about to be flanked. On the right two more Confederate brigades were advancing, and withdrawal would mean a double envelopment and sure destruction. He badly needed support. His next move was to bring up the remainder of the brigade. Cutler's 6th Wisconsin scrambled up the bank and came into action on the far right. Taking advantage of a Confederate error, Cutler was able to flank the 21st North Carolina and drive it off.

With the sun setting, and no wind, heavy clouds of powder smoke began to cover the grim scene on the ridge. The Union line, with the 19th Indiana its anchor on the left in the orchard, faced north. The 2nd and 7th Wisconsin held the center, and the 6th Wisconsin covered the right. Campbell had silenced the Confederate artillery and was now firing canister. Gibbon's 2,000 men opposed more than 5,000 Confederates—the divisions of Taliaferro and Major General Richard S. Ewell. And Jackson had more available. No one was more aware of the desperate nature of the situation than Gibbon. He had already sent Frank Haskell to Doubleday, begging for help. But Doubleday wanted orders, and Rufus King was too ill to provide them. Hatch's brigade was beyond reach. Patrick's brigade did not want to advance against those guns.[57]

Help, however, arrived from an unexpected quarter. Major General John F. Reynolds, a splendid soldier and never one to shirk responsibility, on his own initiative had marched his Pennsylvania Reserve division toward the sound of the firing and then ridden ahead. Once Doubleday had a superior present to tell him what to do, he acted. Two of his regiments immediately moved up to the woods and into the line of Gibbon's brigade.[58]

This was a battle without sublety—purely a straight infantry fight. Gibbon later wrote that it was "the most terrible musketry fire I have ever listened to." There was almost no cover. At places the two lines were less than a hundred yards apart. Neither side could advance, and neither would retire.

There was at least one bad moment, but Doubleday's 76th New York came up just in time to steady the 6th Wisconsin, repulsing three separate charges. Casualties among the officers were high. O'Connor was dying, Major Thomas S. Allen of the 2nd Wisconsin had been twice wounded, Major Isaac May of the 19th Indiana was dead, and Lysander Cutler was wounded. Almost 40 percent of the blue ranks was down, dead or wounded. On both sides the battle lines were marked by well-ordered ranks of the dead. Taliaferro had been struck three times; Ewell's leg had to be amputated; the Stonewall Brigade sustained 40 percent casualties.[59]

When darkness fell the firing died away, and as if by mutual consent, the two forces drew apart. The surgeons and the stretcher parties came in among the exhausted, powder-blackened infantry to carry off those they might be able to help. John Gibbon moved up and down the ranks of his men, thanking them for the fight that they had waged. As the Westerners shook his hand, they noted with amazement that his cheeks were wet with tears.[60]

NOTES

1. Catharine L. Gibbon to Fannie Lardner, 28 April 1861, MHS (hereafter cited as CLG to FL); journal of Nicholas Gibbon; file on Lardner Gibbon as Confederate officer, NA.

2. John Gibbon, "Life Among the Mormons," *American Catholic Quarterly Review*, October 1879, 664.

3. John Gibbon, *Personal Recollections of the Civil War* (New York, 1928), 7.

4. Monthly Returns, 4th Artillery, October 1861, AGO, NA, RG 94; Gibbon, *Recollections*, 8–9; Augustus Buell, *The Cannoneer* (Washington, 1890). (The authors are aware that the authenticity of Buell's claim to authorship of this oft-cited source has been called into question (James I. Robertson, Jr., "The War in Words," *Civil War Times Illustrated*, July 1977, 35.) Such questions notwithstanding, the book demonstrates a remarkable knowledge of events which occurred in Battery B, 4th U.S. Artillery, during the period that *The Cannoneer* covers. For example, the incident at Antietam in which Gibbon personally manned a gun of the battery is described in Buell's book on page 34. Gibbon tells the story himself on page 83 of his *Recollections*, which was not published until 1928. The authors have not found any other account in print. For another example, it is possible to corroborate, in Gibbon and in various unit histories, the details recited by Buell on the recruiting for the battery of volunteers from the Iron Brigade and from other regiments. For these reasons *The Cannoneer* has been accepted and utilized as a source for *Iron Brigade General*.)

5. Buell, *Cannoneer*; Gibbon, *Recollections*, 9.

6. Gibbon, *Recollections*, 10; U.S. War Department, *The War of the Rebellion: A Compilation of the Official Records of the Union and Confederate Armies* (Washington, 1887), I, Pt. 5, 21 (hereafter cited as *OR*).

7. Gibbon, *Recollections*, 14–15; John Gibbon to Adjutant General, 12 January 1862, File 766G, Letters Received, AGO, NA, RG 94.

8. George G. Meade, Jr., editor, *The Life and Letters of George Gordon Meade, Major-General, United States Army* (New York, 1913), II, 125; Bruce Catton, *Grant Moves South* (Boston, 1960), 170.

9. Gibbon, *Recollections*, 14, 38.

10. John Keegan, *The Face of Battle* (New York, 1976), 173.

11. Keegan, *Face of Battle*, 35.

12. *Harper's Weekly*, 22 February 1862, 119; John Gibbon to Fannie Gibbon, 17 January 1862, GP, HSP (hereafter cited as JG to FG.)

13. JG to FG, 20 January 1862.

14. *OR*, I, Pt. 5, 708; JG to FG, 13 February 1862.

15. CLG to John Gibbon, 16 January 1862, GP, HSP.

16. JG to FG, 20 February 1862.

17. Gibbon, *Recollections*, 18; *OR*, LI, Pt. 1, 821.

18. Gibbon, *Recollections*, 16–17.

19. JG to FG, 25, 28 March 1862.

20. *OR*, V, 21; JG to FG, 12 April 1862.

21. JG to FG, 16 April 1862.

22. JG to FG, 12 April 1862.

23. *OR*, XII, Pt. 1, 427–430, 432–437; JG to FG, 19, 21 April 1862.

24. Gibbon, *Recollections*, 15, 27.

25. JG to FG, 8 May 1862.

26. Gibbon, *Recollections*, 27; JG to FG, 22 April 1862; *OR*, LI, Pt. 1, 605.

27. Letters Received File 220G CB62, WD, AGO, NA.

28. Alan T. Nolan, *The Iron Brigade* (New York, 1961), 51; Rufus R. Dawes, *Service with the Sixth Wisconsin Volunteers* (Madison, 1962), 43.

29. Nolan, *Iron Brigade*, 11, 15–17, 51–52.

30. Gibbon, *Recollections*, 27; Nolan, *Iron Brigade*, 53–54.

31. Gibbon, *Recollections*, 27.

32. Gibbon, *Recollections*, 35–36.

33. Unidentified clipping, Gibbon scrapbook, p. 3., GP, HSP.

34. Gibbon, *Recollections*, 59; Dawes, *Sixth Wisconsin*, 44; Lucius Fairchild to Libbie Gordon, 1 July 1862; to father, 15 June 1862, Fairchild Papers, SHSW; Jesse Roberts to brother and sister, 11 May 1862, Roberts Letters, SHSW.

35. JG to FG, 23 May 1862.

36. Ibid.

37. *OR*, XII, Pt. 1, 282; Dawes, *Sixth Wisconsin*, 45–46.

38. JG to FG, 5, 7 June 1862.

39. Gibbon, *Recollections*, 35; Fairchild to father, 20 June 1862, Fairchild Papers, SHSW; Dawes, *Sixth Wisconsin*, 51–52.

40. JG to FG, 25 (?) June 1862. "Miss Scott" may possibly have been Mary Helen Scott, Fannie's attendant at their wedding.

41. *OR*, XII, Pt. 1, 102.

42. *OR*, XII, Pt. 1, 503–504, 519–520.

43. The account of the Frederick's Hall raid is based on *OR*, XII, Pt. 3, 523, Pt. 2, 121–125; Dawes, *Sixth Wisconsin*, 53–54; Nolan, *Iron Brigade*, 64–67.

44. Kenneth P. Williams, *Lincoln Finds a General* (New York, 1949), I, 254–258.

45. Williams, *Lincoln Finds a General*, I, 261–263.

46. JG to FG, 12, 18 August 1862.

47. JG to FG, 15 August 1862.

48. OR, XII, Pt 2, 591; JG to FG, 20 August 1862; Gibbon, *Recollections*, 44; Dawes, *Sixth Wisconsin*, 56.

49. Dawes, *Sixth Wisconsin*, 59.

50. *OR*, XII, Pt. 3, 684.

51. John C. Ropes, *The Army Under Pope* (New York, 1882), 66–67: Williams, *Lincoln Finds a General*, I, 299, 311–312.

52. *OR*, XII, Pt. 2, 337.

53. Dawes, *Sixth Wisconsin*, 61; William B. Taliaferro, "Jackson's Raid Around

Pope," in Charles C. Buel and Robert U. Johnson, eds., *Battles and Leaders of the Civil War* (New York, 1956), II, 509–510.

54. Gibbon, *Recollections*, 51; Taliaferro, "Jackson's Raid," 509–510.

55. Gibbon, *Recollections*, 52.

56. Nolan, *Iron Brigade*, 87.

57. Dawes, *Sixth Wisconsin*, 67, 68; Gibbon, *Recollections*, 52–54, 57; *OR*, XII, Pt. 2, 380 ff.

58. *OR*, XII, Pt. 2, 369, 371.

59. Gibbon says he took 1,800 men into action (*Recollections*, 55.) The brigade returns, August, 1862 (AGO, NA, RG 94), show 2,735 present for duty on 15 August and 1,704 on 31 August. Gibbon may be counting only numbers engaged, not noncombatants and stragglers. The 2nd Wisconsin alone lost 298 out of about 500 engaged. For Confederate losses, see *OR*, XII, Pt. 2, 811–813.

60. Letter of J. A. Watrous, *Chicago Sunday Times-Herald*, 27 October 1895, clipping in GP, HSP.

4 East Wood, West Wood, Dunker Church

As darkness enveloped the battlefield, Gibbon ordered the 19th Indiana to fall back and protect the Federal left. Then he rode off to find King. By this time Hatch had come up with his brigade, retracing his steps when he heard the sound of the firing. Gibbon, outraged at the failure of his command to receive support when it stood on the edge of destruction, freely expressed his anger toward Patrick, Doubleday, and his superior, the increasingly infirm and ill Rufus King. His inaction and that of Patrick "was apparently not explained and is inexplicable today."[1]

While the wounded were collected, the commanders tried to decide what to do. The order to march to Centerville was still in force, but Jackson's presence made it illogical to continue in that direction. Where McDowell was remained anyone's guess. Pope's current orders and dispositions were unknown. Gibbon pointed out that the remaining alternative was to go to Manassas Junction, Pope's last known headquarters. The discussion vacillated and Gibbon, exasperated, took a sheet of paper and wrote out a proposal to go to Manassas Junction. To this the others agreed, and King wrote a note to McDowell advising him of the situation. A staff officer set out to find the corps commander.[2]

Unfortunately, Gibbon did not have all the facts. Previously King had agreed to the suggestion of John Reynolds to concentrate their forces and remain where they were. This would have kept a large force between Jackson and Lee, and it is possible that the division of Brigadier General James B. Ricketts, which had left Thorofare Gap, would also have joined King. When Reynolds learned of King's unilateral withdrawal, King could not be found. Gibbon's suggestion was unfortunate; what was even worse, however, was King's failure, through illness or incompetence, to advise his subordinates of all the alternatives available.[3]

The decision to retreat kept the troops from burying the dead or loading all of the wounded on wagons. Some had to be abandoned to become prisoners, and others had to walk. Brawner Farm was left by Gibbon's brigade with no regrets; as Rufus Dawes said it, it "eradicated our yearning for a fight." For Gibbon the battle marked an end and a beginning. No longer did he look upon his men as well-drilled but green amateurs; he now referred to them as the brigade "I have the honor to command." [4]

Very early in the morning of 29 August, an angry John Gibbon finally found Pope at Centerville. After reporting on the Brawner Farm action, he remained for orders. Pope then decided to plan a general assault on the Confederates by the 30th, having seriously underestimated the speed of the rebel advance and being unaware that Lee and General James Longstreet were about to join Jackson. [5]

Gibbon's tidings that the turnpike was now open to Lee and Longstreet did not bother Pope, who had his own mental picture of the situation. He believed Jackson to be withdrawing. With three corps now on hand, McDowell coming up, and Fitz John Porter's V Corps approaching, Pope decided to have Porter march to Gainesville, and asked Gibbon to deliver the orders. [6]

Porter's men, with King's division in company, started for Gainesville and a head-on collision with the freshest portion of the Army of Northern Virginia. When Porter reached a point three miles from Gainesville he called a halt, and remained there, inactive, all of 29 August. Gibbon deployed his 1,250 officers and men on the high ground northeast of the turnpike. There they stood on the defensive all day and night, although other portions of Pope's army engaged in heavy but inconclusive fighting during the afternoon. [7]

By the 30th Pope's delusions led him into fatal error. Not yet realizing the strength of the force that he faced, and believing Jackson to be in full retreat, he ordered a final assault by Porter and McDowell. Unfortunately, Lee's preparations for a counterattack were almost mature. Jackson was strongly positioned on an unfinished railroad embankment, a short distance north of the Brawner farm where the battle of the 28th had taken place. Lee's other corps, under Longstreet, had come on the scene to join Jackson's; it was posted on Jackson's right, with its line extending across the turnpike. [8]

McDowell jumped off in attack at about 4:00 P.M., with Hatch's and Patrick's brigades in line and V Corps on their right. Gibbon and Doubleday formed the second wave of the assault, with Gibbon deploying his brigade in two lines, then into a single one as it entered dense woods below the railroad grade. As the trees became thick enough to force Gibbon to dismount, he noted that his regiments were starting to lose formation in the thickets. When the railroad embankment came into view, an incredible storm of artillery fire erupted on the left; Longstreet had launched a counteroffensive, catching the Union troops in the flank. The

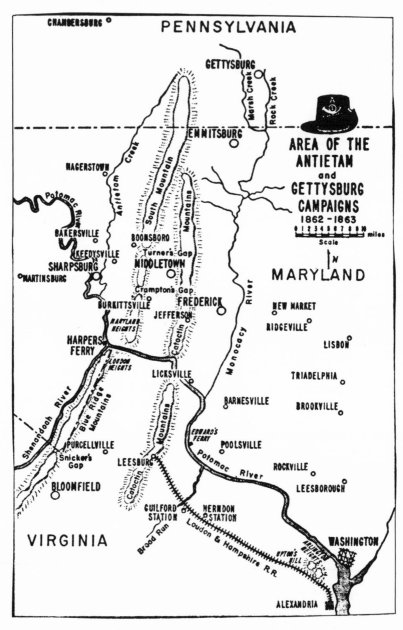

Antietam and Gettysburg Campaigns, 1862–1863. Courtesy Alan T. Nolan, *The Iron Brigade: A Military History.*

leading Union brigade panicked and fled, running into Patrick's men. The retreating regiments soon became a mob that threatened Gibbon's line.

At this, his first sight of battlefield panic, Gibbon took charge. Drawing his revolver, he rushed into the mass of fugitives, shouting at the 6th Wisconsin to fix bayonets, and to "stop those stragglers! . . . Make them fall in! Shoot them if they don't!" Gibbon's steady lines slowed down the flight and his troops held their formation. But even as he sent a company of the 6th out as skirmishers, Confederate shells began to fall around his men, and the whole situation started to come apart. When Porter was repulsed, the withdrawal of his troops sucked Hatch away with them. Gibbon and his lone regiment were isolated. Still exchanging fire with the Confederates, Gibbon withdrew. As he led his unit out of the woods, he removed his hat in salute.[9]

With the Union left now threatened with envelopment, Gibbon's brigade moved back to a line across the Warrenton-Sudley road; Battery B followed the infantry. Here Gibbon found McDowell, who ordered him to stand as the rearguard. Along with General Philip Kearny he watched as the artillery shelled the Confederates. Kearny commented sadly on the situation, and when Gibbon demurred, responded, "It's another Bull Run . . . Reno is not stampeded, I am not stampeded, you are not stampeded. My God, that's about all." Kearny later paid tribute to the Westerners, telling his wife, "The army ran like sheep, all but a General Reno and a General Gibbon."[10]

Undeniably it was a bad defeat. As Gibbon withdrew his regiments over the Bull Run bridge, he saw the detritus of disaster: upset supply wagons, stragglers, columns of confused troops, littered fields. On 31 August the brigade left for Germantown and then Upton's Hill, arriving there on 3 September. On the 1st Gibbon saw Kearny's body being carried back toward Washington. In a fight with Jackson's troops at Chantilly, this good soldier had ridden into the Confederate lines during a rainstorm and had been killed.[11]

On 1 September Gibbon was finally able to get word of his safety to Fannie. Confessing to her that he had felt "personal fear" at Second Bull Run, he said that it had disappeared, "swallowed up by one of anxiety for the result of the battle." And at Upton's Hill the men heard of McClellan's return to command of the Army of the Potomac. "I do not know," Gibbon wrote, "what would have become of us had not McClellan been put in charge." He was quite happy over the conduct of his brigade. "My men behaved splendidly and by their coolness and courage set a good example to some less inclined to be steady."[12]

When Gibbon received orders to take the brigade into Maryland, he had 1,427 officers and men under arms. Marching over the Long Bridge into Washington on 7 September, the troops rested in front of the White

House, then tramped on to Rockville for the night. By 13 September they were approaching Frederick.[13]

McClellan had begun moving the Army of the Potomac toward Frederick when Lee invaded Maryland. On 5 September the two wings of Lee's army crossed the Potomac. Exactly what Lee's plans and dispositions were was unclear, but McClellan maneuvered to keep his army between Lee and Washington. Gibbon thought that Lee was trying to return to Virginia, and that a battle was unlikely. There had been a division command shuffle after Bull Run, with Hatch now permanently replacing Rufus King. Gibbon's predecessor drifted into the backwaters of the war, and then out of the service altogether. McDowell's corps, redesignated I Corps, had a new commander, General Joseph Hooker.[14]

As the brigade went into camp just east of Frederick, Gibbon took the opportunity of a break in the march to visit McClellan at his headquarters. John Gibbon admired no general more than McClellan, and to the end of his life he remained McClellan's partisan and defender. What is more important, he made no effort to keep his views on "Little Mac" out of the public eye. Although he was not as unwise or unfortunate as Fitz John Porter, it is probable that John Gibbon's support of this still-controversial general had a deleterious effect on his career, during the war and afterward.

Gibbon's call on McClellan was not social; his brigade had already sustained heavy casualties, and with few recruits coming into the ranks, he needed reinforcement. He also wanted to maintain its distinctive Western character and spirit. In the company of his West Point classmate, McClellan unbent and readily agreed that the next Western regiment to come into the army would go to Gibbon. Then he revealed an intelligence coup. McClellan took from his pocket a folded paper, showed Gibbon the signature, and said, "It gives the movement of every division of Lee's army. Tomorrow we will pitch into his center, and if you people will only do two good, hard days' marching, I will put Lee in a position he will find it hard to get out of." Lee's Special Order 191, lost by a messenger, had been found by two Union soldiers. It revealed the disposition of Lee's army, now divided into three separate forces, a division that gave McClellan a tremendous opportunity to destroy the Army of Northern Virginia piecemeal.[15]

Gibbon had been particularly impressed by McClellan's handling of his army's march to Frederick. "Little Mac" had "his team well in hand," and was "very quiet, not even a vexed tone in his voice . . . his mind clear and ready to receive and digest the impressions made upon it." South Mountain, a short distance west of Frederick, was now the key to Lee's plan. If he was to concentrate his forces before the Union army fell upon them, he had to hold the passes into western Maryland. His task was further complicated by the multiplicity of routes over the mountain. Four highways provided entry; from south to north, they were the old National Road, at Turner's Gap; the old Sharpsburg Road, at Fox's Gap; the Burkittsville Road, at Crampton's Gap; and the Hagerstown Road, parallel to the National Road.[16]

As Hooker's I Corps crossed into the area below South Mountain, now rising steadily before them, they could hear the crash of artillery and see powder smoke. Major General Jesse L. Reno's corps had already clashed with the Confederate units holding the passes along the old Sharpsburg Road. In front of Hooker stood D. H. Hill's division, five brigades, emplaced in Fox's and Turner's Gaps. If the Union troops had pitched into their opponents at this point, Lee would have had an even worse situation. But Ambrose Burnside, commanding this wing of the army, ordered Reno to halt until Hooker was ready to make a parallel assault north of the National Road. This delay gave Longstreet's corps a chance to come up from Hagerstown.

On the afternoon of 14 September Hooker deployed his three divisions for attack. Brigadier General George G. Meade's Pennsylvania Reserves took position on the right; Hatch's command was stationed nearest the turnpike to his left, with Ricketts' division in support. Burnside ordered Gibbon to return to the National Road and wait. Now the brigade constituted the link between the corps of Hooker and Reno, and an advance would take it directly through the gorge of Turner's Gap.[17]

This was a bad place to attack, because terrain completely favored the Confederates. The ground rose continuously, and the clear zone was only 150 to 300 yards wide. Heavy woods and stone fences crisscrossed the front of the advance, and two masses of hills cut Gibbon off from the remainder of I Corps. From a vantage point in the rear Burnside and McClellan could see all of Hooker's field of combat.[18]

With Battery B unlimbered on the road, Gibbon had his men lie down while he waited for the order to go forward. For about an hour, while Reno assaulted, the men relaxed. Just as the sun began to slip behind the western ridges, Gibbon was ordered to attack the Confederate center. He immediately deployed two companies as skirmishers and broke the brigade into a double line, with the 7th Wisconsin and 19th Indiana in front. This allowed rapid movement over the obstructions, and also permitted Gibbon to re-form quickly into a single line of battle.[19]

Not only was the geography against Gibbon's men; now the setting sun shone in their eyes. When the Confederate pickets opened fire, the Union skirmishers went into action. For a full half-mile these two opposing lines played a deadly game of advance and retreat. A farmhouse provided shelter for enemy riflemen until a shell from one of Battery B's Napoleons sent them out its back door. Gibbon, from horseback, constantly urged the lines on with the orders "Pass forward the skirmishers! Push on, the Seventh! Push on, the Nineteenth! Forward! Forward!"[20]

With dusk rapidly falling, Gibbon's troops reached Hill's main position, held by the brigade of Colonel A. H. Colquitt. As the four regiments assaulted, the terrain forced a maneuver that opened the left flank to a punishing fire from nearby woods. The Southerners were also strongly emplaced behind a stone wall. Against the troops in the woods the 6th Wisconsin went into action. Lieutenant Colonel Edward S. Bragg, commanding in Cutler's absence, formed the regiment into two wings, placed them in tandem, and advanced his left wing through his right, firing volleys. Four such discharges cleared the woods, and the line continued to move forward. Meanwhile the Hoosiers had flanked the Confederates out of their position along the wall.[21]

Gibbon now found that he had three problems: the growing exhaustion of his men, the gathering darkness, and an alarming shortage of ammunition. Cartridge boxes of the dead and wounded were ransacked, and a renewed fire from the Confederates sharply returned. When Bragg's men cheered, no response came; the opposition had gone. About 9:00 P.M. the action ended.[22]

Although the gorge was now securely held, the cost had been high. Hatch's division suffered 496 casualties; Gibbon's brigade accounted for over 300 of those. Thirty-seven men were dead, 251 wounded, and thirty missing. Another 28 percent of the roster was gone. The affair at Turner's Gap showed once again that Gibbon was a good troop leader, fully in control of the situation. The advance had been aggressively pressed, and the drill and training of both officers and men paid off handsomely. Effective use of the artillery helped considerably, and the restrictive nature of the ground kept the units from becoming too dispersed, a constant problem in Civil War combat. Gibbon called it "a pretty heavy fight. . . ." The brigade, he told Fannie, "again distinguished itself very much." But it remained for Joseph Hooker to make what may be his most lasting contribution to the Army of the Potomac. After seeing the relentless advance of the Westerners, he crowed to McClellan, "What do you think now of my Iron Brigade?"[23]

Unable to hold South Mountain any longer, Lee withdrew toward Sharpsburg on Antietam Creek. Gibbon marched the brigade on to Boonesboro on the 15th, then to Keedysville, where the men were finally able to boil coffee and cook some breakfast. As they neared the Confederate defenses, shells began to burst overhead. Doubleday, now commanding the division (Hatch had been wounded at South Mountain), turned his column to the right, up Antietam Creek and beyond artillery range. There the division camped.[24]

The aftermath of the South Mountain fight brought John Gibbon news of his family. From a prisoner he learned of the temporary capture of his brother Robert, now surgeon of the 28th North Carolina. Following the battle at Hanover Court House on the Peninsula in the preceding May,

Robert Gibbon had fallen into Federal hands while tending the Confederate wounded. On the day following he managed to elude his captors and rejoin his regiment. What John Gibbon did not know was that only a couple of days prior to South Mountain his brother Nicholas—captain and commissary officer of the regiment to which Robert belonged—had narrowly escaped a similar fate. While buying a hat in a Boonesboro shop, Nick had nearly been apprehended by a detachment of Federal cavalry; he escaped by hiding in the bushes and vines of the back yard until a countercharge by Gray horsemen routed his pursuers.[25]

Throughout the 16th McClellan examined the ground, wasting another precious day of the advantage that Lee's lost order had given him. This delay provided Lee with further opportunity to complete his army's concentration.

About 4:00 P.M. Hooker received orders to deploy I Corps on the northern flank of Lee's line, which was anchored on the ridge that ran north-to-south to the east of Sharpsburg. Doubleday led the division through the shallow waters of Little Antietam Creek and then turned it south on the Hagerstown-Sharpsburg Road. As darkness began to fall, rifle fire erupted ahead; Meade's skirmishers had struck Confederate pickets from Stonewall Jackson's corps. Continual firing kept Gibbon's troops from sleep until about 9 P.M., when they were allowed to make camp on the farm of Joseph Poffenberger. Gibbon had them lie down in close ranks, muskets loaded. A slight rain began to fall. Without fires, wet, tired, his men must have been cold and apprehensive.[26]

At earliest light a roll of drums aroused the ranks of infantry, and their sergeants called the companies into formation. The rain had stopped, and a slight mist crept over the ground. On that day the whole I Corps did not have 10,000 rifles in the ranks; Gibbon was taking approximately 800 infantrymen into battle. When the 6th Wisconsin formed, Confederate artillery fire found the range. A shell burst in the ranks of the regiment, killing or wounding about a dozen men.[27]

With the casualties removed, the brigade dressed ranks and moved off toward battle. As Gibbon looked south from astride his horse, he saw a prosperous farming region. On the left of the road an enormous cornfield stood ready for the harvest. On its left was a stand of trees, the East Wood. On the right of the turnpike was another, the West Wood, fronted by a split rail fence. Among these three features the ground was slightly open, distinguished by the whitewashed church of the pacifist Dunker sect. A high rail fence ran along both sides of the Hagerstown Turnpike.[28]

Of all the Army of the Potomac's battles, Antietam perhaps stands out as the most confused and the one that wasted the most opportunities. McClellan's battle plan was very unsophisticated; his corps commanders made no real effort to coordinate their assaults, and army headquarters no effort to force them to do so. Hooker's examination of the Confeder-

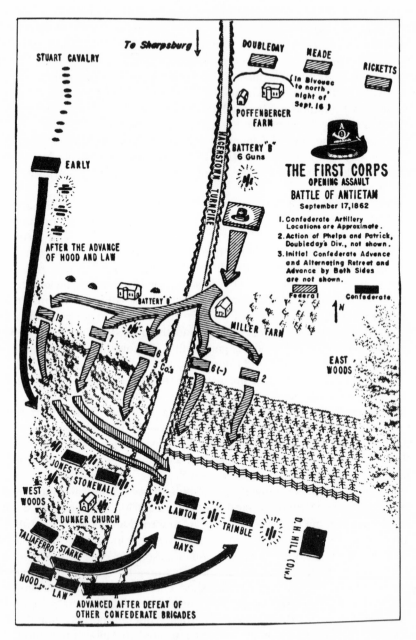

First Corps, Opening Assault at Antietam, 1862. Courtesy Alan T. Nolan, *The Iron Brigade: A Military History.*

ate positions had been desultory. He knew the enemy lay ahead in some strength, but had no exact knowledge of their posting. He also failed to place guns on a height that would have dominated Jackson's flank and rear, and did not consult with his right flank neighbor, Major General Joseph K. F. Mansfield of XII Corps. This meant that Hooker's under-strength corps went into action alone.[29]

The Iron Brigade deployed astride the turnpike just south of the D. B. Miller farm buildings. Gibbon placed the 2nd and 6th Wisconsin on the east side of the road, the 7th Wisconsin and 19th Indiana on the west. Battery B, now under the command of Lieutenant James Stewart, took position just to the left of the Seventh. As firing began, Captain John Kellogg of the Sixth took two companies forward as skirmishers. Hooker then ordered Gibbon to attack, with his objective the Dunker Church. At the edge of the woodlot the Union advance troops began to drive the Confederate pickets back on their main body. The brigade surged for-ward, and the artillery opened fire with shell on the Southern positions. Ahead of the Sixth and Second lay the cornfield; when the sun came out and burned off the mists, its rays reflected off the rifles and bayonets of an entire division of Confederate infantry concealed there.[30]

Gibbon's men came forward at regular walking pace, their rifles held at the charge, making no sound or cheer. Now the battle opened. Rick-etts' division entered the East Wood to cover Gibbon's left flank; the 7th Wisconsin and 19th Indiana climbed a fence and advanced into the West Wood. The other two Wisconsin regiments ran toward the cornfield. The Confederate line, with a sudden convulsive movement, exploded into a storm of projectiles and smoke. Under this fire—what that grim soldier Jubal Early called "a terrible carnage"—Gibbon's lines began to dissolve as he started to lose control over the rapidly separating units. This was not unusual; communication depended on word of mouth and messenger, easily disrupted links. Moreover, the Iron Brigade was moving forward on two distinct axes of advance.[31]

The entire force took a punishing fire from the Confederate infantry. Stewart saw fourteen of his men go down in ten minutes. Bragg and Fairchild fell wounded; command of the Sixth devolved on Major Rufus R. Dawes. Nevertheless, Battery B and the infantry maintained a return fire into the cornfield and drove Jackson's troops back. Now an addi-tional brigade and Meade's division surged forward behind the Western-ers. The church was but one hundred yards away. At about 6:45 A.M., Ewell's division, trying to rally, was shattered by powerful volleys from the brigade and driven off, losing nearly 50 percent of its men engaged.[32]

By now the full fury of the battle had gripped Gibbon's force. Dawes described them as "loading and firing with demoniacal fury and shouting and laughing hysterically." Gibbon, accompanying the two regiments on the east side of the road, had by this time probably lost effective tactical control of the rest of the brigade. As the advance continued, the formations became more spread out and harder to direct. The battlefield now resembled an overturned checkerboard.[33]

Confederate reinforcements began to arrive; a line of enemy infantry, the brigades of E. M. Law and John B. Hood, came sweeping into the ground behind the church. The Union troops were exhausted, short of ammunition, their muskets fouled, with many officers now casualties; they began to fall back. At the northern edge of the cornfield Rufus Dawes managed to rally his Wisconsin men. Gibbon dismounted and came running over to Dawes, shouting, "Here, major, move your men over, we must save these guns." The old artilleryman took personal charge of their defense, firing round after round of canister into the Confederate infantry, while Dawes directed musketry into the advancing lines. The Southerners did not quite reach the guns; whole ranks went down before the whirlwind of shot.[34]

Gibbon now realized that he was unsupported and had to withdraw. Battery B—minus thirty-three dead horses—limbered up and went to the rear of the Poffenberger farm. The Iron Brigade followed as I Corps withdrew. Gibbon, later helping to rally Major General John Sedgwick's division, discovered that his sword hilt had been shot off. Considering the heavy officer losses, it is remarkable that this was as close as he came to a wound.[35]

Out of approximately eight hundred men, the Iron Brigade suffered 335 total casualties, plus thirty-eight in Battery B—losses of nearly 42 percent. Lieutenant Colonel Alois O. Bachman of the 19th Indiana was dead and the commanders of two Wisconsin regiments were out of action. The 6th Wisconsin had lost the most: 152 out of 312. The Second had eighty-six killed and wounded.[36]

Both the state of the Iron Brigade and its performance were characteristic of infantry fighting during the Civil War. At first Gibbon had his men well in hand. But as resistance increased and the crescendo of violence mounted, the brigade lost cohesiveness; as individual units, its regiments fought doggedly on. Gibbon showed the same courage and pugnacity that his men displayed, and if South Mountain had given them a reputation, Antietam reinforced it. Gibbon characterized the experience very well: "We knew very little of what was going on in our immediate vicinity. We were in the hottest of hornet's nests and had all we could do to attack what was in our front whilst the sounds of a severe battle struck our ears from all directions."[37]

The battle ended in stalemate. Once Lee had been allowed to withdraw into Virginia on 18 September, some of the brigade's members took the opportunity to look over the battlefield. From their camps they saw wagonloads of human limbs being moved from field hospitals to burial pits. In the now-leveled cornfield, along the Hagerstown Turnpike, and especially before the spot where Battery B had made its stand, the dead lay in rows and piles. Rufus Dawes saw a grisly sight in the Miller barnyard: a horse, killed while trying to rise, frozen in a sitting position.[38]

The Army of the Potomac remained inactive around the vicinity of Sharpsburg until the end of October, drawing replacements and immense quantities of new equipment. Some of Gibbon's regiments gained strength with the return of wounded from hospitals and men from detached service, but none, he told Fannie proudly, from stragglers or deserters. Between 17 September and 21 October the 6th Wisconsin's effective strength increased from 250 to 313 men.[39]

In addition, McClellan kept his promise to give Gibbon a new Western regiment. On 8 October 1862 the 24th Michigan Volunteers joined the brigade. Gibbon inspected the new unit on the 16th and was pleased with its size and bearing. The seasoned veterans of the Iron Brigade gave the newcomers a cool welcome. Gibbon's men were aware that they were shock troops, and they withheld acceptance until the new men might have an opportunity to come under fire. Gibbon quickly sensed the atmosphere of the ceremony, and wrote to Fannie that "it will not be long before it will be a worthy member of the 'Black Hats.' "[40]

Hooker left I Corps at this time. Wounded in the foot, he turned over command to Major General John F. Reynolds. A superb soldier, Reynolds built the corps into a great formation until it was shattered and he was killed on the first day at Gettysburg.[41]

In the midst of all this reshuffling, Gibbon celebrated his seventh wedding anniversary on 16 October. Unfortunately, he and his wife were separated, but he told her that, if the army remained in Maryland much longer, he would ask for leave to go to Baltimore. However, on 26 October the troops moved out to Virginia during heavy rains. McClellan, whose days with the army were numbered, told Gibbon that he had recommended his promotion to major general. But at Bloomfield a more concrete advancement materialized.[42]

Summoned to Reynolds, Gibbon learned from the corps commander that Ricketts was leaving and was asked if he wanted command of the 2nd Division. Stunned, Gibbon later wrote, "My first feeling was one of regret at the idea of being separated from my gallant brigade." Some of this distress must have showed, because Reynolds responded, "Well, if you don't want it, I will offer it to. . . ." Then ambition triumphed over sentiment and Gibbon accepted. Frank Haskell went along as a personal aide, as did his brother-in-law, Ned Moale.[43]

Unquestionably, Gibbon created the Iron Brigade. With tact, rigorous discipline that never dipped into brutality, and a keen appreciation for morale, he prepared it for its terrible introduction to combat on 28 August and the cauldron of fire that was Antietam. Following his example of personal bravery, his men stood fast in battle and developed into one of the most cohesive and legendary units in American military history. A quarter century after the end of the war Rufus Dawes assessed in retrospect the impact of Gibbon on the brigade:

He soon manifested superior qualities as a brigade commander. Thoroughly educated in the military profession, he had also high personal qualifications to exercise command. He was anxious that his brigade should excel in every way, and while he was an exacting disciplinarian he had the good sense to recognize merit where it existed. His administration of the command left a lasting impression for good upon the character and military tone of the brigade, and his splendid personal bravery upon the field of battle was an inspiration. . . . Beyond a doubt, it was [his] preparation that brought the brigade to its high standard of efficiency for battle service.

If the brigade had done well, its commander marched apace. Less than a year before he had been one of many captains of artillery. Now he was a general of reputation and proven ability, with a sturdy character and a promising future. As he sat his horse beside the road on 5 November and watched his old command move out, John Gibbon had cause for both regret and pride.[44]

Gibbon had little time to become acquainted with his new command, and no attempt to establish his imprint on it was possible. But the division was solid enough, with three brigades and fourteen regiments, plus four batteries of artillery. They came generally from New York and Pennsylvania, with a few units from New England. However, the question of subordinate commanders presented a problem. If no brigadier general was assigned to a brigade, command devolved upon the senior of the various regimental commanders. On assuming his new post Gibbon found that, at the head of two of his brigades, he had inherited colonels in whom he had little confidence. He met the problem in characteristic Gibbon fashion, head on. Reshuffling the division organization, he put the regiments commanded by the colonels to whom he objected into the brigade commanded by the lone brigadier general assigned to him, thus clearing the way for the seniority system to place at the heads of the other brigades men whom he wanted there.[45]

The jump in command was not the only change Gibbon experienced in the winter of 1862. On 5 November Lincoln, exasperated beyond endurance by McClellan's eternal maneuvering, continual requests for supply, and lack of aggressiveness, removed him from command; Ambrose E. Burnside replaced him. Gibbon was stunned. "The Government has gone mad," he exclaimed to Fannie. It was the worst possible thing Lincoln could have done, in his opinion, "worth to the South as much as a victory." Burnside, he thought, would not last long, because ambitious Joseph Hooker would soon follow him. McClellan's removal impelled John

Gibbon to take an action that went far beyond his usual common sense approach to trouble. He tried to persuade his superiors to send a dispatch to Lincoln, advising him to permit McClellan to conclude his present campaign. Very fortunately, this went no further than discussion.[46]

Burnside moved immediately to revise the organization of the Army of the Potomac. With seven corps generals reporting directly to him, the command structure was unwieldy. Under the Burnside reorganization three two-corps Grand Divisions were created, XI Corps being designated as an independent reserve. I Corps found itself, along with VI Corps, in Major General William B. Franklin's Left Grand Division. Burnside also secured Lincoln's acceptance of his plan to cross the Rappahannock at Fredericksburg and deploy in Lee's rear before the Army of Northern Virginia could concentrate and oppose the move. On 11 November the Union forces took the road for Fredericksburg, and Gibbon's division arrived at Bealton's Station the same day. There it sat for five days. Although able to reach the river before Lee deduced what was going on, Burnside could not cross.

At Fredericksburg the Rappahannock was not fordable, and a crossing depended on the army's engineers providing pontons for bridges. Thanks to a monumental misunderstanding among Burnside, the ineffectual General-in-Chief Henry W. Halleck, and the engineers, the bridging materials remained behind until 25 November, when they finally arrived. On 19 November Franklin's Grand Division began moving into the Fredericksburg area; I Corps reached the Rappahannock on 11 December. Gibbon's division made the march to Fredericksburg on very short rations, apparently because the army's transportation was occupied in forwarding ponton bridge equipment to the area. Upon its arrival on 19 November at Brooks's Station, where it remained for a number of days, the 12th Massachusetts of Gibbon's division found that there was no food for it; the regimental history records that "this was the normal condition during the stay." The Twelfth aptly named its camp "Starvation Hill."[47]

Two weeks before the disastrous attack on Fredericksburg, Gibbon urged a plan on Burnside that might have avoided the useless bloodshed of 13 December, and that bore a startling resemblance to Grant's operation plan of June 1864. Gibbon advised Burnside to reject trying to bull his way across the Rappahannock and through the enemy fortifications, but to leave a holding force there to pin Lee down. By using his command of the area's rivers, Burnside could transport the bulk of his army to the south of Richmond and seize Petersburg. This city, Gibbon pointed out, was the key to all communication between Richmond and the South. Once it was taken, all railroads in the area would fall under Union control, forcing the evacuation of the Confederate capital.

For a young brigadier, Gibbon revealed a keen appreciation of the advantages offered to the Union by its holding command of the Confederacy's waterways. Such a move in winter might have been too risky. But he recognized the strategic impasse that Lincoln was trying to explain to Burnside (and earlier, McClellan): that the Army of Northern Virginia, and not Richmond, was the proper objective. Gibbon wrote to Burnside, "If the enemy gets there first, he must fight us below Richmond . . . where he has . . . few fortifications, and where we shall be between him and his reinforcements."[48]

The proposal undoubtedly came to Burnside's attention, as he received it directly from Gibbon, but Burnside took no heed of the suggestion. Although now opposed by Lee's entire army on the opposite bank of the Rappahannock, he adhered to his original plan, determined to fight his way over the river and drive the Confederates from their defensive position. The worst experience of the Army of the Potomac was about to begin.

NOTES

1. Alan T. Nolan, *The Iron Brigade* (New York, 1961), 92. Sixteen months later Gibbon could still write, "Patrick's brigade remained immovable, and did not fire a shot." U.S. War Department, *The War of the Rebellion: A Compilation of the Official Records of the Union and Confederate Armies* (Washington, 1887), Vol. XII, Pt. 2, 381, (hereafter cited as *OR*).

2. John Gibbon, *Personal Recollections of the Civil War* (New York, 1928), 56–57; *OR*, Vol. XII, 381, Pt. 3, 717–718; John C. Ropes, *The Army Under Pope* (New York, 1883), 81–82.

3. Gibbon wrote a letter to King, which he authorized King to publish, accepting full responsibility for the decision. Even then Gibbon did not know about King's activities. The letter is in Charles King, "Gainesville," War Papers, Wisconsin Commandery, Military Order of the Loyal Legion, Vol. III, 277–278.

4. Rufus Dawes, *Service with the Sixth Wisconsin Volunteers* (Madison, 1962), 70; *OR*, Vol. XII, Pt. 2, 379.

5. Gibbon, *Recollections*, 57–60; *OR*, Vol. XII, Pt. 2, 76.

6. Gibbon, *Recollections*, 59.

7. Gibbon, *Recollections*, 60.

8. Nolan, *Iron Brigade*, 103.

9. Gibbon, *Recollections*, 63; Dawes, *Sixth Wisconsin*, 70–73; *OR*, Vol. XII, Pt. 2, 368.

10. Gibbon, *Recollections*, 68; *OR*, Vol. XII, Pt. 2, 416, 379.

11. Gibbon, *Recollections*, 70.

12. John Gibbon to Fannie Gibbon, 1, 2, 3 September 1862, GP, HSP, (hereafter cited as JG to FG.)

13. *OR*, Vol. XII, Pt. 2, 745; Gibbon, *Recollections*, 71; JG to FG, 8 September 1862. The differing figures on Iron Brigade numbers can probably be explained by realizing that Gibbon was referring to men actually carrying muskets, not total muster roll numbers.

14. *OR*, Vol. XII, Pt. 1, 169–180.

15. Gibbon, *Recollections*, 71–73; Silas Colgrove, "The Finding of Lee's Lost Order," R. U. Johnson and C. C. Buel, eds, *Battles and Leaders of the Civil War* (New York, 1956), II, 603.

16. Gibbon, *Recollections*, 72; James V. Murfin, *The Gleam of Bayonets: The Battle of Antietam and the Maryland Campaign of 1862* (New York, 1965), 167.

17. Gibbon, *Recollections*, 76.

18. Frank A. Haskell letter to brother and sister, 14 September 1862, Haskell papers, SHSW.

19. Haskell, letter, 14 September 1862; *OR*, Vol. XII, Pt. 1, 417.

20. Dawes, *Sixth Wisconsin*, 81; Haskell, letter, 14 September 1862.

21. *OR*, Vol. XII, Pt. 1, 247–248, 250–252.

22. *OR*, Vol. XII, Pt. 1, 254.

23. Gibbon, *Recollections*, 79; JG to FG, 15 September 1862; *Indiana at Antietam* (Indianapolis, 1911), 111; Nolan, *Iron Brigade*, 335–336, has the best discussion of the origins of the brigade's name. Gibbon later wrote, "How or where the name of the 'Iron Brigade' was first given, I do not know, but soon after the battle of Antietam the name was started and ever after was applied to the brigade." Gibbon, *Recollections*, 93.

24. Gibbon, *Recollections*, 73–76; Dawes, *Sixth Wisconsin*, 85–86.

25. JG to FG, 16 September 1862; journal of Nicholas Gibbon; family tradition, related to Mark H. Jordan by the late Mrs. Bancroft Hill.

26. Dawes, *Sixth Wisconsin*, 85–86; *OR*, Vol. XII, Pt. 1, 217–218, 135.

27. Dawes, *Sixth Wisconsin*, 88; Murfin, *Bayonets*, 212; Gibbon, *Recollections*, 81–82. Bruce Catton, *Mr. Lincoln's Army* (New York, 1964), 370, has a good discussion of numbers on this part of the Union line. Meade, for example, reported less than 3,000 effectives, Ricketts 3158, and one brigade of Doubleday's division never fought. All of this makes I Corps' record that much more impressive.

28. Warren W. Hassler, Jr., *General George B. McClellan: Shield of the Union* (Baton Rouge, 1957), 273, 276; Jacob Cox, "The Battle of Antietam," *Battles and Leaders*, 635–637.

29. If anything saved Lee from destruction on that day, it was this lack of coordination. He was continually able to shift troops from one part of his shredded line to another all day.

30. *OR*, Vol. XII, Pt. 1, 248, 254–255, 218.

31. *OR*, Vol. XII, Pt. 1, 968.

32. *OR*, Vol. XII, Pt. 1, 229, 269–270; Dawes, *Sixth Wisconsin*, 90.

33. Dawes, *Sixth Wisconsin*, 90–91.

34. Gibbon, *Recollections*, 88–89; *OR*, Vol. XII, Pt. 1, 229; Dawes, *Sixth Wisconsin*, 90.

35. Gibbon, *Recollections*, 84–85.

36. *OR*, Vol. XII, Pt. 1, 189–191.

37. Gibbon, *Recollections*, 89.

38. Dawes, *Sixth Wisconsin*, 95–96.

39. JG to FG, 2 October 1862; *OR*, Vol. XII, Pt. 1, 877.

40. JG to FG, 9 October 1862.

41. On Reynolds, see Edward J. Nichols, *Toward Gettysburg* (University Park, 1958).

42. JG to FG, 16 October 1862.

43. Dawes, *Sixth Wisconsin*, 50; Gibbon, *Recollections*, 95–96.

44. Gibbon, *Recollections*, 95–96; Dawes, *Sixth Wisconsin*, 43.

45. Gibbon, *Recollections*, 100–101.

46. JG to FG, 9 November 1862; Gibbon, *Recollections*, 98.

47. OR, Vol. XXII, Pt. 1, 452–453; Benjamin F. Cook, *History of the 12th Massachusetts Volunteers*, 79 (Boston, 1882).

48. *OR*, Vol XXI, 812; Mark H. Jordan, "Gibbon's Plan for Taking Petersburg in '62," *Civil War Times Illustrated*, June 1962, 17.

5 A Little Grove of Trees

Although now a divisional commander, Gibbon retained a close interest in and affection for his old brigade, and after his promotion attempted to influence the selection of the new Iron Brigade commander. Combative in battle, John Gibbon's aggressive and impetuous nature also manifested itself in the area of Army of the Potomac politics. His tendency to involve himself without hesitation in affairs not properly his concern was becoming more pronounced. Gibbon favored Lysander Cutler of the 6th Wisconsin to succeed him as brigade commander, but he also believed Lucius Fairchild of the 2nd Wisconsin to be a good choice. Cutler, on the grounds of seniority, was the favorite. However, Joseph Hooker, while still I Corps commander, recommended the 19th Indiana's colonel, Solomon J. Meredith, as Gibbon's replacement. The War Department promoted Meredith to brigadier general and confirmed Hooker's recommendation. Gibbon was furious. He considered Meredith unfit for brigade command, and rejected the appointment because of its political nature.

Meredith's military incapacity was a matter of conjecture. However, Gibbon was on firmer ground when he charged that Meredith's political friends had engineered the promotion. The new commander was a prominent figure in the Indiana Republican Party, and a known intimate of Governor Oliver P. Morton, a powerful national figure, a friend of Secretary of War Stanton, who had close contacts with the members of the Joint Committee on the Conduct of the War. Hooker, who was seeking the Army of the Potomac command, knew of these connections. In addition, Gibbon may have harbored a personal grudge. Meredith had protested the assignment of a Regular Army officer and a non-Westerner to command the all-volunteer, all-Western Iron Brigade.

Gibbon's attempts to intervene were fruitless. His request to Hooker that Meredith be transferred to his Grand Division, away from I Corps, was rejected out of hand. Gibbon, who apparently had forgotten his own path to promotion as brigadier general, lashed out in private at Hooker, describing him as one who "sacrificed his soldierly principles whenever such sacrifice could gain him political influence to further his own ends."[1]

The impending attempt to break General Robert E. Lee's lines above Fredericksburg now forced John Gibbon to focus on more immediate concerns. Major General William B. Franklin's Left Grand Division was designated by Burnside to drive through Lee's right flank below Fredericksburg, turning him out of the formidable Marye's Heights position. On 11 December I Corps marched down to the crossing point over the Rappahannock River, and moved skirmishers to the right bank over a ponton bridge laid by the engineers. These men held a bridgehead until the remainder of the troops crossed the following morning. A heavy fog hampered preparations on the 12th, as the 2nd Division led I Corps over the bridges. Some Confederate artillery fired sporadically on the crossing, ineffectively.[2] Gibbon led his men to the left, away from Fredericksburg, and took his column of three brigades along the river and across fields toward the Bowling Green Road, which paralleled the Rappahannock. By late afternoon he had deployed the division on the extreme right of the I Corps line, linking that formation with VI Corps. Brigadier General George G. Meade placed his small division on Gibbon's left. Doubleday was placed in reserve behind Meade. Gibbon had his men, deployed in two lines of brigades, lie down and get what rest they could. A damp chilling fog and a bitterly cold night, coupled with orders for no fires, made the wait very long.[3]

Although Burnside's orders seemed to imply that Franklin should have moved further south and turned the Confederate right flank, Franklin emphasized to Meade that he was to attack the heights in front of his position, supported on the right by Gibbon and with Doubleday backing him up as a reserve. Gibbon's position was between the Bowling Green road and the railroad.[4] However, dense fog delayed the advance. About 11:00 the visibility became better, clear enough for Confederate horse artillery to begin an enfilade fire on Meade's and Gibbon's ranks. Both commanders had their men lie down while Union artillery dealt with this distraction. Meade's attack went in about noon, accompanied by Gibbon's brigades on the right.[5]

The Confederates had left a gap between two brigades, and Meade pushed his men into it, driving a wedge into the Confederate line. At the same time, Gibbon led his troops beyond the railroad tracks and up to a crest where they collided with two and possibly three brigades of Southern infantry. His advance stalled, and, as his men returned musketry fire, Confederate cannon poured canister into Gibbon's ranks. However, Gibbon deployed Colonel Adrian Root's brigade into column formation and drove it at the Southern line. Root's assault disorganized several Confed-

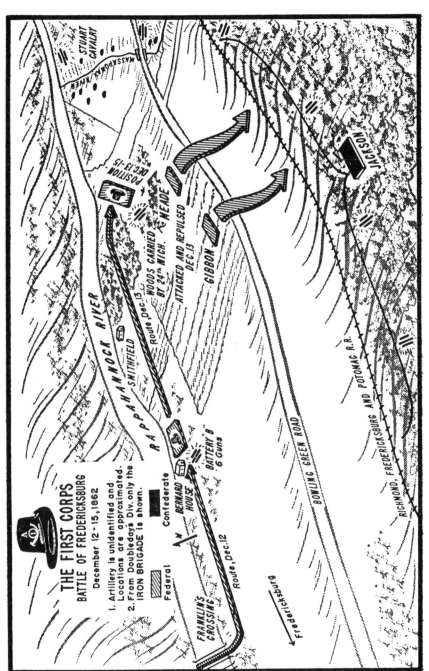

First Corps, Battle of Fredericksburg, 1862. Courtesy Alan T. Nolan, *The Iron Brigade: A Military History.*

erate units and took 180 prisoners. By this time, however, Meade's pre-
diction that he would be unable to hold any gains unless supported came
true. The intense fighting exhausted Meade's small division and, as Stonewall Jackson brought up his reserves, Meade started to drift away from
Gibbon, forcing him to fall back.[6] The withdrawal threatened to become
a stampede, until Brigadier General David Birney's III Corps division came
forward in support of Meade. Eventually Birney, Meade, and Gibbon reorganized the position and turned back the Confederate counterattack.[7]

Gibbon was standing by one of his batteries, directing its fire when, at
about 2:30 P.M., a shell exploded nearby, driving a fragment into his right
hand and wrist. The wound was painful, but not serious. A surgeon at an
aid station bandaged the wound, but Gibbon's part in the Fredericksburg
battle was over.[8]

Franklin sacrificed a considerable number of men in his futile and ill-
considered attack. Gibbon's brigades lost 141 killed and 924 wounded.
The division fought well, but had been badly used. Not knowing what he
wanted to do, Franklin failed to support the attack. Fighting in difficult
terrain, without an objective, and with a commander who held superior
numbers but failed to use them in support of his attack, Gibbon's troops
were almost certain to fail.[9]

The wound justified a grant of sick leave, and Gibbon turned over command to the ranking brigadier and left for Washington by steamboat. On
15 December he arrived at the home of John Potts, senior clerk of the
War Department, where his family was staying. By this time an infection
in the wound forced Gibbon to bed. There he was visited by President
Abraham Lincoln on the 16th. Although Gibbon never revealed to anyone
what they discussed, Lincoln doubtless wanted firsthand news of the battle and any information about the Army of the Potomac that could assist
him in dealing with the command crisis in that army and the developing
political crisis within his own party.[10]

Gibbon's wound made his enforced leave a prolonged one. On three
separate occasions, testimony from army doctors at Baltimore and Philadelphia allowed him to obtain certificates keeping him from active duty.
As late as 17 February 1863 he was certified as "unfit for active service
in the field," because "active use of the hand would probably be attended
by loss of the thumb."[11] The Gibbon family made good use of the time
together, calling on family and friends in Baltimore and Philadelphia.
Eventually, however, Gibbon had to return to the Army of the Potomac.
On 22 March 1863, he and a group of other officers boarded a steamboat
at Alexandria, Virginia, and made the trip down the Potomac to Aquia
Creek. At Falmouth, Gibbon reported to Major General Joseph Hooker,
now commander of the Army of the Potomac, who promised him a divisional command when one could be arranged. Gibbon would not be returning to I Corps.[12]

For a week the matter lay in abeyance. Frank Haskell, still acting as Gibbon's aide, wrote in his diary on 24 March "We shall probably know today or tomorrow what command JG will get." Shortly afterward, Hooker referred Gibbon to Major General Darius N. Couch, the new commander of II Corps and a West Point classmate of Gibbon's. Couch's offer of the 2nd Division in his corps was immediately accepted.[13]

Gibbon assumed command on 3 April. The 2nd Division was an excellent formation, typical of all the II Corps units. His predecessors in command, Charles P. Stone, John Sedgwick, and O. O. Howard, were all capable men, and even the critical Frank Haskell noted that "the appearance of the Division was remarkably good." Its fifteen regiments were organized into three brigades, commanded by Brigadier Generals Alfred Sully and Joshua T. Owen and Colonel Norman J. Hall. With an effective strength of about 6,000, including two batteries of artillery, it was larger than his old command. Gibbon pronounced himself "well pleased with the new command, for it is larger and under better discipline." [14]

Gibbon's pleasure over his new command did not extend to the Army's commander. He joined most of the regular officers in their disapproval of Joseph Hooker and the path he had taken to high command. "Hooker," Gibbon later wrote, "was a strange composition . . . a great deal of his attractive frankness was assumed and he was an intriguer." No one was sure of his capacity to command a large army against Robert E. Lee.[15]

Pleasure over a new command was spoiled, however, when part of a regiment in Gibbon's division mutinied on 29 April 1863.[16] Six companies of the 34th New York Volunteer Infantry, in Sully's brigade, insisted that their enlistment time was up and they wanted to go home before the next battle. By dating their two years of obligated service from when they had been assembled by the State of New York, instead of when the War Department had accepted them for federal service, they hoped to shave six weeks from their service time. Although the dispute had been brewing for some time, when ordered to assemble for drill on 29 April, the New Yorkers refused. Sully did not take any immediate action, and Gibbon came down on him as hard as he would the mutineers. Removing Sully from command, Gibbon wrote in his order that

Brigadier General Alfred Sully, having reported to the general commanding the division that it was not in his power to enforce discipline in his command, he is hereby relieved from duty with the division. He will as soon as the division rejoins the rest of the Corps, report to Major General Couch in person.[17]

After disposing of Sully, Gibbon moved against the recalcitrant troops. He had the 15th Massachusetts assembled with loaded rifles and deployed around the disaffected six companies of New York men, and appealed to the mutineers to do their duty and await action on their dispute

by the War Department. No one present doubted that Gibbon would ruth-
lessly order the soldiers to fire if the mutineers refused to obey orders.
The six companies yielded to Gibbon's persuasion or the threat of naked
force that lay behind it. Once again, John Gibbon had analyzed his volunteers correctly. The next day, when he called for men to lay a ponton
bridge over the Rappahannock in the face of enemy fire, eighteen of the
erstwhile mutineers stepped forward.[18]

Gibbon's action produced immediate results, but the subsequent court
of inquiry, convened by Couch at Sully's request, did not view Gibbon's
removal of his subordinate favorably. When the court issued its findings
after the Chancellorsville campaign, the report agreed with Gibbon's actions in restoring discipline, but it also stated that Gibbon was unjustified
in removing Sully, since that officer probably doubted his authority to
order extreme measures in suppressing the disobedience. Shortly after,
however, both Sully and the New Yorkers left the Army of the Potomac.[19]

Hooker's plan to defeat Lee did not include a large role for John Gibbon. His division, along with Sedgwick's VI Corps, was left behind to hold
Fredericksburg and pin down the troops Lee had there, while Hooker
crossed the Rapidan River upstream to catch Lee between his main body
and the Union forces at Fredericksburg. Sedgwick planned to cross the
Rappahannock at Franklin's Crossing, while Gibbon remained at Falmouth, above Fredericksburg. On 29 April 1863, Sedgwick moved two
infantry divisions over the river. The next day, the Union troops could
hear sounds of gunfire from the direction of Chancellorsville and could
see Confederate infantry moving away from their positions on Marye's
Heights to reinforce Lee.[20]

Sedgwick had not succeeded in keeping the Confederate forces opposing him pinned down, and on 2 May Jackson's flank attack on Hooker
forced the Union army onto the defensive near Chancellorsville Court-
house. Hooker now ordered Sedgwick to attack, hoping that some pressure would be taken off his forces. On the night of 2 May Gibbon moved
troops, artillery, and engineers down to the river, and began bridge construction shortly after midnight. Hall's and Owen's brigades crossed at
sunrise. Sedgwick hoped that Gibbon would be able to flank the Confederates out of their defensive position, thus avoiding an assault on Marye's
Heights.[21]

Gibbon's attempt to mount an attack was thwarted by a combination
of difficult ground and dogged Confederate opposition. He and Brigadier
General G. K. Warren, the army's chief engineer, found, on examining the
ground to the right, that any advance would mean the crossing of two
canals. Hall's brigade, supported by artillery, failed to dislodge the Confederates guarding the bridge over the first canal. When Gibbon attempted to move farther to the right to flank the Confederates out of
their position behind the second canal, he found even stronger defenses,

and gave up the attempt. Gibbon reported his failure to Sedgwick and retreated into Fredericksburg.[22] At 11:00 A.M. Sedgwick stormed Marye's Heights, by then very lightly held, and pushed on toward Salem Church. Gibbon was left behind to hold the bridges. Sedgwick fought a defensive battle with Lee on 5 May, withdrawing over the Rappahannock afterward. At 3:00 A.M. the next day Gibbon evacuated Fredericksburg, crossed to the north bank and moved to Falmouth.[23] The dismal and barren Chancellorsville campaign was over. Haskell's subsequent characterization said it all: It was, he wrote, "the most magnificent farce that was ever enacted."[24]

Gibbon's opinion of Joseph Hooker, already low, was reinforced by information obtained from talking with Meade and Major General Winfield S. Hancock, a fellow II Corps divisional commander. From them he learned that Hooker had allowed the Army of the Potomac to be defeated in detail, and that only XI Corps had performed badly. Hooker, seeking a scapegoat, tried to place some of the blame for the defeat on Meade and Major General John F. Reynolds, both friends of Gibbon. At the same time Darius N. Couch requested to be relieved from command of II Corps and subsequently left the Army of the Potomac. Gibbon wrote to Fannie that "no one whose opinion is worth anything had now any confidence in General H. and the Prest. has been told so." But he could not say if a change in the Army command was going to take place.[25]

With the army once again in camp, Gibbon could attend to some more personal matters. He asked his wife to send him a box of good cigars, since he had exhausted the present supply, and they were "much more convenient to smoke on a horse than my pipe." Later he requested that she furnish him with a keg of whiskey, declining to draw on the low-quality item furnished by the commissary stores. But most of all he wanted to be with his family. He wanted to "get my harness off and settle down into a quiet place for the rest of my life." Even Fort Crittenden would be satisfactory, if he could have his family around him.[26]

As a divisional commander, Gibbon had to spend a great deal of time on the administration of his division. Since the U.S. Army had functioned largely as a garrison force prior to the Civil War, its bureaucratic routines were designed for a force that did not move around very much. This allowed the leisurely completion of many reports and returns, something that a field army found highly inconvenient. By 1863 Gibbon had had a surfeit of it. In an attempt to simplify matters, Gibbon made a reasonable suggestion regarding the inventory of worthless or damaged property. As he wrote in his letter to the War Department,

The present system of Accountability for property . . . gives rise to too great a Multiplicity of papers. Every Company in the Service has more or less property worn out, which has to be inspected and condemned by the Division Inspector

Gen'l. . . . Each Co. Comd'r must make out triplicate inventories of each kind of property, so that to get rid of a few worthless muskets and a few pieces of damaged clothing or Camp or Garrison Equipage in each Company from 750 to 900 papers must be prepared. . . . In this way the mere labor of preparing for inspection and condemnation becomes interminable. . . .[27]

As an improvement, John Gibbon proposed that worthless property be inspected and certified by the regimental commander or his representative and then turned in to the division ordnance officer or brigade quartermaster; when these individuals had collected a sufficient amount of junked arms and equipment, the required triplicate inventories could then be prepared on the consolidated mass of material, and not on each individual item. This sensible suggestion was quickly brushed off by the functionaries in the Quartermaster and Ordnance Bureaus. They pointed out that the duty only had to be done once a month, unless the reporting unit was relocated. It apparently escaped them that the Army of the Potomac was not a garrison force. In addition, the 1827 law allowed company commanders an extra allowance of $10.00 per month for doing the paperwork. This might have been a factor in not adopting the suggestion.

By the first week of June, II Corps had settled down under its new commander, Major General Winfield S. Hancock. Once Couch had left the Army of the Potomac, Hancock became his undisputed successor. His abilities as a troop leader were recognized throughout the army and, as his chief of staff said, the appointment "was a matter about which there could be no question."[28] Doubtless his elevation was as popular with John Gibbon, a close friend, as it was with the men of II Corps. Hancock's appointment was well-timed, because, just a week before, on 3 June 1863, Lee began to move the Army of Northern Virginia away from Fredericksburg toward Culpeper Court House and the Shenandoah Valley. Not until the end of the second week of June did Hooker realize that Lee had stolen a march on him, and ordered his troops away from the Rappahannock. During the daylight hours of 13 June II Corps broke camp and went back on the Virginia roads, traveling toward Centreville, Virginia, by way of Aquia Creek, Dumfries, Wolf Run Shoals, and Sangster's Station. The hot, dry weather quickly debilitated the men. By the time the corps had reached the Fairfax Court House area, stragglers littered the roads. Gibbon felt compelled to issue a stern order that "in the vast majority of cases the straggler is a skulking cowardly wretch who strives to shift his duties upon the shoulders of more honest and better soldiers."[29] This was quite unfair, and contrary to the view of Hancock, who deployed the corps ambulances to pick up those who had fallen out and bring them forward. Perhaps the fact that Gibbon's division had the rearguard and so received the worst of the dust from the infantry columns provoked his uncharitable comment.[30]

At Centreville, on 17 June, Gibbon received shocking news. Hancock drew him aside to report that Gibbon's little son had died in Baltimore. Although John Jr. had been ill throughout the winter and early spring, he had apparently recovered by May. Hancock, with Lee on the march, could allow Gibbon but two days leave. He left immediately by train from Fairfax to Washington and then to Baltimore. With time so short, he was unable even to stay for the funeral, leaving Fannie to bear the burden of arrangements herself.[31] Fannie took the loss very hard. Life in Baltimore for her could not have been easy. It was a city full of secessionist sympathies, and as the wife of a Union general, and one who had not remained with his adopted southern state, she became the target of gibes from Confederate supporters. After the Chancellorsville campaign she implored her husband to abandon what she saw as an unwinnable war and come home. Only a month later, her only son died. Gibbon, who was not feeling well himself, tried to console her after his return to Centreville. Their loss, he wrote, "comes to me now with even more reality than ever, but we must try to reconsile [sic] ourselves to it and think it is all for the best." He went on to urge her not "to grieve too much . . . and recollect that you still have two children and a husband who loves you dearly, very, very dearly."[32]

Hooker's indecisiveness in determining Lee's intentions led II Corps on a series of back-and-forth marches. On 21 June, Gibbon, along with the other II Corps divisions, led his unit to Thoroughfare Gap through the Bull Run Mountains. He and Hancock, both now ill, shared an ambulance. After remaining in the gap until 25 June, totally undisturbed by any enemy activity, the troops broke camp and returned to Gainesville by way of Haymarket. Gibbon's division underwent personnel changes during the march.[33] Gibbon removed Brigadier General "Paddy" Owen, commander of the Philadelphia Brigade, from his command because of a recurring drinking problem. Hancock then assigned the brigade to Brigadier General Alexander S. Webb, who had just arrived in camp.[34]

At Edwards' Ferry, on 26 June, Gibbon led the 2nd Division over the Potomac via a ponton bridge and in a steady downpour. The welcome rain provided much relief from the heat and dust, but it quickly turned the roads into a quagmire as the troops moved off toward Frederick, Maryland. The twenty-five-mile march on the 28th, with a minimum of straggling, and through country untouched by the war and populated by Union sympathizers, lifted the mens' spirits.[35]

At Frederick, Gibbon learned that Hooker had resigned his command. By provoking a dispute over the control of the Harper's Ferry garrison, and threatening to resign if his wishes were not followed, he presented Lincoln with an opportunity to remove a commander in whom he had no confidence. On the 28th Gibbon learned that his friend, George G. Meade, commander of V Corps, was now Hooker's successor. Gibbon was "delighted" to hear of the change, but when he and Hancock rode over to Meade's headquarters to congratulate him, they found Meade "very anxious" and not totally in accord with Gibbon's enthusiasm. Meade jokingly threatened to have Gibbon shot for suggesting him earlier for the position.[36] Meade was no military genius, but he was a competent commander, respected by his subordinates and unlikely to panic under stress. Moreover, he was wary but not afraid of Robert E. Lee.

While Meade accustomed himself to his new situation, Gibbon began moving his troops from the Frederick area toward Uniontown. Morale was high, and Gibbon rewarded those who marched well. Earlier he had excused the 15th and 19th Massachusetts from picket duty for their exemplary march discipline. Now, as the division neared the little town of Liberty, he had the 19th's glee club lead the division through the town. It struck up "Marching Along" with a stirring effect: "The division fell into step and the chorus could be heard ringing along the entire line."[37]

At 8:00 A.M. on 30 June, the 2nd Division began heading for Uniontown, Maryland, and then Pennsylvania. Morale was high despite the long marches and hot weather. The next day Confederate and Union forces clashed at Gettysburg, Pennsylvania. Meade precipitated the meeting by ordering Brigadier General John Buford and his cavalry division to occupy the town, assigning Major General John F. Reynolds, with I, III, and XI Corps, to support him. Confederate General A. P. Hill's corps engaged Buford, and Reynolds' infantry came up just in time to save the cavalry from overwhelming defeat. Heading Reynolds' advance was the Iron Brigade, going into its greatest battle. Along the Chambersburg Road it mauled the Confederate advance, knocking it out, and fought on until it was but a shell of its former self. Reynolds, directing his corps into the fight, was killed.

On 30 June Meade decided that at least some of the Confederate forces in Pennsylvania would probably advance to Gettysburg. Because of this assumption, he ordered Hancock to move II Corps to Taneytown, strengthening the army's left flank. By 11:00 A.M. on 1 July Gibbon and the other II Corps divisions were at Taneytown. In the early afternoon news from Gettysburg changed the entire situation. Union and Confederate forces had clashed there and were even then battling for possession of the town and its roads. Word came that Reynolds, commanding in Meade's behalf, had been badly or even mortally wounded and as a result, Meade went to Hancock and directed him to go personally to Gettysburg, assume command of the Union troops there and advise Meade whether or not to accept battle.[38]

Meade was fortunate in having a subordinate such as Hancock on whom he could rely. Hancock, in turn, had in Gibbon a divisional commander who was, he judged, fully capable of handling a corps. In the circumstances, neither Gibbon nor Hancock was entitled by seniority to command, but Meade did not hesitate in placing each of them in a position of responsibility. In his order directing Hancock to take control of the battlefield, Meade specifically ordered him to turn command of II Corps over to Gibbon. Since this order was drafted in Hancock's presence, it obviously reflected his concurrence. Gibbon had come a long way from the command of an artillery battery.[39]

Hancock had but a few minutes to brief Gibbon before he got into an ambulance, spread out some maps of the Gettysburg area to study, and rattled away. Gibbon and his small staff began issuing the orders necessary to move II Corps forward. During the afternoon, the troops set out via the Taneytown road to Gettysburg. Around 11:00 P.M. Gibbon allowed the men to make camp and sleep for a few hours. No sooner had Gibbon gone to bed than Meade and his staff rode past. The army commander consulted with Gibbon, probably seeking news from Gettysburg, and ordered him to press on at first light. Gibbon did better than that. The three divisions were on the move at 3:00 A.M., marching down the sides of the poor and rutted Taneytown road, while the vehicles and artillery took the center.[40] While the men moved on, Gibbon rode ahead to Gettysburg and reported to Meade at the Leister House, where Meade had made his headquarters. Meade told him to place his divisions south of the hill known as Big Round Top. This would guard against any possible turning movement by the Confederates.[41] In the morning Gibbon led II Corps up to Cemetery Hill, where he turned over command to Hancock at 6:00 A.M.[42]

Gibbon's division, when posted, occupied the heart of the II Corps line. On his right was Hays' 3rd Division, with its right flank near the cemetery in Ziegler's Grove and its left ending near a stone wall, where Gibbon's position began. Here his men were supported by an artillery battery, and to the left of this unit was Lieutenant Alonzo Cushing's Battery A, 4th U.S. Artillery. From there Gibbon's line ran south until it struck the line of Cemetery Ridge and the troops of Brigadier General John Caldwell's division. Gibbon established no fixed headquarters, but remained in the general area of the right flank.[43]

Although Gibbon's division was not large, its brigade commanders and regiments were of excellent quality. Alexander Webb and Norman J. Hall were both West Pointers and men marked out for further advancement. William Harrow, the only nonprofessional, was ill, but would not relinquish command and "play safe" during the Gettysburg campaign.[44]

Gibbon's front furing the morning and early afternoon of 2 July remained quiet. Only some fire from skirmishers and intermittent artillery exchanges broke the stillness. About 4:00 P.M. he met Hancock near Cushing's battery and learned that there was some activity on the III Corps front off to his left.[45] Major General Daniel Sickles, the III Corps commander, had been both uncertain of what position he should occupy and wary of the danger of being flanked by Confederates attacking near

Big and Little Round Tops. A total misunderstanding of Meade's intentions coupled with Sickles' natural aggressiveness led him to push his entire corps forward into a salient open to attack from both sides.

When Gibbon and Hancock saw Sickles' men move forward with drill field precision, the latter remarked to Gibbon, "That is a splendid advance. But those troops will be coming back very soon."[46] Sickles also managed to break all connection with II Corps on his right. In order to maintain contact and to support III Corps, Hancock had Caldwell's division, on Gibbon's left, move into the gap.

Gibbon was astonished by Sickles' move. He later wrote, "We could not conceive what it meant as we had heard of no orders for an advance and did not understand the meaning of this break in our line."[47] On his own initiative, Gibbon took the 15th Massachusetts and 82nd New York from Harrow's brigade and moved them up along the Emmitsburg Road above the Codori Farm buildings. Later he posted a battery of twelve-pounder Napoleons in the right rear of the 15th Massachusetts. As Hancock became more and more involved in the effort to shore up the Union left flank, Gibbon's role became one of providing reinforcements. At Hancock's order, Gibbon had Colonel Hall send two of his regiments in aid of the III Corps right flank. This, along with other dispersals of II Corps units, left only half of II Corps holding its positions along Cemetery Ridge.

The Confederate attack on III Corps, which began about 4:00 P.M., quickly demonstrated that Sickles' position was untenable. The entire Union left flank was put in danger, and once again Meade called upon Hancock to retrieve the situation. He ordered him to take over command of III Corps from Sickles, who had been wounded. Gibbon again assumed command of II Corps, just as the last Confederate assault of the day came charging against his positions along Cemetery Ridge. Two Confederate brigades struck the forward elements of II Corps around the Codori Farm buildings, overran a battery, and captured two guns from another before it could be moved. They then swept into a gap on the right of Hall's brigade. Gibbon, who had an excellent view of this action, later wrote that the Confederates came on with "impetuosity." As they moved up the slope of Cemetery Ridge like a wave, Gibbon and now Hancock were desperately trying to gather enough reinforcements to stem the enemy advance. Although the situation seemed desperate, the ascending ground and mounting casualties robbed the rebel attack of its strength.[48] Despite these factors, and the heavy cannon and rifle fire poured into them, the Confederates did drive through the Union line at Hall's position and occupied a portion of the Cemetery Ridge crest.

By this time the sun was setting, and its diminishing light combined with the clouds of powder smoke to make vision uncertain. The poor visibility almost cost Hancock his life, when he mistook Confederate infantry climbing Cemetery Ridge for a retreating Union regiment. Gibbon, along with other officers, was busy rallying forces for a counterattack. Webb's brigade, now close at hand, assailed the rebel front and flank, ousting it from the crest of the ridge and driving it toward the Emmitsburg Road. With the arrival of other Union reinforcements, Gibbon's position was secured. Darkness now covered the battlefield, and the second day's fighting at Gettysburg ended.[49]

As the medical teams of both sides moved through the night to gather up the wounded, Meade and his commanders, including Gibbon, gathered at Meade's headquarters to discuss the army's situation and exchange opinions.[50] About 9:00 P.M. Generals Henry Slocum, Hancock, Gibbon (II Corps), A. S. Williams (XII Corps), David Birney (III Corps), George Sykes (V Corps), O. O. Howard (XI Corps), John Sedgwick (VI Corps), and John Newton (I Corps) crowded into the front room of the little house that served Meade. Also present with Meade and Major General Dan Butterfield, his chief of staff, were Major General Alfred Pleasonton, the cavalry commander, and Warren, the army's chief engineer. These officers stood around for a time, discussing what had happened on their respective fronts. Gibbon's aide, Frank Haskell, described his commander:

Not weighing one hundred fifty pounds, he is compactly made . . . with ruddy complexion, chestnut brown hair, with a clean shaved face, except his moustache, which is decidedly reddish in color, medium-sized, well-shaped head, sharp, moderately jutting brow; deep blue, calm eyes, sharp, slightly aquiline nose, compressed mouth, full jaws and chin, with an air of calm firmness in his manner. He always looks well dressed.[51]

Gibbon said little until Newton remarked that Gettysburg was "no place to fight a battle in." Gibbon challenged him on this point, and Newton engaged in a discussion on whether Lee would attempt to turn the Union left flank. After a rambling discussion, Butterfield brought the talk to a close by asking each commander to vote on whether the army should shift its position. Gibbon, as the junior officer present, voted first, with the remark, "Remain here, and make such correction in our position as may be deemed necessary, but take no step which even looks like retreat." Along with the majority, he thought the army should stay where it was for at least another day. Meade agreed, and Gibbon heard him say, quietly, "Such then is the decision."[52] Meade went up to Gibbon after the meeting and told him that Lee would probably attack II Corps next, because he had tried and failed on both flanks.[53] Meade's forecast proved accurate.

Exhausted, Gibbon, accompanied by Newton and Hancock, crawled into a II Corps ambulance to snatch a few hours of sleep. At 4:00 A.M. Gibbon got up, awakened Haskell, and the two sat and listened in the growing light to the rattle of musketry and boom of cannon from Culp's Hill, in the rear of the Union position. Once there was light enough to see by, Gibbon and the other II Corps officers began to prepare their positions for any attack. Hancock resumed command of the corps about noon and Gibbon returned to his duties with the 2nd Division. His men had continued to make their positions more defensible by piling up fence rails and earth as breastworks. Gibbon's division and that of Alexander Hays, to his right, occupied a line of about 2,000 feet, with about 5,500 men as rifle strength. On Gibbon's immediate left was Doubleday's division of I Corps. Between seventy and eighty cannon backed up the Federal units. Gibbon placed Webb on the right around the angle in the stone wall, Hall in the center, and Harrow on the left.[54] From their position, Gibbon's men could see a large concentration of Confederate artillery being arrayed across the valley.[55]

Gibbon encountered Meade at about 11:00 A.M., just as he was settling down to do some paperwork, and persuaded him to join the II Corps mess for lunch. Gibbon's mess staff had found two chickens, "in good running order," and, "no doubt without due process of law," proceeded to stew them. An old mess chest served as a table. Gibbon and Hancock had stools to sit on; when Meade arrived, an old cracker box served as his seat. The late arrivals sat on the ground. With the chickens went potatoes, toast, and coffee. Meade managed to relax a little. After a time he went off to visit Hays. The others drifted away, and Hancock started dictating orders. Several officers lit cigars or dozed. Silence deepened, and the day grew hotter.[56]

At approximately 1:00 P.M., the mess group heard a single cannon fire from near the Peach Orchard, then another. There was a sudden movement along the line of Confederate guns, and then they fired, almost simultaneously, in a long, rippling crescendo of flame and smoke. In on the lunch group came a cyclone of exploding shell, smoke, and noise, as the crest of Cemetery Ridge was plastered with explosives.

Gibbon seized his sword and ran for the stone wall, calling for his horse. His orderly had been killed already, but another man brought the animal. Then Gibbon realized what a conspicuous target he would be on horseback and remained dismounted.[57] As he approached the crest, Gibbon encountered Hancock, who sought his opinion on what Lee intended. Gibbon answered that Lee either intended a full-scale assault or was covering a retreat. By this time he had noticed that the Confederates were firing just a little too high. Along the Taneytown Road the shells fell thickly, turning that area into a killing zone. But few struck the stone wall or the ground immediately behind it.

In the interval between the start of the Confederate bombardment and the commencement of Pickett's advance, an event occurred that arguably had a significant impact on Gibbon's later career. It involved the employment during that period of the Union artillery. In the Army of the Potomac, the guns were divided between the Artillery Reserve and the artillery batteries organic to each corps. Brigadier General Henry Hunt, a gunner unsurpassed in ability on either side, was Meade's Chief of Artillery; as such, he was responsible for the supply and organization of all batteries and controlled the Artillery Reserve. In theory his control extended also to the corps' organic artillery, but the corps commanders could and sometimes did override his orders to corps batteries.

During the bombardment of Cemetery Ridge, Hunt ordered the return fire of the Union guns to be at first deliberately paced and then stopped, in order to conserve ammunition for the infantry charge to come. Insofar as II Corps artillery was concerned, Hancock countermanded that order, on the premise that the morale of the infantrymen subjected to the rebel barrage would be enhanced if they could hear their own cannon replying. Consequently, when the Confederate foot troops came forward II Corps guns were short of everything but canister, useful only at short range. Moreover, many batteries, having by their activity drawn Confederate response, had been wrecked by counterbattery fire and had been pulled out of line. Hunt later argued that if his plan had been followed, the artillery would have stopped Pickett's charge before it even reached the Union line.[58]

Gibbon clambered over the wall and proceeded to walk up and down in front of it, to encourage his men. Haskell joined him, and Gibbon commented rather loudly and acidly on the poor quality of the Confederate gunnery.[59] He could see that the shell fire was having little physical effect on his men, as long as they kept under cover, and even less psychological damage was being done. Gibbon could see Confederate skirmishers across the valley, but no infantry columns. Intercepting two soldiers looking for cover, Gibbon told them to return to their ranks, remarking that "All these matters are in the hands of God, and nothing you can do will make you any safer in one place than another." The men went back to the wall.[60]

The fire began to slacken about 2:30 P.M., as the Confederate batteries ran short of long-range ammunition, and Gibbon and Haskell returned to the infantry line. They were approaching the left of the 2nd Division when Captain Francis Wessels, a staff officer, came up with their horses. He said to Gibbon, "General, they say the enemy's infantry is advancing." Gibbon mounted and rode up to the crest, from which he could see a large mass of Confederate infantry leave the woods and form for assault.[61] As soon as they came within range, the Union guns opened fire, but they continued to advance, closing ranks. Gibbon rode down his line and told his men, "Do not hurry and fire too fast; let them come up close before you fire, and then aim low and steadily." No one knew better than he the power of that first, unhurried volley.[62] Alexander Webb, whose brigade would be struck first, advanced three guns from Cushing's battery down to the wall as the Confederates crossed the Emmitsburg Road.

The right flank of the Confederate column, battered by Union guns, had drifted to its left, and now the spearhead of the assault was aimed at the grove of trees behind the wall, the heart of Gibbon's position. Webb had the 71st Pennsylvania in the angle, and the 69th Pennsylvania behind the wall to the left of Cushing's guns. As these guns fired one last barrage of canister, the Confederate divisions, now one mass, gave the rebel yell and broke into a charge. A few Union soldiers ignored Gibbon's admonition to hold fire, but most waited until the Southerners were just 400 feet away. A storm of rifle and artillery fire erupted, and the pressure grew on the Union line. In the 19th Massachusetts, stationed in the grove, the file closers linked hands in order to hold the ranks in place, countering the natural instinct of a rifleman with a muzzle loader to step backward while reloading.[63]

Gibbon pulled the 19th Maine and 20th Massachusetts out of line and moved them at the double-quick toward the trees. At that moment he felt a hard impact on his shoulder, then burning pain. A bullet had gone completely through the shoulder, fracturing the shoulder blade. He saw that his left arm was covered with blood. Gibbon started to faint. He dismounted and, assisted by Captain Wessels, made it to an aid station.[64] Webb had also been wounded, and Hancock was struck in the thigh by a bullet and was down with a wound that would take months to heal. Frank Haskell found Gibbon at II Corps' field hospital, having his wound dressed. He told Haskell that, in his opinion, a Confederate sniper concealed by the bushes along the wall had shot him.[65] On 4 July, as a cold rain drenched the battlefield, Gibbon boarded a train at Westminster for Baltimore, where he joined Fannie and the children.[66]

Gibbon's performance at Gettysburg always loomed large in his career. He had a key role at the very crux of the fighting; in his report, Gibbon stated, "The division went into action about 3800 strong; lost in killed and wounded over 1600, and captured more prisoners than it had men on the ground at the end of the conflict."[67] Along with Hancock and others, Gibbon helped his men keep their courage during Lee's bombardment and his tough, hard-headed realism and imperturbability lent steadiness to the Union defense when it was badly needed. The army largely acted as a team and, with a commander in Meade whom they could respect, the Union forces came through their greatest trial to date.

Gettysburg was a poignant example of the divisions forced upon Gibbon and his family by the Civil War. George Pickett and Harry Heth, both Confederate commanders, had been classmates of Gibbon at West Point. Johnston Pettigrew, who took over command of Heth's division when he was wounded, was Gibbon's cousin, and had entertained John and Fannie Gibbon in Charleston, South Carolina, just three years previously. Most tragic of all, fifteen of the regiments that crossed the valley to strike Gibbon's line came from North Carolina; one of them was the 28th North Carolina, among whose officers were Robert and Nicholas Gibbon.[68]

NOTES

1. The Meredith episode is detailed in John Gibbon, *Personal Recollections of the Civil War* (New York, 1928), 107–109, and Alan T. Nolan, *The Iron Brigade* (New York, 1961), 172–173. Gibbon discusses the entire episode without mentioning Meredith's name.

2. U.S. War Department, *The War of the Rebellion: A Compilation of the Official Records of the Union and Confederate Armies* (Washington, 1887), Vol. XXII, Pt. 1, 132 (hereafter cited as *OR*); Gibbon, *Recollections*, 102.

3. Gibbon, *Recollections*, 103; *OR*, Vol. XXII, Pt. 1, 453.

4. *OR*, ibid., 453–455.

5. *OR*, ibid.

6. Gibbon, *Recollections*, 103–106.

7. *OR*, ibid., 362.

8. Gibbon, *Recollections*, 104.

9. *OR*, ibid., 129–142.

10. Gibbon, *Recollections*, 106.

11. The records of the surgeons, dated 6 and 26 January and 17 February 1863, are found in AGO, NA, RG 94.

12. John Gibbon to Fannie Gibbon, 23 March 1863, GP, HSP (hereafter cited as JG to FG.)

13. JG to FG, 30 March, 1 April 1863, GP, HSP; Haskell Diary, Haskell Papers, State Historical Society of Wisconsin.

14. Frank A. Haskell to brother and sister, 4 April 1863, Haskell Papers, State Historical Society of Wisconsin.

15. Gibbon, *Recollections*, 107.

16. Gibbon, *Recollections*, 110. Gibbon did not identify the regiment involved, nor mention Sully by name.

17. Special Orders, No. 122, Headquarters, 2nd Division, II Corps, Army of the Potomac, 1 May 1863, *OR*, Vol. XXV, Pt. 1, 351.

18. Andrew A. Ford, *The Story of the Fifteenth Regiment Massachusetts Volunteer Infantry* (Clinton, Mass., 1898), 245; *OR*, ibid., 302.

19. *OR*, Vol. XXV, Pt. 1, 352.

20. Gibbon, *Recollections*, 111; JG to FG, 2 May 1863, GP, HSP.

21. *OR*, Vol. XXV, Pt. 2, 340; Gibbon, *Recollections*, 115–116; JG to FG, 3 May 1863, GP, HSP.

22. *OR*, Vol. XXV, Pt. 1, 350–351; Gibbon, *Recollections*, 116.

23. JG to FG, 6 May 1863, GP, HSP.

24. Frank A. Haskell to brother and sister, 12 May 1863, Haskell Papers, SHSW.

25. Gibbon, *Recollections*, 120; Bruce Catton, *Glory Road* (New York, 1964), 226–227; JG to FG, 10, 25 May 1863, GP, HSP.

26. JG to FG, 1, 3, 17 June 1863, GP, HSP; Catton described the commissary whiskey in *Glory Road*, 134–135.

27. JG to Brigadier General Seth Williams, Assistant Adjutant General, Army of the Potomac, 20 April 1863, Letters Received File, WD, AGO, NA, RG 94.

28. David M. Jordan, *Winfield Scott Hancock: A Soldier's Life* (Bloomington, 1988), 79 (hereafter cited as *Hancock*).

29. Ford, *15th Massachusetts*, 256.

30. Jordan, *Hancock*, 77; Gibbon, *Recollections*, 125.

31. Gibbon, *Recollections*, 125.

32. JG to FG, 28 June 1863, GP, HSP; FG to JG, undated (May 1863?), GP, HSP.

33. JG to FG, 22, 23, 24 June 1863, GP, HSP.

34. George R. Stewart, *Pickett's Charge* (Boston, 1959), 59, 74–75.

35. Francis A. Walker, *History of the Second Army Corps in the Army of the Potomac* (New York, 1886), 260–261; *OR*, Vol. XXVII, Pt. 3, 338.

36. JG to FG, 29 June 1863, GP, HSP.

37. JG to FG, 30 June 1863, GP, HSP; History Committee, *History of the Nineteenth Regiment Massachusetts Volunteer Infantry 1861–1865*, 221 (Salem, 1906).

38. Catton, *Glory Road*, 287–300, has perhaps the most dramatic picture of the Iron Brigade's last fight. For a more detailed treatment, see Nolan, *Iron Brigade*, 223–259. The Iron Brigade took 1,883 men into action and suffered 1,212 casualties, with the 24th Michigan taking 80 percent losses.

39. *OR*, Vol. XXVII, Pt. 1, 367–368; Pt. 3, 461; George Meade, *The Life and Letters of George Gordon Meade* (New York, 1913), II, 77–78.

40. *OR*, Vol. XXVII, Pt. 1, 367–368; Frank L. Byrne and Andrew T. Weaver, editors, *Haskell of Gettysburg: His Life and Civil War Papers* (Madison, 1970), 98–99.

41. Byrne and Weaver, *Haskell*, 103; Edwin B. Coddington, *The Gettysburg Campaign: A Study in Command* (New York, 1968), 327–328; U.S. Congress, Second Session, Thirty-Eighth Congress, Report of the Joint Committee on the Conduct of the War (Washington, D.C., 1865), Vol. I, 405.

42. Byrne and Weaver, *Haskell*, 100; Gibbon, *Recollections*, 133; *OR*, Vol. XXVII, Pt. 1, 416.

43. Coddington, *Gettysburg*, 343–345, unravels this entire scene.

44. Harry W. Pfanz, *Gettysburg: The Second Day* (Chapel Hill, 1987), 74; *OR*, Vol. XXVII, Pt. 1, 370, 416, 419, 423, 426; Committee, *19th Massachusetts*, 229.

45. John Gibbon to George G. Meade, 24 June 1866, Meade, *Life and Letters*, II, 95.

46. Pfanz, *Gettysburg*, 267.

47. Gibbon, *Recollections*, 136; Committee, *19th Massachusetts*, 226–232, gives a detailed account of this action.

48. *OR*, Vol. XXVII, Pt. 1, 478.

49. Pfanz, *Gettysburg*, 422.

50. The main source for the 2 July conference is Frank Haskell, reprinted in Byrne and Weaver, *Haskell*, 132, but also see Gibbon, *Recollections*, 141–145.

51. Byrne and Weaver, *Haskell*, 134.

52. Frank A. Haskell, *The Battle of Gettysburg* (Boston, 1958), 76.

53. Gibbon, *Recollections*, 145.

54. Coddington, *Gettysburg*, 481.

55. Byrne and Weaver, *Haskell*, 163.

56. Meade, *Life and Letters*, II, 105.

57. Gibbon, *Recollections*, 147–148.

58. This difference on the appropriate employment of the II Corps artillery was to surface in the post-war disputes. Kenneth P. Williams, *Lincoln Finds a General* (New York, 1949), Vol. II, 710, 713–715, 722–723. John Gibbon's subsequent involvement in the issue probably had a significant effect on his later career.

59. Haskell, *Gettysburg*, 89–92; Kenneth P. Williams, *Lincoln Finds a General*, Vol. II, 713–714.

60. Haskell, *Gettysburg*, 91.

61. Byrne and Weaver, *Haskell*, 158; Haskell, *Gettysburg*, 91.

62. Byrne and Weaver, *Haskell*, 159.

63. Thomas L. Livermore, *Days and Events: 1860–1866* (Boston, 1920), 262.

64. Catton, *Glory Road*, 336; *OR*, Vol. XXVII, Pt. 1, 428–429, 431–435; Gibbon, *Recollections*, 153; Byrne and Weaver, *Haskell*, 161, 174; Haskell, *Gettysburg*, 101–102; J. D. Smith, *History of the Nineteenth Regiment of Maine Volunteer Infantry* (Minneapolis, 1909), 124.

65. Haskell, *Gettysburg*, 118.

66. Byrne and Weaver, *Haskell*, 193.

67. *OR*, Vol. XXVII, Pt. 1, 176, 421. The official count of casualties in the 2nd Division, II Corps, was 344 killed, 1,202 wounded, and 101 captured or missing, for a total of 1,647. The highest divisional loss in the Army of the Potomac was 2,155 by the 1st Division, I Corps, which included the Iron Brigade. The 3rd Division, I Corps, suffered almost as heavily. In their overall totals both divisions counted 500 or more men lost as prisoners or otherwise missing. Excluding the captured or missing category, the highest casualties were sustained by the two divisions of III Corps, with totals in killed and wounded of 1,655 and 1,876 respectively. Gibbon's division took 3,773 men into the battle. It was very nearly decimated in the literal sense of the word. On the regimental level, the highest level of casualties experienced was in all likelihood that of the 1st Minnesota of Gibbon's division. In a sacrificial charge on 2 July which checked the Confederate advance on Cemetery Ridge, it took losses of 82 percent; from an initial strength of 262 men, 47 remained unharmed after the engagement. Catton says that this figure constitutes a record for the Union Army *(Glory Road*, 322). The 24th Michigan of the Iron Brigade suffered almost as heavily, losing 80 percent on 1 July *(Glory Road*, 303–304).

68. USMA Register, 1846, 1847; Williams, *Lincoln Finds a General*, Vol. II, 715; records of Robert Gibbon and Nicholas Gibbon as Confederate officers, National Archives. The authors have not been able to establish beyond doubt that Surgeon Robert Gibbon was present at Gettysburg on 3 July 1863, but the available evidence supports that interpretation. Captain Nicholas Gibbon, the regimental commissary officer, was absent on leave in North Carolina. (Typescript copy of Nicholas Gibbon's war journal, lent to Mark H. Jordan by the late Dr. James W. Gibbon of Charlotte, North Carolina.)

West Point, circa 1860. Courtesy Special Collections Division, United States Military Academy Library.

Irvin McDowell. Courtesy Library of Congress.

Winfield S. Hancock, Francis C. Barlow, David B. Birney, and John Gibbon, 1864. Courtesy The State Historical Society of Wisconsin.

General Grant and party, Fort Sanders, 1868. Included in photo are *(left to right)*: Sidney Dillon, Union Pacific board of directors, later president; unknown *(behind Sheridan)*; Major General Philip H. Sheridan; Mrs. Joseph H. Potter; Brigadier General Frederick Dent; Mrs. John Gibbon; Colonel John Gibbon; John Gibbon, Jr.; General U. S. Grant; Katherine Gibbon; Mrs. Kilburne *(nursemaid?)*; Grenville M. Dodge, Union Pacific chief engineer *(in back of Frances Gibbon)*; Frances Gibbon; Lieutenant General William T. Sherman; Lieutenant Colonel Adam L. Slemmer *(behind Sherman)*; Major General William S. Harney; Thomas C. Durant, Union Pacific vice president; Lieutenant Colonel Joseph H. Potter. Photograph courtesy The Oakland Museum.

Edward Bragg, Lucius Fairchild, and John Gibbon. Courtesy The State Historical Society of Wisconsin.

Chief Joseph and John Gibbon, 1889. Courtesy Smithsonian Institution National Anthropological Archives.

6 Into the Wilderness

Recovery from the shoulder wound Gibbon had suffered at Gettysburg took the remainder of the summer and fall of 1863. Finding hot and crowded Baltimore not to their liking, the Gibbons took advantage of an invitation from John H. Latrobe and moved to his summer home in rural Maryland. Although the wound became infected, Gibbon's iron constitution came to his rescue. By the first week of August he was well enough to visit Washington and call on his West Point classmate, Provost Marshal General James B. Fry; and on the following day, 6 August 1863, he sent a proposal to Fry, asking that it be forwarded to Secretary of War Edwin M. Stanton. Gibbon seems to have discussed the matter with General-in-Chief Henry Halleck on the 5th. What Gibbon wanted was the creation in the army organizational structure of a department of artillery (distinct from ordnance), with status comparable to that of the separate engineer bureau. The object of this new organization would be, inter alia, to have artillery officers control artillery operations. In the field they would not have to tolerate interference with their decisions from anyone but the army commander.

Given the timing of this recommendation, it is impossible not to conclude that it reflects the events of 3 July, when Hancock overrode Hunt's order to the Federal batteries to withhold their fire and conserve their ammunition for Pickett's charge. Plainly, Gibbon was siding with his fellow artilleryman against his close friend and immediate superior in the chain of command.[1]

The suggestion went nowhere. The controversy did not reach the public's attention until Hunt wrote in *Battles and Leaders* two decades later. Nonetheless, given the close-knit world of the Regular Army of 1863, it is hard to imagine Hancock's not hearing about it soon after it was made.

Gibbon's implied but obvious criticism of Hancock in this action goes far to explain the full-grown feud that later developed between the two.

By October he was able to return to semiactive duty as commander of the draftee depot in Cleveland. His aide, Frank Haskell, joined him there, and in November they obtained leave to attend the dedication of the National Cemetery at Gettysburg.[2] In their self-guided tour of the battlefield, he and Haskell almost missed Lincoln's dedicatory remarks, and Gibbon never made any comment on them. From Gettysburg Gibbon went to take charge of the Philadelphia draftee depot, and there his family joined him. They spent the winter in Pennsylvania.[3] The next several months were taken up with supervision of the depot, an unsuccessful search for promotion, and involvement in the controversy over Meade's conduct of the Gettysburg battle.

Gibbon was an ambitious man and, as has already been seen, sought advancement. His friends tried to do something for him, but circumstances kept him from command above divisional level. Meade attempted to secure Gibbon's promotion in September 1863, when he wrote to General-in-Chief Halleck to ask that Gibbon and John Buford be promoted to major general of volunteers for their services at Gettysburg. Meade was aware that there were no vacancies in this rank at the time, but he wanted to place himself on record as favoring the promotions.[4] In addition, the proposed reorganization of the Army of the Potomac opened up the possibilities of a corps command. Meade and the War Department recognized that I and III Corps, now very under strength, would have to be deactivated. Moreover, Meade did not have five competent corps commanders. The five army corps of the Army of the Potomac were consolidated into three: II Corps, under Hancock; V Corps, under Major General G. K. Warren; and VI Corps, under Sedgwick.[5] Gibbon came very close to obtaining the command of VI Corps. Sedgwick, although able and beloved by his troops, was not favored by various Republicans nor by Secretary of War Stanton, who wanted him replaced. Meade held them off for a time, and then agreed to assignment of Sedgwick to the Shenandoah Valley command. Gibbon was to be his replacement. However, for political reasons, Lincoln intervened to place Major General Franz Sigel in the Valley command. Sedgwick stayed with VI Corps, and Gibbon returned to his II Corps division.[6]

Hancock's slow recovery from his serious Gettysburg wound also complicated matters, as Meade held up the reorganization of the army until Hancock's return. As late as 15 March 1864 he was writing to Gibbon to request news as to when Hancock would return to active duty. For a time Major General David Birney, whose division had been transferred to II Corps upon the breakup of III Corps, was proposed as the new corps commander. Gibbon disliked Birney, and told Fannie that he would not serve under him. He may have been put off by Birney's abolitionist view-

points, his lack of a West Point background, his cold and ambitious personality, or a combination of all three. Hancock's return to command on
23 March ended that possibility.[7]

Gibbon did not help himself by becoming involved in the controversy
over Meade's decisions during the Gettysburg battle. Although Meade
generally stayed away from the argument over whether he intended to
retreat at Gettysburg, the action of Daniel Sickles drew other officers into
a defense of their commander. Sickles was the author of the wholly fic-
titious story that Meade proposed to retreat after the battle of 2 July, but
was stopped that night by a near mutiny of the corps commanders. Sickles' main medium for this tale was a series of articles he wrote for
various newspapers under a pen name. Both Gibbon and Hancock wrote
to Meade, assuring him of their confidence. Hancock supported Meade in
testimony before the Committee on the Conduct of the War, and Gibbon
wrote a letter to the *Philadelphia Evening Bulletin* disputing the story.
The letter, which was published on the front page, stated that "There is
no truth . . . that one of the corps commanders had . . . an order from
General Meade directing the army to retreat." Gibbon furnished Meade
with copies of all his correspondence on the subject.[8] Meade thanked
Gibbon for his support, but warned him to be careful. Meade's "political
adversaries" would "punish those who have made themselves conspicuous on my side." Gibbon, Meade went on to say, did not realize how
"things are managed nowadays."[9] Eventually, the public controversy died
down, but Gibbon, a quarter-century later, was still writing in defense of
his friend's actions.[10]

Gibbon had no enthusiasm for the coming campaign. The more time
he spent with Fannie and the children, the less he wanted to leave them.
As he later wrote:

I must confess that I was not enthusiastic about taking the field again . . . twice
recommended for promotion by army commanders, but the promotion did not
come, although others got it, and I began to lose heart. . . . This view of the
matter was, I am free to admit, not patriotic but it was human.[11]

Gibbon returned to the Army of the Potomac changed in appearance;
he was now bearded. He had grown beards twice previously, during his
time as a West Point instructor, and after Fredericksburg. The self-por-
trait caricatures with which he decorated his letters in 1862 show only a
mustache. In April 1863, shortly after joining II Corps, he told Fannie that
he had "shaved my beard and put myself in fighting trim." From 1864 to
the end of his life he wore a neat, close beard.

Gibbon was still on the road to Virginia when Hancock resumed command of II Corps. He left Philadelphia on 29 March 1864, arriving in
Washington on the 31st. After giving testimony in support of Meade be-

fore the Committee on the Conduct of the War, he and Meade shared a special train to Culpeper, the headquarters of the Army of the Potomac.[12] He found his 2nd Division altered by the army reorganization. The three brigades were commanded by Alexander Webb, Joshua Owen, and Colonel Sprigg Carroll. Additions from dismantled units brought the roster manpower to 11,367 officers and men, but detachments, sickness, and other deductions reduced the effective strength to about 60 percent of the total. Gibbon's fellow divisional commanders were Brigadier General Francis C. Barlow, Major General David Birney, and Brigadier General Gershom Mott.[13] The remaining five weeks were spent in bringing the new troops up to the high II Corps standards of drill and command. Grant reviewed the entire corps on 22 April, and Gibbon felt that his division was in good condition. However, he missed his family. That night he wrote to Fannie, "My whole soul is wrapped up in you and in my dear children, and however I may be occupied I am never satisfied unless I hear constantly from you." Until the war ended, Gibbon's mind remained preoccupied with his enforced separation from his wife and family. The war was now mere duty to him. Discouragement over promotion, lack of sympathy with war aims, and personality conflicts with men whose friendship he valued made Gibbon's next twelve months generally unhappy ones.[14]

All preparations over, Gibbon sat in his tent on the night of 3 May, waiting for the approaching departure time. As the cavalry units moved toward the fords of the Rapidan River, he wrote Fannie a brief note, saying that the march would begin at midnight and that he would have to leave with his mess bill unpaid. The royalty check from D. Van Nostrand for sales of *The Artillerist's Manual* had not arrived. In the dim light just before sunrise on 4 May, the divisions of II Corps rumbled over the ponton bridges at Ely's Ford. Further upstream, V and VI Corps crossed at Germanna Ford. II Corps did not march much farther that day; Meade ordered it to halt at the clearings around the old Chancellorsville battlefield, where the men made camp between 1:00 and 2:00 P.M.[15]

Union numbers would not be much of an asset in the Wilderness. Grant and Meade did not intend to fight a battle there, but wanted to move through as fast as possible, gaining a march on Lee and possibly getting on his flank. Dense with scrub pine and undergrowth, it was an area of little light, few and poor roads, and vegetation that crept close to every path. Two east-west roads, the Orange and Fredericksburg Turnpike and the Orange Plank Road, a few miles south of it, were the main highways to Fredericksburg in the east. The Germanna Plank Road was the only north-south road suitable for a large body of troops. It crossed the turnpike at Wilderness Tavern. Another ran from the turnpike, crossed the Orange Plank Road, and then went to Todd's Tavern and Spotsylvania Court House. This was the Brock Road. All of these were hard-surface dirt roads, rutted and in poor condition. The worst stretch was between the Orange Plank and upper Brock Roads.[16]

Using the Catharine Furnace Road on the morning of 5 May, the II Corps divisions moved toward Todd's Tavern. Gibbon's division took the lead, followed by Birney (3rd Division), Mott (4th Division), and Barlow (1st Division). Progress was extremely slow, and Gibbon took four and one-half hours to cover seven miles. The heat, for so early in the year, was oppressive, and the insects a nuisance. As his division neared Todd's Tavern, a rider came pounding the road to Hancock, with a dispatch, telling him to halt his corps and await further instructions. The dispatch, written at 7:30 A.M., did not reach Hancock until 9:00 A.M., and was prompted by the appearance of Confederate troops advancing up the Orange Turnpike toward the Union forces on the Germanna Plank Road. The Confederate II Corps of Lieutenant General Richard Ewell was moving to intercept the V Corps line of march.[17]

At about the same time, Lieutenant General A. P. Hill's Confederate I Corps appeared on the Plank Road near Hancock's flank and rear, and threatened to drive a wedge between II Corps and the remainder of the Army of the Potomac. To thwart this move, Meade ordered Union forces to the Brock Road–Plank Road intersection and, by his 7:30 A.M. dispatch, had Hancock countermarch his four divisions, seize the intersection, and attack the head of Hill's column. Turning II Corps proved to be a slow business, and not until 11:00 A.M. did the troops manage to turn about and begin to retrace their steps, with Gibbon's division now in the rear.[18]

The poor roads forced Hancock's divisions to spread out and almost lose contact. Birney and Mott forged ahead with their divisions, while Barlow and Gibbon dropped behind. Not until 2:40 P.M. did Birney make contact with the VI Corps division of Brigadier General George Getty, which had arrived at the intersection and was attempting to hold off the Confederate advance. About 4:00 P.M. Hancock ordered an assault on the leading brigades of Hill's corps. Gibbon, who could see virtually nothing of the fighting, struggled to reach the sound of musketry, which was steadily growing in intensity. Fortunately, he and Barlow arrived at the Brock Road intersection just as the crisis of the first day's battle appeared. Hancock had sent Getty's and Mott's divisions forward in a counterattack, but the extreme fatigue of Getty's men, the lack of visibility and poor ground, and a shortage of ammunition kept his attack from having much power.

Mott's men fared no better. Encountering a line of unseen Confederate infantry, the Union troops were shattered by a number of close-range volleys and broke, running back toward the spot where Hancock had established his field headquarters.[19] As Mott's men appeared from the woods, Hancock spurred his horse into their midst, crying for them to rally and sending his aide, Major W. G. Mitchell, spurring down the road to order Gibbon up on the double-quick.[20] Carroll's brigade was the first to appear. Hancock sent it into action up the Plank Road while Gibbon began feeding his other brigades into the battle as rapidly as they appeared. Owen moved to back up Carroll, and Webb relieved the battered troops of Mott's division.[21]

Gibbon's arrival ended the crisis. Hancock tried to start a counterattack against the Confederate flank with Barlow's division, but confusion and growing darkness put an end to the first day's fighting. All that night Hancock and his subordinates prepared for the next day's battle. In the process, Gibbon's brigades were temporarily assigned to other divisions, rather than moving them, while Hancock placed him in command of a provisional corps assigned to watch the Union left flank. Exposed flanks were much in the minds of the Union commanders that night. Lieutenant General James Longstreet's III Corps had not yet come up, although Grant and Meade knew it was approaching the battlefield. No one knew when it would be available to Lee. The Union army was fighting in the area where, just a year before, Stonewall Jackson had slipped around and flanked Hooker's forces. Meade had already warned Hancock "to look out for his left."[22]

Hancock sent Gibbon, now commanding all of Barlow's brigades and the corps artillery, back down the Brock Road with orders to guard against the chance that Longstreet would attack up that road or the Catharpin Road to the south. Gibbon's position on the Brock Road was too far down to maintain contact with Hancock. A gap now existed between the Union troops clustered around the intersection and Gibbon's units. Facing his men south, Gibbon had them construct a line of crude breastworks and positioned a brigade out to block the Brock Road. The other brigades extended in a line to the east, ending near a large hill. There the terrain cleared, and Gibbon was able to position the corps artillery in battery.[23]

These preparations took all night. At 5:00 A.M. Hancock launched his assault. The exhausted troops of A. P. Hill collapsed and broke toward the rear.[24] Gibbon, obeying his orders, stayed put, while Hancock, even though busily directing the assault, sent him several messages urging him to look out for the left flank. These alarms must have heightened Gibbon's awareness of the importance of his guard post and put him on increased alert.[25] What happened next became a subject of controversy and played a major role in destroying the relationship between Gibbon and Hancock. By 7:00 A.M. Hancock's advance was starting to stall, because of collisions of Union formations in the dense underbrush and the impact of Longstreet's counterattack coming up the Orange Plank Road. Hancock sought, according to his report, to bring renewed power to his attack by calling upon Gibbon's troops.[26] As he later wrote in his report,

At 7:00 A.M. I sent a staff officer to General Gibbon, commanding the left of my line, informing him of our success on my right, and directing him to attack the enemy's right flank with Barlow's division, and to press to the right toward the Orange Plank Road. This order was only partially carried out.[27]

To the end of his life Gibbon insisted that he never received an order to advance, whether from Hancock or anyone else, and that he remained where he was while Longstreet's counterattack developed because he never saw the staff officer Hancock insisted he had dispatched with the order.[28] Although no evidence exists that Hancock reprimanded Gibbon that day, or even shortly after, for his supposed disobedience, the presumed tardiness on the part of his subordinate festered, and by the time Hancock came to write his official report on the Wilderness fighting in November 1864, it had grown into a matter he thought should be placed on the record. Unfortunately, Hancock's recollections of the events of 5–6 May 1864 had become confused, and did Gibbon a grave injustice.

Aside from Hancock's report, the only documentation for the charge that Gibbon failed to carry out Hancock's order exists in the memorandum book kept by Major W. G. Mitchell, Hancock's aide-de-camp and the man supposedly entrusted with the order. Mitchell recorded in the memorandum book that he was dispatched to Gibbon at 7:05 A.M.[29] The book gives the appearance of being a "real-time" record of events. But it was actually put together days or even weeks afterward, using whatever notes or scraps of written and remembered information were available. As a source it is very suspect. The book does not record other equally important orders; for example, there is no account of the message Mitchell carried to Gibbon on the previous day, ordering him to come up and relieve the hard-pressed division of George Getty.[30] What may have happened is this: Hancock, when writing his report, simply confused some of the events of the two days. A specific example is the wounding of George Getty; Hancock speaks of this as happening on 5 May, although it actually occurred on the 6th. Such confusion would be easy to happen to a man who, some months later, was tired, ill, disappointed with the course the war had taken, and discouraged by the supposed failure to destroy a large part of Lee's army in the Wilderness. Hancock was quite sure this had been in his grasp. As he later wrote, "Had my left advanced as directed by me in several orders, I believe the overthrow of the enemy would have been assured."[31]

In addition, still another factor may have influenced Hancock's attitude toward Gibbon and unconsciously encouraged his allegations that Gibbon had failed to perform as ordered. Hancock can hardly have been unaware of Gibbon's proposal on independence for artillery commanders, a suggestion which he could only view as a criticism of his handling of the II Corps artillery at Gettysburg. It would have been more than human of Hancock not to resent this action of Gibbon as a perceived betrayal of their friendship.

When Gibbon began to write his memoirs in the 1880s, he attempted to refute Hancock's charge. This prompted a letter from Hancock, stating that there had been such an order, carried by Mitchell, and that Hancock had also sent a follow-up order, carried by another aide, Captain W. D. W. Miller. This officer confirmed Hancock's assertion in a letter to Gibbon in 1884. Miller also testified that he met Mitchell coming back from delivering the first order. After twenty years, and with Mitchell dead, this testimony deserves no comment.

Putting aside the weakness of the documentation on Hancock's side, there is another point in Gibbon's favor. A reluctance to attack on his part is totally out of character. Gibbon had always displayed a driving pugnacity and fearlessness on the battlefield, at Brawner Farm, South Mountain, Antietam, Fredericksburg, and Gettysburg. His attention to detail and his belief in faithful obedience to and prompt execution of orders were part of his very nature. He expected no less from his subordinates. It is very hard to imagine Gibbon deliberately ignoring a direct command from a commander whom he admired and who was his friend.

In addition, Hancock's first biographer and historian of II Corps, Francis A. Walker, doubted the story. Walker, who had been an assistant adjutant general in II Corps and an intimate of Hancock's, later went on to a distinguished career as president of Harvard University. In his biography of Hancock, he wrote, "The history of war abounds in such misunderstandings. No one who knew Gibbon can possibly believe that this accomplished officer consciously failed to do anything that was required of him." In his history of II Corps, Walker stated that "With the warmest affection and admiration for General Hancock, I feel free to say that my mind has always inclined toward Gibbon's view of the occurrence." If Grant knew anything about this, he attached no importance to it. One week after the Wilderness, he recommended Gibbon for promotion to major general, a move that eventually gave him the two stars that had been so long in coming. Hancock raised no objection, and that would have been the time to do so.[32]

Gibbon played little part in the winding down of the Wilderness battle. By the morning of 7 May, the fighting had died away to picket firing, and neither side showed much inclination for further combat. Of the 6,799 men in Gibbon's division, 164 men were dead and 937 wounded.[33]

Grant now decided to turn Lee's right flank by advancing the army to Spotsylvania Court House. The bridges across the Rapidan at Germanna Ford were taken up and relaid further down the river, and Union cavalry began to probe toward Todd's Tavern and Spotsylvania Court House. An immense train of wounded was dispatched to rear area hospitals. V Corps, leading the march, moved down the Brock Road, followed by VI and IX Corps. Hancock's task was to follow them to Todd's Tavern, entrench, and hold the Catharpin Road against the Confederates.[34]

As Grant's headquarters moved toward Spotsylvania, passing troops still in position, Colonel Theodore Lyman glimpsed John Gibbon, standing by the roadside, "and a tower of strength he is, cool as a steel knife, always, and unmoved by anything and everything. . . ." Two days later he rode with Meade to a conference at Hancock's headquarters, and had another opportunity to record his impressions: ". . . and thither came steel-cold General Gibbon, the most American of Americans, with his sharp nose and up-and-down manner of telling the truth, no matter whom it hurts. . . ."[35]

Gibbon learned of the new move through a circular from Hancock to all division commanders, advising them that II Corps would start after 11:00 P.M. However, daylight came before Barlow's division moved out. The troops took up their blocking positions between 9:00–10:00 A.M. and Gibbon had his men dig a line of rifle pits along the Catharpin Road. There they remained until Meade ordered Hancock to send a division halfway between Todd's Tavern and the area around Spotsylvania Court House. Hancock dispatched Gibbon, who held his position until the entire II Corps moved onto the high ground overlooking the Po River on 9 May.[36]

Grant expected to find a way behind Lee's left flank here, because he ordered Meade to have Hancock cross the Po and push forward to determine Confederate strength in this area. The river, about three feet deep at the crossing, presented no major obstacle, and the crossing was unopposed by Lee's army. Between 4:30 and 6:00 P.M., the divisions of Barlow, Birney, and Gibbon moved over the river. Engineers began to construct ponton bridges while Hancock hurried his forces south, hoping to put his army corps on or behind Lee's flank. He was very impatient and when Gibbon's division, moving in battle formation, slowed the advance, he ordered Gibbon to give way to Barlow. However, by 10:00 P.M. darkness had halted the movement.[37]

During the night Lee moved troops up to guard his flank in such strength that Hancock realized the impossibility of continuing the maneuver. At the same time a change in Grant's plans brought about a Union withdrawal. Gibbon took his division back over the river at 10:00 A.M. and marched, along with Birney, to the V Corps sector. There Meade had planned to assault Lee's lines at 5:00 P.M. This attack was a total failure. Gibbon sent in the brigades of Webb and Carroll, in line together, and held Owen in reserve. The Union troops had had ample opportunity to observe the strength of the rebel trenches, and they attacked with little enthusiasm. Strong enemy fire soon halted the assault.[38] A second attack, which was mounted about 7:00 P.M. by Webb's and Owen's brigades, was also a failure. According to postwar testimony by a member of Owen's brigade, only the divisional commanders even bothered to examine the ground in front of the Southern trenches. And here Gibbon and his commanders saw firsthand evidence of weariness on the part of the troops. Webb was unable to keep his regiments together, had to place one officer under arrest, and discovered the troops who had left their units gathered in the rear, making coffee.[39]

Grant, encouraged by Colonel Emory Upton's partial success that afternoon with a closely massed assault column, now proposed to throw Hancock's entire corps, arranged as an infantry column, at Lee's center. This attack would strike the northern part of the salient, or horseshoe, that formed the center of the Confederate line. On Meade's order, Hancock withdrew Barlow's and Birney's divisions for the approach march. Gibbon was left in position until dark, because Meade believed that a withdrawal by him would alert Lee. He promised to send Gibbon later.[40]

Guided by engineers, Gibbon reached the assembly area around the Brown house at approximately 1:00 A.M., 12 May. Rain, fog, and cold kept discomfort at a maximum and visibility at a minimum. No fires were allowed. Neither Grant nor Meade's officers were able to plot a line of assault, and it is likely they did not know the exact position of the salient apex. Despite this lack of information, Hancock formed his corps for the assault. Marshaled in a rectangular formation were Barlow and Birney on the left and right, supported by Gibbon and Mott, respectively. About 4:35 A.M. the darkness and fog began to lift, and Hancock ordered the men forward. Gibbon had about 1,500 yards to cover before his men struck the Confederate line. During the approach, Hancock ordered Gibbon to advance as support for Barlow's left, and Gibbon moved Owen's and Carroll's brigades forward.[41]

Gibbon, along with the other commanders, was probably having difficulty by this time keeping his formations in order. As the soldiers in front halted to clear the obstacles placed by the Confederates, the rear and front units pressed together until II Corps formed one solid mass of 19,000 infantry. The men surged forward when they saw the Confederate lines, cheering loudly, and crashed into the salient, capturing thousands of prisoners. Carroll's and Owens's brigades entered the line on the east side, occupied some abandoned trenches, and turned two captured guns on the retreating Confederates. Webb, following them, was badly wounded and taken to the rear.[42]

The initial attack was enormously successful, but the Union commanders began to lose control of events as units lost cohesion and the impetus of the attack died. Gibbon's troops, although continuing to occupy captured Confederate positions, took little part in the ghastly deadlock known as the "Bloody Angle." He was repelled and sickened by the carnage. To Fannie he wrote that it "looks like a slaughter pen, and is a sight to make anyone sick of war."[43]

During 12 May the Confederates withdrew to a new line at the base of the salient. Gibbon's division was ordered on the following day to make an attempt to determine the new rebel line. The only result was another bloody repulse and the loss to a serious wound of Carroll, arguably the best of Gibbon's brigade commanders after Webb. Gibbon was, by this time, feeling the strain of almost continual fighting. Lacking confidence in his division, he hoped Grant would not attack again, and that "we will leave it to the enemy to attack." Moreover, his hopes of promotion had dimmed.

There were no vacancies on the major general's list to which he could be posted, and he told Fannie, "I shall believe my promotion when I see it." He was not feeling well: "too busy or anxious to eat," as usual under such excitement he ate "but little and smoke a great deal which does my stomach no good and I feel pretty well worn out."[44] And the war had drawn Gibbon into nearness with his family. A captured North Carolina officer told Gibbon that Robert Gibbon was his regiment's surgeon.

One more assault remained for Gibbon. Since most of the Confederate army had moved off to counter Grant's flanking movement, he felt that any attack on Lee's new line might be productive. Gibbon and Barlow led their brigades forward, passing over the same ground covered by Hancock's grand assault, but struck heavy field fortifications. With his lead brigades pinned down by canister fire, Gibbon could not even advance his reserves. After 2,000 casualties and no results, Hancock withdrew. On 20 May II Corps left Spotsylvania.[45]

Maneuvering replaced heavy fighting. While Gibbon led his division over the North Anna and then the Pamunkey Rivers, he watched his old division drain away. When the campaign had begun on 3 May, the division had approximately 6,800 officers and men. During May it suffered 4,359 casualties. The draft and bounty systems had provided 3,940 replacements, but they were not trained veterans. With these changes the division declined in discipline and performance, and sometimes Gibbon had to take drastic action to curb desertions under fire. The fate of Private John D. Starbird of the 19th Massachusetts, regarded by Gibbon as one of his best regiments, was a case in point.

Starbird had previously deserted and returned to duty. He was on probation when he deserted again during the fighting of 18 May. Captured on the 19th, he was tried summarily by court martial, convicted, and sentenced to be shot at 7:00 A.M. the following morning. Justice moved swiftly in the field. Gibbon approved the sentence that night and forwarded it immediately to Meade's headquarters, which in turn also approved it and quickly returned the papers. A terse entry appeared in Gibbon's diary: "May 19th—a straggler summarily tried today and sentenced to be shot at 7 A.M. May 20th, 7:08 A.M. He is just shot." The firing party consisted of eight men, seven with live ammunition and one with a blank load. The weapons were loaded by the officer in charge and distributed at random. The captain initially detailed for the task could not carry it out; he preferred to take the risks of picket duty instead, and exchanged with a less squeamish fellow officer. In reporting this sad event the regimental historian remarked that the horrible example had a salutary influence on the men who had enlisted for a money bounty, and that its effect on II Corps was the equivalent of receiving another full regiment.[46]

Gibbon dealt swiftly with other offenses. Private Thomas R. Dawson of the 20th Massachusetts, condemned for rape, was hanged during May. He had gotten drunk while on picket duty, deserted the post, and assaulted an old woman. The entire division, formed in square, witnessed his hanging. Dawson rode into the square seated on his coffin in an open wagon, behind the divisional band playing the Dead March. Accompanied by the provost marshal and a chaplain, and surrounded by files of fellow soldiers with arms reversed, the man stood while the noose was placed about his neck. A ghastly error then occurred. The rope was too long, and when dropped, the man touched the ground. The provost marshal had to shorten the rope and repeat the task. At the end, the men were marched past the open grave with Dawson's coffin in it.[47]

Many changes occurred in the Army of the Potomac at this time. Three-year regiments raised in the Spring of 1861 were leaving at the end of their enlistments; their replacements were newly recruited regiments and troops drawn from the defensive fortifications of Washington, which was no longer seen as under a serious Confederate threat. In II Corps Mott's division had developed a reputation for unreliability. At the end of May it was broken up and its units distributed among the three remaining divisions. Along with the other changes, Gibbon had lost some of his most trusted subordinates. Webb and Carroll, who had been wounded, were gone, and Owen was the only brigade commander familiar with Gibbon's methods and style. The first and third brigades, commanded by Colonels H. Boyd McKeen and Thomas A. Smyth, were largely composed of bounty enlistees and drafted men, neither of whom the veterans rated highly. The fourth brigade, under Brigadier General Robert O. Tyler, was made up of former heavy artillerymen, who had spent the war, until now, in the forts that guarded Washington. Although its regiments were large, their capabilities were quite unknown.[48]

Grant's steady advance around Lee's right had placed the Army of the Potomac in a geographical box. The Union army was running out of maneuvering room. Only two alternatives were available to Grant: either break through Lee's lines, or sweep south to and over the James River, abandoning his new supply base at White House. Grant chose the former, and it was this decision that led to the disastrous assault at Cold Harbor.

On 31 May, Union cavalry took the area around Old Cold Harbor from the Confederates, and held their positions until infantry came up to support them. Another attack the next day managed to seize part of the rebel trenches. This encouraged Grant to try for a breakthrough, and he ordered Meade to launch a full-scale assault. He immediately commanded Hancock to move II Corps to the west of Old Cold Harbor, and carry what was thought to be a weak position. The attack was set for 2 June and this meant that II Corps would have to undertake a night march.

The march was a fiasco. Made in intense heat, over dusty roads that covered the troops with white powder, it left the men exhausted for the planned attack on 2 June. A staff officer took one entire division down a narrow path through woods so dense that cannon lodged between trees, and the division became so lost that it was forced to countermarch back the way it had come. The head of the column did not reach Cold Harbor until 6:30 A.M., and the remainder arrived about four hours later. Meade was forced to postpone the attack until 2:40 P.M., and then until the morning of 3 June.[49]

Hancock put his corps into position on the extreme left of the Union line, with his left flank on the Chickahominy River. Once in place, he spent the night deploying the men. The cramped position only permitted the deployment of two divisions for the attack, and Hancock chose his shock troops, those of Barlow on the left, and those of Gibbon on the right. Birney he held in reserve. Gibbon, in turn, formed his men into two parallel columns of two brigades each. Tyler's and Owen's brigades made up the left column, and Smyth's and McKeen's the right. Gibbon ordered Owen and McKeen to keep their brigades in column of regiments until the first line of Union infantry had occupied the enemy's trenches. Then, and only then, were they to deploy into line of battle, pass through the first line, and exploit the breakthrough.[50] Unfortunately, neither Gibbon nor any other of the Union commanders made any attempt to examine the ground or even analyze whether such an assault would be successful. Gradually, but visibly to the naked eye, the ground in front of the Union position sloped upward toward a ridge, giving the Confederates the advantage of the high ground. Lee and his subordinates laid out their front so cunningly as to cover every approach with a devastating crossfire.

At precisely 4:30 A.M., 3 June, the Union guns opened with a bombardment that did nothing but alert the Confederates. As Barlow and Gibbon led their men forward, they encountered musketry fire that one veteran described as the Wilderness and Gettysburg combined.[51] Both Barlow and Gibbon commanded from on foot, realizing what a target a mounted man would make. The uneven nature of the ground caused Gibbon's brigades to strike the enemy line piecemeal. Moreover, as they neared the Confederate trenches, they found a swamp barring their path. It forced the leading brigades to separate to pass around it. As the swamp widened, so did the gap between the brigades. Owen completely forgot his orders and deployed into line of battle, Tyler ran into the same problems, and the whole attack column dissolved in confusion and slaughter. The 164th New York managed to gain control of some trenches, but its colonel was killed and his men driven out. McKeen was also killed and Tyler badly wounded. Smyth, with his brigade isolated, was forced to retreat. However, the Union troops withdrew only a short distance, dug in and remained in place. Barlow, his assault halted, had his men entrench about ninety to 200 feet from the Confederate lines; Gibbon's were closer. The 19th Massachusetts were able to throw stones into the rebel positions, and could bring no rations up until the next night.[52]

The entire battle probably did not last thirty minutes, and in terms of the time involved and the losses, was Gibbon's worst experience of the war. Of his division, sixty-five officers and 1,032 enlisted men were casualties. More depressing to Gibbon than anything else, his "poor friend Haskell," whose regiment, the 36th Wisconsin, had just joined the division, was shot through the head and died a few hours later. Gibbon had already marked him out for brigade command.[53] Although some minor readjustments of the line took place between 3 and 12 June, no real fighting occurred. Picket firing and skirmishing drained another 522 dead and wounded from the divisional ranks during this period. The trenches became pestilential holes to the point where Gibbon called this period "the most trying campaign."[54] The only bright spot for him came on 12 June, when Meade told him that the Senate had confirmed his nomination to be major general of volunteers. Major General Don Carlos Buell, a regular army colonel, had been mustered out of his volunteer rank in order to make a vacancy.[55]

That evening, the Army of the Potomac began to disengage from the Cold Harbor area and fade away toward the James River. Grant's strategic objective was Petersburg. Over its railroads came food and munitions for Lee's army and the Confederate capital. The fall of the city would render Richmond untenable, and Lee would be forced into open country, where Grant's superior numbers could be brought to bear against him. However, there was a great risk involved. If Lee realized what was happening, he could catch the Union army on both sides of the James River and defeat it in detail. Also, if he reached Petersburg ahead of Grant, its immense fortifications would make a direct assault by the Army of the Potomac futile. Grant managed to slip away unnoticed. As darkness came on 12 June the 2nd Division, along with the rest of II Corps, left for the Chickahominy River. During the afternoon of 13 June it crossed on a ponton bridge and arrived at Willcox's Landing, on the James, that night. There Gibbon ordered his men to make camp on the plantation of former President John Tyler. From there he could see the engineers building a

2,000-foot ponton bridge over the river. Warships protected the structure from Confederate gunboats as the clumsy pontons were maneuvered into place and the approaches to the bridge prepared.

Gibbon's division did not use the bridge. Rather than wait for its completion, Meade had steamers assembled to ferry Hancock's men over to the opposite bank. During the morning of 14 June, II Corps crossed, with Birney's division the first over, and Gibbon following. By 15 June the entire II Corps had crossed, except for one regiment of infantry and some artillery.[56] But Hancock delayed the advance toward Petersburg in order to wait for 60,000 rations that Meade had ordered delivered. The morning hours of the 15th were taken up waiting for this food, which never arrived, and not until 10:30 A.M. did Birney's division lead II Corps toward Petersburg. The entire body of troops did not clear the landing area until nearly noon.[57] Terrible heat and dusty roads made the march a trial of endurance. Many men, because of sunstroke or exhaustion, were forced to fall out and rest or find water. A faulty map delayed the advance. In addition, Hancock was confused as to his objective. Not until 5:25 P.M., when a message arrived from Grant, did he understand that he was to assist Major General William F. Smith in his XVIII Corps attack on the Petersburg lines.[58] Birney's and Gibbon's were the only divisions available, but when Hancock finally made contact with Smith, he learned that the latter intended to halt for the night, and only desired II Corps to take possession of the ground he held, so that his men could withdraw and rest. Hancock, although the senior commander on the field, declined to intervene, and the fighting died away. By the next day Confederate reinforcements were filling the trenches, and a great opportunity had been lost. Over the next two days, Gibbon led his men in unsuccessful attacks against the Petersburg lines, until their impregnability became manifest. Grant called off the offensive, and the Army of the Potomac settled down for a siege that would last for eight months.[59]

NOTES

1. JG to Colonel James B. Fry, 6 August 1863; JG to Hon. Edwin M. Stanton, Secretary of War, 6 August 1863. RG 94, Old Army Branch, National Archives.

2. John Gibbon, *Personal Recollections of the Civil War* (New York, 1928), 170–173; Frank L. Byrne and Andrew T. Weaver, eds., *Haskell of Gettysburg: His Life and Civil War Papers* (Madison, 1970), 232–233.

3. Gibbon, *Recollections*, 184.

4. George Gordon Meade, Jr., ed., *The Life and Letters of George Gordon Meade*, Major General, United States Army (New York, 1913), II, 184. (Buford died in December 1863 and was posthumously promoted to major general.)

5. John Gibbon to Fannie Gibbon, 1 April 1864, GP, HSP (hereafter cited as JG to FG.)

6. Gibbon, *Recollections*, 209–210.

7. JG to FG, 4 April 1864, GP, HSP; David Jordan, *Winfield Scott Hancock: A Soldier's Life* (Bloomington, 1988), 106–107.

8. Edwin B. Coddington, *The Gettysburg Campaign: A Study in Command* (New York, 1968), 348, 721–722; Meade, *Life and Letters*, 186; Gibbon, *Recollections*, 185–186.

9. Gibbon, *Recollections*, 185–186.

10. John Gibbon, "The Council of War on the Second Day," in Robert U. Johnson and Clarence C. Buel, editors, *Battles and Leaders of the Civil War* (New York, 1956), III, 313–314.

11. Gibbon, *Recollections*, 198.

12. Byrne and Weaver, *Haskell of Gettysburg*, 240–242; JG to FG, 1, 4 April 1864, GP, HSP; Gibbon, *Recollections*, 209. Gibbon and Meade had written to the governor of Wisconsin recommending Haskell for this promotion. From the Secretary of War Gibbon also obtained for Haskell an appointment as assistant adjutant general with the rank of major. (Haskell file, Adjutant General's Office, RG 94.)

13. Francis A. Walker, *History of the Second Army Corps in the Army of the Potomac* (New York, 1886), 401–403.

14. JG to FG, 22 April 1864, GP, HSP.

15. Andrew A. Humphreys, *The Virginia Campaigns of 1864 and 1865* (New York, 1883), 18–19; JG to FG, 3 May 1864, GP, HSP; Gibbon, *Recollections*, 211.

16. George A. Agassiz, editor, *Meade's Headquarters, 1863–65. Letters of Colonel Theodore Lyman from the Wilderness to Appomattox* (Boston, 1922), 89.

17. U.S. War Department, *The War of the Rebellion: A Compilation of the Official Records of the Union and Confederate Armies* (Washington, D.C., 1887), Vol. XXXVI, Pt. 1, 318 (hereafter cited as *OR*); Gibbon, *Recollections*, 211; Edward J. Steere, *The Wilderness Campaign* (New York, 1965), 104–106; *OR*, Vol. XXXVI, Pt. 2 403.

18. *OR*, Vol. XXXVI, Pt. 1, 318. Gibbon's division later moved to third place in the column. Gibbon, *Recollections*, 211.

19. Agassiz, *Meade's Headquarters*, 92.

20. Agassiz, ibid.

21. Agassiz, *Meade's Headquarters*, 92; *OR*, Vol. XXXVI, Pt. 1, 320.

22. Jordan, *Hancock*, 118.

23. *OR*, Vol. XXXVI, Pt. 1, 321–323; Gibbon, *Recollections*, 214–215.

24. Gibbon, *Recollections*, 214.

25. Steere, *Wilderness Campaign*, 339–341.

26. Steere, ibid.

27. *OR*, Vol. XXXVI, Pt. 1, 321.

28. Gibbon, *Recollections*, 394.

29. Mitchell's note is in *OR*, Vol XXXVI, Pt. 1, 351.

30. Agassiz, *Meade's Headquarters*, 92.

31. Quoted in Gibbon, *Recollections*, 402n–403n.

32. Ulysses S. Grant to Secretary of War Edwin M. Stanton, 13 May 1864, in Ulysses S. Grant, *Personal Memoirs* (New York, 1885), II, 234–235; for a thorough discussion from Hancock's point of view, see Jordan, *Hancock*, 120–122.

33. Agassiz, *Meade's Headquarters*, 103, 107; Walker, *Second Army Corps*, 441–443; *OR*, Vol. XXXVI, Pt. 1, 434.

34. *OR*, Vol. XXXVI, Pt. 1, 329. Mott's division was now operating under Sedgwick's VI Corps.

35. Agassiz, *Meade's Headquarters*, 103, 107.

36. William D. Matter, *If It Takes All Summer: The Battle of Spotsylvania* (Chapel Hill, 1988), 123–125.

37. Matter, *Spotsylvania*, 150.

38. Matter, ibid., 153.

39. Matter, ibid., 184.

40. Matter, ibid., 192; Gibbon, *Recollections*, 219–220; *OR*, Vol. XXXVI, Pt. 2, 409–410.

41. Gibbon, *Recollections*, 219–220; JG to FG, 13 May 1864, Gibbon Papers, MS 1284, Maryland Historical Society (hereafter "GP, MHS"); Bruce Catton, *A Stillness at Appomattox* (New York, 1954), 118–122.

42. Gibbon, *Recollections*, 219–220; *OR*, Vol. XXXVI, Pt. 1, 431, 448; JG to FG, 13, 14, 15 May 1864, GP, MHS.

43. Meade, *Life and Letters*, II, 197; JG to FG, 7 May 1864, GP, MHS.

44. *OR*, Vol. XXXVI, Pt. 1, 340–343; Gibbon, *Recollections*, 224.

45. Gibbon, *Recollections*, 223–224; History Committee, *History of the Nineteenth Regiment Massachusetts Volunteer Infantry 1861–1865*, 315 (Salem, 1906).

46. John G. B. Adams, *Reminiscences of the Nineteenth Massachusetts Regiment* (Boston, 1899), 94; Committee, *19th Massachusetts*, 315.

47. *OR*, Vol. XXXVI, Pt. 1, 434; Adams, *19th Massachusetts*, 84–86; Committee, *19th Massachusetts*, 300–301.

48. Charles H. Porter, "The Battle of Cold Harbor," *Military Historical Society of Massachusetts Papers* (Boston, 1905), IV, 327–329; Walker, *Second Army Corps*, 506–507; *OR*, Vol. XXXVI, Pt. 1, 344, 432; Catton, *Stillness at Appomattox*, 238. Gibbon said that his division, which had nine miles to cover that night, ultimately marched fifteen miles.

49. *OR*, Vol. XXXVI, Pt. 1, 345; Gibbon, *Recollections*, 232–233.

50. John D. Billings, *History of the Tenth Massachusetts Battery of Light Artillery in the War of the Rebellion* (Boston, 1881), 200.

51. Porter, "Cold Harbor," 344–345; *OR*, Vol. XXXVI, Pt. 1, 345; Adams, *19th Massachusetts*, 98.

52. Walker, *Second Army Corps*, 512–513; *OR*, Vol. XXXVI, Pt. 1, 433; JG to FG, 4 June 1864, GP, MHS; Adams, *19th Massachusetts*, 99; Committee, *19th Massachusetts*, 319.

53. Walker, *Second Army Corps*, 521; Agassiz, *Meade's Headquarters*, 146; *OR*, Vol. XXXVI, Pt. 1, 434.

54. JG to FG, 12 June 1864, GP, HSP; Gibbon, *Recollections*, 240–243; OR, Vol. XL, Pt. 1, 303; Grant, *Memoirs*, II, 279–290.

55. Gibbon, *Recollections*, 243; *OR*, Vol. XL, Pt. 1, 366, 303.

56. Jordan, *Hancock*, 143.

57. Gibbon, *Recollections*, 243; *OR*, Vol. XL, Pt. 1, 303–305; James M. Aubery, *The Thirty-Sixth Wisconsin Volunteer Infantry*, 82–83 ([no place of publication or publisher], 1900).

58. *OR*, Vol. XL, Pt. 1, 366, 303–304.

59. *OR*, Vol. XL, Pt. 1, 167, 174, 206; Aubery, *36th Wisconsin*, 84–91. The events of 15 June 1864 and the failure of the Federals to capture Petersburg were a Union tragedy. Bruce Catton estimates that the mistakes of that day added eight months to the Civil War. (Catton, *Stillness at Appomattox*, 189.)

7 A Winter of Discontent, and Glorious Summer

Although the opening of the siege lines around Petersburg signaled the end of full-scale fighting, Grant's strategy of extending his lines and seeking to cut Lee's communications meant that the troops would be involved in a series of corps-level battles along the vital railroads. Not all of these were Union victories, but they did serve the purpose of further grinding down the already weak Confederate forces. Also, they revealed just how deeply deterioration had set in among some of the best units of the Army of the Potomac.

The first of the small battles was precipitated when Grant sent General Horatio Wright's VI Corps and II Corps (now temporarily under David Birney) out to cut the Weldon Railroad. Along the Jerusalem Plank Road they clashed with A. P. Hill's veterans, and were humiliated. The Confederate commander held Wright in place with one division while mauling Birney's three divisions with his other two. Not particularly severe in terms of killed and wounded, the defeat was most disheartening for the mass of II Corps men taken as prisoners. Whole regiments went down virtually without firing a shot, and one six-gun battery was lost with no attempt to recapture it.

Gibbon recognized that some of his best regiments were simply burnt-out cases, full of half-trained or untrained men, lacking cohesion or drive. Losses of proven leaders in the preceding weeks had taken their toll. The 15th Massachusetts—the crack troops on whom Gibbon had relied a year previously to face down the mutineers of the 34th New York—had surrendered at Jerusalem Plank Road after little more than token resistance. The night after the battle Gibbon poured out his disillusionment in a letter to Fannie. Part of the trouble, he believed, could be assigned to the fact that the enemy knew the country better than their opponents. But the main reason for failure was the condition of the soldiers, "who are thoroughly worn out and exhausted with marching, fighting, and loss of sleep, and it is not much to be wondered at." They had "been thro' some fearful scenes lately."

June of 1864 was a sad time for John Gibbon. In the "quite heavy fight" of 16 June he thought of "poor little Johnny," dead a year previously. Fannie was in an advanced state of pregnancy, and the prospect of his being absent from her coming confinement made him almost desperate— "but," he wrote, "I serve a hard master."[1]

In his report to Meade, Gibbon laid out the cold facts. Starting with an effective strength of 6,799 on 5 May, the division had taken 7,970 casualties by the end of June; these losses amounted, in net terms, to 72 percent of original strength plus replacements. In effect, the 2nd Division had been recycled. Officer turnover was particularly heavy. Seventeen brigade commanders had passed through the table of organization. Of the officers killed or wounded, forty were regimental commanders, including among them some outstanding leaders. Haskell, heading the 36th Wisconsin, had died atop the enemy's works at Cold Harbor; for another instance, the 20th Massachusetts had been led in the Wilderness by Major Henry Abbott, "the *best* officer in the division," who had been mortally wounded there.

As a result, brigades were sometimes led by lieutenant colonels, regiments by captains, companies by lieutenants of very little experience. This situation was potentially disastrous for an army of the character of the Army of the Potomac, which depended for victory upon mutual confidence between officers and men. Now, neither knew what to expect from the other. Some superiors had lost the trust of their subordinates. A good many officers probably had lost confidence in themselves. What II Corps needed was a long period of rest, discipline, and training. Gibbon doubtless remembered with fondness the Iron Brigade days, when the unity was so deep that response in battle was instinctive.[2]

At the top, too, things were not the same. Hancock had not been present at the Jerusalem Plank Road fight; his Gettysburg wound had reopened and was sloughing out bone, forcing him to go on leave. Several minor clashes with his superior convinced Gibbon that "General Hancock was suffering from the wear and tear of the campaign, increased probably . . . by the opening of his Gettysburg wound, or that he no longer desired the continuation of the cordial relations heretofore existing between us, and I reached this latter conclusion with a very considerable degree of regret."[3] Hancock was not the same man he had been. In the postwar Army his relationship with Gibbon would become one of open antagonism.

If Gibbon's relations with Hancock were unpleasant, those with his troops were not much better. He had previously clashed with "Paddy" Owen of the Philadelphia Brigade during the march to Gettysburg, as already noted. Now, after Cold Harbor, Gibbon preferred court-martial charges against him for deploying the brigade too soon during the attack, in defiance of orders. Owen was not tried but was sent back to civilian life. At the end of June the 15th, 19th, and 20th Massachusetts, once the cream of the division but now shrunken down to a total of one thin battalion, were consolidated. Owen's famous brigade was totally broken up. Its men jeered Gibbon when they saw him.[4]

Gibbon himself was feeling the "wear and tear" of continuous fighting. On 5 July he wrote "I wish sensible men would get together and put a stop to this war. . . . We had best now to conclude to make peace and live together amicably." Wear and tear notwithstanding, there had been one bright spot in the recent grim weeks. In the interim between the Petersburg and Jerusalem Plank Road debacles, his commission as major general had at long last arrived, and even as he wrote of stopping the war, he gave a dinner party in celebration of his added star. Meade, Hancock, Burnside, and Birney were among the guests, a band provided music, and all present enjoyed a merry time. Shortly thereafter he was able to take leave to be with Fannie in Baltimore for the delivery of a new son, also named John.[5]

During this time of frustrated hopes Gibbon and Hancock clashed in two petty squabbles that hastened the collapse of their friendship. On 25 July, during operations near Deep Bottom, Major General Philip H. Sheridan and his cavalry became hotly engaged by Confederate infantry. Hancock ordered Gibbon to hold his division ready to move on short notice and prepare to support the horsemen. While Gibbon waited for further orders, Hancock approached and demanded to know if his division was in motion. Gibbon, surprised, replied, "No, sir, I have received no orders to move it." Hancock then claimed he had so ordered half an hour before. Gibbon responded by quoting his previous orders from his superior.

The discussion grew heated, and Gibbon told Hancock, "General Hancock, either I am very stupid this morning or you unintelligible, for I certainly did not understand you to give any such order." When Hancock called upon Mitchell, a man for whom Gibbon had considerable respect, for confirmation, Mitchell agreed with Gibbon. The 2nd Division then went forward to support Sheridan.[6]

The next day Gibbon had his troops throw up breastworks, and Hancock told him he would be up to inspect the line. While Gibbon was talking with Sheridan, Hancock approached, "evidently under considerable excitement." With an oath, he demanded to know who had laid out Gibbon's line. Gibbon answered that he had. Hancock told him loudly that he should be ashamed of such dispositions, and ordered Gibbon to follow him. "Get on your horse," he said, "and come with me; I will show you where it is defective!"[7]

When they reached the line Hancock indicated an area where the terrain would provide an approaching enemy with concealment from the men behind the breastworks. Gibbon pointed out that he had placed an artillery battery on the left that would thoroughly enfilade, long before it reached Gibbon's works, any attacking force which tried to take advantage of the ground. Hancock, taken aback, retorted, "Well, I will hold you responsible for your line and everything that may happen here."

Gibbon said, "General, I am perfectly willing to be so held responsible and I regret you had not come to that conclusion before insulting me in such a way before half a dozen general officers of the Army." Hancock then apologized to Gibbon and to the officers present, but nothing could ever take back the sharp words between the two former friends.[8]

After a short sick leave at home in August, Gibbon returned to his troops just in time for another railroad-cutting expedition, this one aimed at the hamlet of Ream's Station, south of Petersburg. The tragedy there completed his break with Hancock. Ream's Station had no effect on the outcome of the war, and was really a rather minor business; its significance is in the way it revealed the state of affairs in II Corps.

Hancock reached the railroad on 23 August. By nightfall on the 24th his men had torn up about three miles of track and done a considerable amount of damage. That night word came of the approach of A. P. Hill's corps. On 25 August, as Confederates advanced, Hancock drew his troops into a square formation, with the east end open. He anchored his front on the railroad embankment, with Brigadier General Nelson A. Miles' division, formerly Barlow's, on the north face and Gibbon's on the south.[9]

The green regiments of Gibbon's division, some of which had never been under fire, became demoralized when Hill's corps opened a severe fire that took them in the rear. As the final Confederate assault of the afternoon came pounding in, first Miles' division broke, and then part of Gibbon's. Gibbon was unable to rally the fugitives or even get them out of their trenches, a brigade in reserve refused to obey Hancock's orders to counterattack, and a large number of troops simply surrendered rather than fight. Gibbon did manage to mount what he called "a feeble effort," but the enemy drove him out, and took two guns. Hancock decided not to wait for reinforcements, and withdrew that night. About 1,700 prisoners, plus nine guns and twelve regimental colors,[10] were among the 2,790 casualties suffered by II Corps.

The 2nd Division returned to camp about 1:00 A.M.; Gibbon collapsed, exhausted. He managed to scribble a brief note to Fannie, saying that "we were somewhat severely handled." Two days later he described it as a "severe and terrible battle, and a mortifying one for the 2nd Corps, which is becoming pretty well used up. . . ." Disgusted and disillusioned, Gibbon turned to his division and to Hancock in resorting to drastic steps. First, he deprived three regiments—36th Wisconsin, 8th New York Heavy Artillery, and 164th New York—of the right to carry colors until they proved their worthiness to have them restored. There was precedent for this action (McClellan had done it to a New York regiment), but it was a slap in the face to the troops involved and was bitterly resented.

Resentment ran particularly strong in the 36th Wisconsin. The regiment had been recruited, trained, and—until his death in battle—led by a genuine hero, Frank Haskell. Unlike their fellow Badgers of the Iron Brigade, who had had a year or more of Army seasoning before their baptism of fire at Brawner's Farm, the 36th had been thrust straight from Wisconsin into the crucible of war. They left Madison on 10 May, and a week later made an all-night march from Belle Plain, below Mount Vernon, to join the Army of the Potomac at Spotsylvania.

At Bethesda Church on 1 June the 2nd Division made a demonstration intended only to divert Confederates attempting to retake a series of rifle pits captured by Birney's 3rd Division the day before. Four companies of the 36th, having misunderstood their orders, charged 100 yards across an open field, drove in the enemy pickets and got into the Confederate main line; of the 240 men who partook, 140 became casualties. At Cold Harbor, unlike their fellows of the noted Philadelphia Brigade, which deployed prematurely and refused to budge, the raw Wisconsin regiment had gone right up to the enemy's works, to its considerable cost. Now its men saw themselves as unfairly singled out in the aftermath of another action in which they had again sustained heavy casualties. They protested that a number of other regiments had also lost their colors without being penalized, suggesting that the more fortunate units had representatives "nearer the throne," that is, on the division commander's staff.

The embattled Badgers did not take their punishment silently, and the resultant furor had high-ranking generals snapping at each other. Second Lieutenant George E. Albee of Company F, captured at Ream's, was soon paroled. As a spokesman for the 36th's prisoners of war in Richmond he made his way to Washington and under the aegis of Assistant Postmaster General Alexander W. Randall, a former Wisconsin governor, obtained an audience with the President. Lincoln referred him to Secretary Stanton with an endorsement requesting that he be given a hearing, and his letter wound its way down through the chain of command to the 36th and back up again.

Meanwhile, someone had challenged Gibbon's authority to assign this penalty, and in consequence he sent forward for review at higher levels his division general order announcing the punishment. Hancock took no exception, but noted that it should apply to all regiments that lost colors. Army of the Potomac headquarters approved the action, and established it as a general rule for the army, but did not make the policy retroactive. This made Gibbon unhappy, in that only the regiments in his division were bearing the stigma, whereas a number of other units had suffered the same calamity. Hancock's endorsement quibbled with Gibbon on semantics, and taxed him for omitting the 20th Massachusetts from the penalty list; Miles, to whose division the 20th had been attached at the Ream's debacle, said that the regiment had surrendered, almost to a man, without doing anything. Meade in his endorsement quarreled with Hancock, supported Gibbon, stood his ground on his own policy, and shipped the entire mass of paper up the line.

Fortunately, a more favorable action at Hatcher's Run at the end of October gave everyone an opportunity to draw the curtain on this brouhaha. On 7 November Meade issued Army of the Potomac General Order No. 41, restoring their colors to the regiments concerned, and on the day following the Adjutant General's Office passed the whole bundle to the Secretary of War. The Battle of the Colors was over.[11]

Gibbon took another step that did not please his superior. He wrote a letter to Hancock urging a complete reorganization and reshuffling of II Corps' divisions, weeding out incompetent officers and even breaking up regiments that were substandard in their performance. This would amount to nothing less than a wholesale purge, and Hancock did not accept the idea. A personal interview with Gibbon on the evening of 27 August degenerated into a sharp verbal exchange, and Gibbon returned to his tent to write Hancock another letter. He offered to agree to the breakup of his division, if it would do some good. Hancock immediately wrote in reply that if Gibbon resigned his command, it would be in the best interests of the service.

The affair had escalated beyond the bounds of reason and common sense. Although Gibbon, infuriated, did submit his resignation and asked Hancock to forward it through channels, eventually both men calmed down. After a two-hour discussion held at the corps commander's initiative, Hancock admitted that "I was mad when I wrote this letter," and agreed to withdraw it. Gibbon in turn asked Hancock not to forward the resignation, and the latter then held his own offending missive in the flame of a candle.[12]

All of this was perfectly consistent with Gibbon's character. In the Fort Crittenden affair, in the circumstances surrounding the removal of McClellan, in his relief of Sully from command, and in his dealings with Owen he bulled ahead, doing what he thought was right, regardless of consequences. This was consistent with the reputation that he held in the army, of speaking out regardless of the consequences, on which Theodore Lyman had remarked to his wife.[13] John Gibbon was no trimmer, and, although he was ambitious and jealous of personal rights, his willingness to take drastic action detrimental to his own welfare is wholly admirable.

Despite the fence mending, and the fact that he and Hancock parted on "reasonably good terms," he realized that the old friendship was gone forever.[14] The formal tie with II Corps was weakened when Grant, on 3

September, ordered Gibbon's temporary transfer to command of XVIII Corps, Army of the James. For two weeks he replaced Major General E.O.C. Ord, who was going on sick leave. Gibbon was glad to depart.

Gibbon took advantage of the XVIII Corps assignment to make an attempt at establishing contact with his family on the other side of the lines. Regular communications between the two opposing high commands were maintained by way of a daily truce boat plying the James River. Having heard that the 28th North Carolina was in the vicinity and having obtained Grant's permission, Gibbon sent a letter via the truce boat to his brother Nick, suggesting that they meet under the truce flag at Aiken Landing. Nick's reply was terse and frosty: "It is not agreeable that I should meet you under the circumstances proposed in your note, although I have no doubt that I could obtain permission from Gen. Lee if I desired it." John was conciliatory in return: "I regret your decision . . . and assure you that under no circumstances could such a meeting with one of my brothers prove disagreeable to me. Should we ever meet hereafter you will find me as ever, your affectionate brother." Nick's hostility apparently was not shared by other family members. At the time of the Wilderness battle Catharine Gibbons managed to pass a letter to her sister Fannie across the lines; in it she spoke of their great anxiety about "our Dear Jack."[15]

Two months later Hancock's wound forced him to go north on a temporary leave which turned out to be permanent. Since he had been for some time II Corps' senior division commander, and since he had twice been called upon to serve temporarily as a corps commander, Gibbon had hoped to succeed Hancock. Meade, however, perhaps aware of the tension which Gibbon's appointment might cause, gave the job to his chief of staff, Major General Andrew A. Humphreys.[16]

Humphreys was a good choice—like Gibbon an exceptionally able man, a fighter and disciplinarian, just the type needed to rebuild II Corps. But at this perceived insult, Gibbon entirely lost his temper. He wrote to Meade, declared the selection of Humphreys to be "a direct slight on me," and went on to say that "I have the honor to request that I may be relieved at once from my present command." This was no offhand reaction; Gibbon wanted out. Disappointed in his hopes for a corps, frustrated by the events of the summer and fall, and perhaps discouraged by the prospect of censure in Hancock's Wilderness report, he was embittered.[17]

Grant pulled Gibbon up short, and told him to stay where he was. A command rearrangement was imminent. Thanks to Butler's failure at Fort Fisher, Grant was finally able to remove that inept general and promote Ord to command of the Army of the James. Gibbon received permanent command of the new XXIV Corps, Army of the James, and with it "hearty congratulations" from Meade. On 14 January 1865 the latter told his wife that Gibbon had been in to say goodbye, and "he was in quite a good humor." [18] The advancement had made a remarkable change in Gibbon's disposition.

All signs pointed toward the spring campaign's being the final one of the war, and with Lincoln remaining firmly in control, there was no doubt that Grant would receive all needed support. Gibbon, whose sympathy had gone to McClellan in the Presidential campaign, did not and never would care for the more radical politics of the Republican Party. He was "delighted" when McClellan accepted the Democratic nomination, and went on to remark that "I don't see how any body [sic] but an unprincipled politician can now accuse him of being in favor of any dishonorable peace or anything short of the restoration of the Union and the Constitution." When Lincoln was returned to power, Gibbon expressed relief that the election was over without any serious disturbance. What he now hoped for was more men from the draft. [19]

Gibbon's new command, one of the two corps in the Army of the James, was a standard formation of three divisions: the First, under Brigadier General R. S. Foster; the Third, under Brigadier General Charles Devens; and an Independent Division, commanded by Colonel T. M. Harris. Another division, led by Brevet Major General Alfred Terry, belonged nominally to the corps, but it was off on detached service at Fort Fisher. [20] Fannie's brother Edward Moale, now a temporary lieutenant colonel, joined Gibbon's staff as assistant adjutant-general. The corps remained inactive on the Petersburg front, north of the James River, during the dwindling months of winter, the only excitement deriving from an attempt by Confederate gunboats on 24 January to pass the river obstructions. As the winter waned, improving weather brought expectations of more serious fighting. [21]

Grant had the army in motion at the end of March, sending Sheridan with the cavalry and a strong force of infantry out to the Union left on a stroke aimed at the Southside Railroad and the turning of Lee's flank. In connection with this move, XXIV Corps was brought from the James front and went into II Corps' old position around Hatcher's Run. In place by the morning of 28 March, Gibbon's infantry beat off an assault on their picket line on 1 April, with the Confederates "handsomely repulsed." [22]

After the Confederate disaster at Five Forks on the same day, Lee realized that his Petersburg lines were untenable. If they broke through the lines Ord and Gibbon, along with Wright's VI Corps, could seize Petersburg and cut the Army of Northern Virginia in two. Lee had to get his army out and over the Appomattox River. In the Confederate defenses opposing the Union forces were two small earthworks, Fort Gregg and Battery Whitworth, held by less than 500 men. Among the defenders were North Carolina troops of Lane's brigade, in which Robert and Nicholas

Gibbon had served. Lee promised the garrisons that if they could hold for two hours, Longstreet would come to their support.

Ord ordered Gibbon to assault and take the forts, and at 5:30 A.M. on 2 April, Gibbon started his preparations. Before the attack could be launched Gibbon received orders to support Wright's VI Corps, which had penetrated the enemy's lines. In response he pushed some of his brigades forward and, seizing the Confederate line in his front, linked up with Wright.

Riding forward, Gibbon met Wright and told him that resistance had collapsed as far as Hatcher's Run. Gibbon wanted to take his still intact corps to Petersburg, but Ord ordered him to envelop the town from the west. Sending Harris off toward Petersburg, Gibbon launched his other infantry toward Fort Gregg. Twice the brigade columns were driven back by very heavy resistance; Gibbon soon realized that success would only be achieved if he could swamp the defense by dint of numbers, accepting the resultant losses. While he was getting his troops into position, his old friend James Longstreet spied him through his field glasses and raised his hat to him. Gibbon was much too busy to see and return the greeting.[23]

Another brigade brought from in front of Battery Whitworth increased his force to 8,000, and Gibbon sent them forward in a single flood. Reaching the walls, the Union troops clambered into the fort, pulling each other up by hand over the parapet. Once inside, the fighting became hand-to-hand, and for twenty minutes a desperate struggle went on until the garrison was overwhelmed. Gibbon's losses of 122 killed and 592 wounded were more than three times those of the defenders.[24]

On the following morning, 3 April, Gibbon's corps marched through Petersburg in pursuit of the fleeing Confederates. During a halt at a clogged road junction Gibbon was overtaken by Grant and his staff, and learned from the General in Chief of the fall of Richmond. As his men formed ranks Gibbon rode down the lines, telling the troops of the capture of the Confederate capital. One man called out, "Stack your muskets and go home!"[25]

Grant's objective was now the pursuit and envelopment of Lee's army, in order to prevent its escape to Lynchburg. While II, V, and VI Corps followed the Army of Northern Virginia directly and forced it into a series of rearguard actions that delayed its retreat, XXIV Corps sought to outrace Lee around his southern flank and secure a blocking position athwart his route.

Fifty-three miles of hard marching in two days brought the corps to Burke's Station on the 5th, and on the 6th it set out for Farmville in the continuing attempt to get across Lee's line of retreat. At Rice's Station Gibbon ran into Longstreet's rearguard, but by the time his columns had deployed for attack, night had fallen. The assault, ordered for the morning of the 7th, was canceled because the Confederates had faded away in the darkness. Pushing down the Prince Edward Court House road, the troops tore "down fences, marching thro' woods, and across streams."

On the same day Gibbon heard of the capture of General Richard S. Ewell and the Confederate rearguard of 8,000 men at Sayler's Creek. Word of the taking of a prisoner by Custer's cavalry gave Gibbon an opportunity for a not-too-gentle gibe at his sister-in-law, Augusta Moale. "Tell Gussie," he wrote to Fannie, "that we have accomplished what she never could, for today we captured Frank Huger." South Carolinian Huger, West Point 1860, had been serving in the Army of Northern Virginia as an artillery colonel. It can be guessed that, during a visit with the Gibbons at the Military Academy in Huger's cadet days, vivacious Gussie had set her cap for him with no success. Gibbon might have added that, far from being on his way to a prisoner-of-war camp, Huger was now riding and tenting with his old West Point friend George Armstrong Custer.[26]

Although the bridges at Farmville were burning when the Union troops reached them, the engineers soon laid a ponton bridge over the Appomattox. While their men bivouacked, Ord and Gibbon called on Grant at his headquarters in the Farmville hotel. The General in Chief remarked to them, "I have a great mind to summon Lee to surrender,"[27] and very shortly thereafter did so. The end was fast approaching.

Next morning XXIV Corps pressed forward toward Appomattox Court House, now some thirty miles away. On the road they were joined by V Corps, now commanded by Gibbon's classmate Charles Griffin, and some of Sheridan's cavalry. At Gibbon's urging, the march continued until midnight.[28] Gibbon began to think that "the men are wound up machines which will run till the spring gives out."

After only three hours sleep, the troops were awakened at 3 A.M. on the 9th, and by 5 A.M. XXIV Corps was astride the road from Appomattox Court House to Lynchburg. Lee was now cut off and forced to make a stand. Foster's division, on the road, and that of Brigadier General John W. Turner (who had replaced Harris in division command) next to it, had started to advance toward the Court House, when the sound of musketry ahead of them grew louder. Union cavalry, disorganized, tore through Gibbon's lines, disorganizing them in turn. With the formations restored, Ord ordered Gibbon forward, and the entire corps in line of battle pushed through a patch of dense underbrush.

Just as the Union artillery prepared to open fire, word came that Grant and Lee were in conference. Putting Foster into a defensive square, Gibbon rode ahead to Appomattox Court House, just too late to witness the departure of Lee. Coming down the steps of the McLean house was Brevet Major General George A. Custer, carrying the table on which Lee had signed his surrender. Gibbon promptly sat down and dashed off a note to Fannie: "When you get this go down on your knees and thank Almighty God for his great goodness to us, for today Genl. Lee's whole army surrendered to us . . . I hope never to hear a gun fired in battle again."[29] The day was one of impromptu reunions among old friends who only hours before had been enemies. Gibbon reminisced with George Pickett and Harry Heth, and his two classmates told him that, had their situations been reversed, he as a traitor to the South could have expected to be hanged.

Although the fighting was over, the Civil War did not wind down immediately for John Gibbon. The ceremonies for the formal parading, surrender, and paroling of the Army of Northern Virginia had to be organized, and for this purpose Grant and Lee each appointed three generals as surrender commissioners. Representing Lee were James Longstreet, John B. Gordon, and W. H. Pendleton. The Union commissioners were John Gibbon, Charles Griffin, and Wesley Merritt of the cavalry.[30] On 10 April the six officers met in the Clover Hill Tavern, but finding this an unattractive site, moved to the surrender room in the McLean house. The commission deliberated over technicalities in perfect courtesy and frankness, following the tone that Grant had set. It was mainly concerned with the issuance of paroles, the surrender and collection of equipment, and the receiving of muster rolls from the Confederates.

At 8:30 P.M., on Gibbon's old camp table, the final documents were signed, and arrangements made for the formal surrender ceremonies. On 12 April, before John Turner's division of XXIV Corps and a division of V Corps, and under the immediate supervision of Brigadier General Joshua L. Chamberlain, the Army of Northern Virginia stacked arms for the last time. Gibbon had his portable printing press strike off the multitude of parole forms needed. After receiving rations, the former Confederate soldiers departed, and Gibbon telegraphed to Grant:

The surrender of General Lee's army was finally completed today. We have paroled from 25,000 to 30,000 men. One hundred and forty-seven pieces of artillery have been received, about 10,000 small arms, and 71 flags. . . . . . I have conversed with many of the surrendered officers and am satisfied that by announcing at once some terms and a liberal, merciful policy on the part of the Government we can once more have a happy, united country.[31]

For a few days Gibbon was occupied with the destruction of military equipment, but by April 17 he was on the road to Richmond, from where he went on to Washington. Gratified by the sentiment which he had found in Virginia toward the end of hostilities, he hoped that "we are now all on the right road to peace."[32]

Gibbon's career as a corps commander was at an end. With the mustering out of the volunteers, his regiments would soon fade away. In order to cut expenses and eliminate maintaining a useless headquarters, Grant recommended the dissolution of XXIV Corps. On 13 June 1865 the corps was mustered out and Gibbon transferred to command of the Military District of the Nottoway, with headquarters at Petersburg. For the time being he retained the rank of major general.

Occupation duty, brief though it was, did not appeal to Gibbon. First, he did not like what he had seen of the freed slaves. At Lynchburg he thought "all they have to do is plunder," and from Petersburg he wrote to John Latrobe that most of his time was spent in trying to reconcile civil and military law in attempting to provide for the "inevitable negro."[33] By winter the blacks would be without food or shelter. He wanted to send them out of the city to some old army camps. As a conservative Democrat, John Gibbon had no great admiration for emancipation policy, and he rather gleefully noted that the blacks were "lazy and disinclined to work, and . . . the negro question is a delicate one to handle without burning one's fingers in these ticklish times of freedom and free suffrage."[34]

One cloud hung over his mind: the uncertainty of the future. Soon all the trappings of rank and increased pay would vanish, when he would leave the volunteer service to become once again Captain John Gibbon, Regular Army. As for going back to command of a company, "the thing is out of the question." He asked Latrobe to look out for something for him. Gibbon simply could not expect to support his wife and three children on a captain's pay and allowances.[35]

Fannie managed to join him at Petersburg in October, and they remained in Virginia until 28 December, when he was mustered out as a major general of volunteers. Finally, the Civil War was over. Brief though it was in years, the 1861–65 period would always be, emotionally, the major phase of his life. For him, as for many sensitive men of North and South, their Civil War memories stretched farther and loomed larger than any other remembrances. And they carried those memories with them to the end of their days.

Gibbon had returned from the West in late 1861 as a good officer who showed promise, but his only notable accomplishment to that date had been the authorship of *The Artillerist's Manual.* By 1865 he had risen in rank as far as he could expect to go; had shown that he could train, administer, and lead large bodies of troops; and had revealed a sturdy, determined character that could be relied on by his superiors. A redoubtable fighter as well as a man ambitious for himself, John Gibbon could look forward to the post-1865 years with some confidence in his future success.

A long career of service lay ahead of him. The transition from war to peace is not always easy, and John Gibbon was to find it a difficult one. Keenly aware in his own mind of what he regarded as his rights, and determined to assert them vigorously against all threats of encroachment by superiors, he was to find that the very trait of stubborn pugnacity that had served him so well in battle would prove less than an asset in the peacetime Army.

NOTES

1. John Gibbon to Fannie Gibbon, 23 June 1864 (hereafter cited as JG to FG), U.S. Military Academy Library.

2. On the losses and Gibbon's assessment of their effect, see U.S. War Department, *The War of the Rebellion: A Compilation of the Official Records of the Union and Confederate Armies* (Washington, D.C., 1887), Vol. XXXVI, 434, Vol. XL, Pt. 1, 368 (hereafter cited as *OR*), and John Gibbon, *Personal Recollections of the Civil War* (New York, 1928), 227–228; JG to FG, 7 May 1864, GP, MHS.

Gibbon's admiration of Henry L. Abbott was reciprocated. In the aftermath of Gettysburg Abbott, writing to his family, characterized Gibbon as "a splendid officer." A month before his death he assessed the leadership immediately above him as follows: "But just think of our getting Gibbon back again. With Webb for brigade commander, Gibbon for division & Hancock for corps, we have got a team that can't be beat." Robert Garth Scott, editor, *Fallen Leaves: The Civil War Letters of Major Henry Livermore Abbott* (Kent, Oh. 1991), 189, 244.

3. Gibbon, *Recollections*, 243–244.

4. *OR*, Vol. XL, Pt. 2, 444–445; Joseph R. C. Ward, *History of the One Hundred and Sixth Regiment Pennsylvania Volunteers* (Philadelphia, 1883), 232; *OR*, Vol. XXXVI, Pt. 3, 435.

5. JG to FG, 5, 26 July, 21 August 1864, GP, HSP.

6. Gibbon, *Recollections*, 248.

7. Gibbon, *Recollections*, 250.

8. Gibbon, *Recollections*, 251.

9. *OR*, Vol. XLII, 293.

10. *OR*, Vol. XLII, 294; James M. Aubery, *The Thirty-Sixth Wisconsin Volunteer Infantry*, 125–131 ([no place of publication or publisher], 1900).

11. JG to FG, 25, 27 August 1864, GP, HSP; Aubery, *36th Wisconsin*, 131; General Orders No. 61, 28 August 1864, and No. 63, 30 August 1864, 2nd Division, II Corps, Army of the Potomac (Aubery, 133). Aubery, 131–153, gives lengthy coverage to the deprivation of the colors issue.

The return of the 36th for 26 August 1864 shows forty-three men present for duty, 143 casualties (fifteen killed and wounded, and 128 prisoners of war (Aubery, 130–131).

12. This account of the episode is drawn entirely from Gibbon, *Recollections*, 258–262. Hancock left no record of it, and apparently never told the story to anyone.

13. George A. Agassiz, ed., *Meade's Headquarters, 1863–1865. Letters of Colonel Theodore Lyman from the Wilderness to Appomattox* (Boston, 1922), 107.

14. Gibbon, *Recollections*, 262.

15. Nicholas Gibbon journal. Family tradition has it that Nick never again spoke to John; CLG to FL, 8 May 1864. It would appear that by 1864 Catharine Gibbons had reconciled herself to the once-despised nickname.

16. JG to FG, 3 September 1864, GP, HSP; Gibbon, *Recollections*, 262–263.

17. Gibbon, *Recollections*, 274–275.

18. JG to FG, 3, 6 December 1864, GP, HSP; Gibbon, *Recollections*, 277; George Gordon Meade Jr., ed., *The Life and Letters of George Gordon Meade, Major-General, United States Army* (New York, 1913), II, 256.

19. JG to FG, 10 September, 11 November 1864, GP, MHS.

20. Gibbon, *Recollections*, 280–282.

21. JG to FG, 25 January 1865, U.S. Military Academy Library.

22. JG to FG, 1 April 1865, U.S. Military Academy Library.

23. Gibbon, *Recollections*, 298; *OR*, Vol. XLVI, Pt. 1, 1174; Shelby Foote, *The Civil War: A Narrative* (New York, 1974), III, 882.

24. *OR*, Vol. XLVI, Pt. 1, 1174; Gibbon, *Recollections*, 301.

25. Gibbon, *Recollections*, 300–302.

26. JG to Mr. (?) Wells, 19 April 1865, GP, MHS; JG to FG, 7 April 1865, GP, HSP; *OR*, Vol. XLVI, Pt. 1, 1174; Burke Davis, *To Appomattox: Nine April Days, 1865* (New York and Toronto, 1959), 269; E. Porter Alexander, *Fighting for the Confederacy* (Gary W. Gallagher, ed.) (Chapel Hill, 1989), 522, cited in Alan T. Nolan, *Lee Considered* (Chapel Hill, 1991), 208.

27. Gibbon, *Recollections*, 306.

28. Gibbon, *Recollections*, 308, 310.

29. JG to FG, 9 April 1865, GP, MHS; to Wells, 19 April 1865, GP, MHS; Gibbon, *Recollections*, 314–317.

30. The roles of Gibbon and Merritt in the closing scene of the war provide an ironic counterpoint to the farcical "treason" affair at Fort Crittenden. The three "patriots" who brought the accusations all had undistinguished war records. None of the accused officers abandoned the Union, and four of them—Gibbon, Merritt, Cooke, and Sanders—became generals.

31. Horace Porter, *Campaigning with Grant* (New York, 1897), 496–497; Gibbon, *Recollections*, 323–339.

32. JG to FG, 14 April 1865, U.S. Military Academy Library; Gibbon, *Recollections*, 346–347.

33. JG to FG, 14 April 1865; to John H. Latrobe, 7 September 1865, GP, HSP.

34. Gibbon, *Recollections*, 346–347.

35. JG to John H. Latrobe, 7 September 1865, GP, HSP.

8 War on the High Plains

In the aftermath of the Civil War the United States Army assumed occupation duties in the South and found itself thrust deep into the politics of Reconstruction. However, occupation could not be expected to last forever, and the Army's high-ranking officers realized that a resumption of its police duties on the Western frontier would eventually require most of the military's time and energy. Meanwhile, many officers remained uncertain of their status while Congress debated the size and structure of the postwar Army. Although he expressed his distaste for remaining a captain of artillery, Gibbon held on to his commission until the situation clarified.

From December 1865 until April 1866 Gibbon remained with his family in Baltimore, serving on various court-martial boards: the brevet promotion board for ranks below general in the cavalry, the artillery, and the staff corps, and on the new Board of Artillery. The latter board, instituted to recommend improvements in the gunnery arm, also oversaw the reestablishment of the School of Artillery at Fort Monroe.[1] In addition, Gibbon found himself embroiled in a minor way with the controversy over the conferring of brevet ranks.

The mid-nineteenth-century Army did not award medals to officers in recognition of exceptional conduct and service; instead, brevet promotions were used as a reward, and were usually granted for bravery in battle. These commissions were not merely honorary; assignments to command could be made on brevet rank basis, and officers wore the uniforms (although not the rank insignia) of their brevet ranks. Congress did however, deflate the system in 1869 and 1870 by ordering that only uniforms of regular rank be worn.

Another feature of the brevet system was that an officer holding a brevet commission was customarily addressed by the title of his brevet rank, rather than the substantive rank in which he was actually serving. A newly married Army bride described the system:

In the Army, lieutenants are called "Mister" always, but all other officers must be addressed by their rank. At least that is what they tell me. But in Faye's company, the captain is called general, and the first lieutenant is called major, and as this is most confusing, I get things mixed sometimes. Most girls would.[2]

Gibbon had long felt that the system of brevet promotions was abused and in August 1864 had taken a strong stand against a recommendation to extend this recognition to officers for purely administrative reasons. Hancock and Meade had agreed with him, and the proposal was dropped.[3] However, the end of the war brought a flood of brevets, in many cases politically inspired; it threatened to demean and dilute the honor which the brevet was intended to convey. In one of his last acts as a major general, Gibbon declined appointment to the brevet ranks of major, lieutenant colonel, colonel, and brigadier general in the Regular Army.[4] Clearly, he meant this rejection to be a protest against the profusion of empty honors.

For brevet commissions to become effective, the Senate had to confirm them in the manner prescribed for regular commissions. The uproar generated in the Army by the indiscriminate award of brevets at this time (1866) led the Senate to refuse to confirm any of them. In response to this reaction and to the widespread criticism of the system, the War Department in the spring of 1866 appointed several officer boards to consider and recommend on all potential Regular Army brevet promotions.

The most senior board, known from its place of meeting as the St. Louis Brevet Board, had the task of making recommendations for brevet promotions to major general and brigadier general. Its members (William T. Sherman, George G. Meade, George H. Thomas, and Philip H. Sheridan) were all major generals by regular commission. (Sheridan never served on the board. In order to force withdrawal from Mexico of the European troops supporting the puppet Emperor Maximilian, the administration stationed Sheridan on the Texas-Mexican border at the head of a strong army; there he remained while the board deliberated.)

The St. Louis board took cognizance of the fact that a brevet holder could be assigned to duty in his brevet rank, if the needs of the service required. Consequently, it envisioned the brevet list as akin to a reserve of generals who could be called on to serve in that rank in the event of a national mobilization. This view led it to limit severely the number of brevets it recommended; it proposed twenty major generals and sixty-six brigadiers. Of the major generals, seven already held the regular rank of brigadier general; John Gibbon, still only a captain in Regular Army rank, was fifteenth on the list. Such was the esteem in which the senior generals of the Army held him.[5]

Other boards were appointed to make selections for brevet promotions to ranks below general. Gibbon, with A. J. Smith and J. G. Parke, served on the board to recommend brevets in the cavalry, artillery, and staff corps.

In the last analysis the view of the St. Louis board did not prevail. When the final list was published in *Army General Orders* late in 1866, the list of new brevet major generals filled nine pages. Nonetheless, Gibbon, possibly mollified by the recognition given him by the St. Louis board, accepted his commission as Brevet Major General, U.S. Army, on 19 December 1866.[6]

Gibbon's decision to remain in the service and await developments proved wise. On 28 July 1866 President Andrew Johnson signed into law an "Act to increase and fix the Military Peace Establishment of the United States." The law made a substantial increase in the size of the regular army, decreed the number and size of regiments, and broke the impasse regarding promotions and assignments. General-in-Chief Grant drew up a list of recommendations for appointment of new colonels and submitted it to Secretary of War Stanton on 7 August; number eight on the list was John Gibbon.[7] Throughout the summer of 1866 many officers waited for announcement of the new promotions. One rumor circulated that Gibbon would be offered the colonelcy of a new black regiment. A friend quoted the story to him in a manner that suggested that of course Gibbon would decline such undesirable duty. The reply was pure Gibbon: "I would take a regiment of monkeys to get a command!" As it developed, the black regiments went to other men. On 7 October 1866 Gibbon sent the Adjutant General his acceptance of appointment as colonel of the new 36th Infantry Regiment, and returned the required oath of allegiance. After passing a physical and professional examination in New York City before a board headed by Colonel Christopher C. Augur, he was ordered to join his regiment on the Western frontier. Except for relatively brief breaks, the West would be his station for the rest of his Army career.[8]

The combined demands of Reconstruction occupation and pacification of the frontier occasioned the expansion of the post-1865 Army. Under the 1866 Act the cavalry grew from six to ten regiments and the infantry from nineteen to forty-five, while the artillery remained static at five. Two regiments of horse and four of foot were to be made of up of black enlisted men led by white officers. Incorporated into the new establishment was John C. Calhoun's concept of an expandable army. At the discretion of the President, each infantry company could have between fifty and 100 privates. This number was eventually set at sixty-four, giving the Army a paper strength of 54,302 officers and men.[9]

Standing at the head of the Army were Ulysses S. Grant, now a full general, and William T. Sherman, lieutenant general. There were also five major generals and ten brigadiers. The generals were distributed throughout the country in command of a system of divisions, departments, and districts, established on a geographical basis. The deployment of the frontier field force was determined by the need to protect from potential Indian assault the railroad construction work and the constantly increasing number of settlers. Sherman commanded the frontier regulars from his headquarters of the Military Division of the Missouri at St. Louis.[10]

Despite its expanded strength, the Army in which John Gibbon now served was little different from the pre-1861 version. Still significant were three main problems: its small size, the inadequacy of its appropriations, and its general neglect at the hands of the public and the Congress. Motivated by reasons of economy and the perennial debate over the propriety of a standing army in a democracy, the national legislature cut away continually at the army establishment. By 1874 it was down to 27,000 officers and men.[11] A general officer list of only three major generals and six brigadiers insured that the scramble among the colonels for promotion to the infrequent vacancies would be intense. In the lower ranks long stagnation in grade was the rule. Arthur MacArthur (father of Douglas), an outstanding regimental commander in the war, became a Regular Army captain in 1866, and remained such until 1889. (An exceptional case produced by the regimental promotion system for lieutenants was that of Ernest J. Garlington, West Point class of 1876. Commissioned a second lieutenant on his graduation, he found himself a first lieutenant two weeks later. He had been assigned to the 7th Cavalry.)

Muster rolls never matched authorized strengths. The 24th Infantry in 1876 had in its largest company seven privates fit for duty. At the battle of the Big Hole in 1877 Gibbon's command averaged twenty-four men per company. The main reasons for this chronic manpower crisis were sickness, desertions, and recruitment failure. Low pay, unattractive service opportunities for enlisted men, and sometimes brutal discipline all combined to deter good men, who might have become long-term professionals, from entering the ranks.[12]

The officer corps stood in no better light. Despite a general scarcity of line personnel, detached service assignments drained away experienced people to staff appointments. As a 3rd Cavalry officer reported, "I am captain of Company D. I am absent on sick-leave; my first lieutenant is absent on recruiting service; my second lieutenant is an aide-de-camp to General Crook, and there is not an officer on duty with the company."[13] When the 7th Cavalry was all but destroyed at the Little Big Horn, fifteen of its forty-seven officers, including Colonel Samuel D. Sturgis (Custer was the lieutenant colonel), were absent.

Low pay and snail's-pace advancement also hamstrung the officer corps.

In 1870, with all pay and allowances, Gibbon earned $3,500 per year. Considering the cost of travel, and the high price of goods on the frontier, this was not enough to support a family and educate children properly. There was no mandatory retirement system. Promotion up to colonel was still by seniority—within each regiment as far as captain, within the branch for the field grades (major to colonel). The President filled general officer vacancies by selection at his own discretion. Frequently this discretion was affected by political considerations. Thanks to various factors, including a steady succession of Republican chief executives, Gibbon remained a colonel from 1866 to 1885.[14]

At the top and throughout its ranks the officer corps grew old and stagnated. Energy declined and interests narrowed. Long range planning among the top men was almost nonexistent until the 1880s. Civil War service still loomed large in memories, and officers defended their past conduct with all the aggressiveness and tenacity they had shown on the battlefield. At times this aspect of Army life became sour and acrimonious, dividing the officer corps into factions. Involvement in national politics proved disastrous to some careers, leading to the exiling of good men to distant posts when they threatened to expose corruption and mismanagement within the War Department. Once again the officer went back to learning all about fifty dragoons, and little else. This was John Gibbon's army, and he was no less a product and symbol of it than any other long-term officer.[15]

Even though his new assignment took Gibbon to a sparsely settled land, devoid of many comforts, he at least had two items that cheered him: a new command to manage, train, and lead; and the presence of his family. Fannie, the two daughters Frances and Katherine, and young John were going to be with him in Nebraska Territory. Moreover, his contacts with North Carolina had been renewed. Soon Catharine Gibbons' letters to Philadelphia resumed, full of news about her children, and especially stories about "Jack." Despite the Civil War, the close-knit Gibbons and Lardners had picked up their ties as if war had never intervened.

Rail transportation carried the Gibbon family to St. Joseph, Missouri, in November 1866; there they found all the steamboats laid up and Missouri River service suspended for the winter. Gibbon promptly bundled his four charges and their baggage into a nine-passenger stage coach and continued onward. After 150 miles they ferried the Platte River and took to an open freight wagon, with the children and Fannie covered with straw for warmth. On the day after Christmas they reached Fort Kearney, Nebraska, headquarters for the 36th.[16]

Gibbon's command was quite typical of old army regiments in both its duties and its manpower characteristics. Part of the Department of the Platte, the forts and camps held by the regiment were sited along the line of the Union Pacific Railroad, and the chief duty of the troops was to provide guards for engineers and working parties. Some companies also watched over the route of the Overland Mail.[17]

At Fort Kearney Gibbon found the 36th in the process of being organized from the former 3rd Battalion, 18th Infantry, the 2nd Battalion of which had been severely handled by Indians in the Fetterman massacre at Fort Phil Kearny, Wyoming, earlier in the winter. In addition to getting his regiment into fighting trim, Gibbon also served during the winter and spring of 1867 as president of the court of inquiry ordered to investigate the Fetterman disaster. After several months of taking testimony the court was disbanded without completing its report. The members were needed at their regular duties and no more time could be devoted to the investigation.

When Gibbon took over the 36th it was still in the throes of organizing. In the expansion from a battalion to a regiment two companies were being added, and the units were not yet up to strength. Of the 600 men carried on the rolls, many had not yet reported. Officers were in short supply. Twelve second lieutenants and one captain remained absent, and Gibbon had to write to the Adjutant General for their addresses so that he could order them to join the regiment. To a man whose recent life had been spent in higher command amid the tumult of the Civil War, the petty details of regimental administration must have been irksome.[18]

Moreover, command of the District of the Rocky Mountains was soon added to his regimental responsibilities. Much of his time was taken up in travel between the widely scattered units of his commands. His troops were constantly on the move from post to post as construction of the railroad progressed and the needs for protection of the work shifted accordingly. As a typical example, in January 1867 Company K and regimental headquarters were at Fort Kearney; I at Fort McPherson, Nebraska; E at Fort Sedgwick, Colorado Territory; G, C, and H at Camp Douglas, Utah Territory; B and D at Fort Morgan, Colorado Territory; and A and F at Fort Sanders, Wyoming Territory. At the end of 1867 only three companies were at the posts that they had garrisoned when the year opened. On the average, during 1867 each company of the regiment moved its base three times. These moves typically were made on foot, and the daily march distances averaged twenty miles or more.[19]

From the isolated posts details went out to guard the railroad line, protect woodcutting parties, watch over the mail routes, and pursue the continual trickle of deserters. They also had construction duties of their own to perform. Although Fort Sanders had been an established post for some time, during the month of April 1867 three of the regiment's ten companies were reported as having construction work on the fort for their primary assignment.

Clashes with Indians were minor; there were no major battles, although in April and May 1867 two sergeants were killed in action. Action of a different sort befell Company E in July of that year when it was dispatched to Julesburg, Colorado Territory, to aid the civilian authorities in establishing order over that turbulent community. Julesburg was the third and most unruly of the "moving towns" that sprang up to provide entertainment of various sorts to the railroad construction forces.

Personnel turnover was high in the 36th, with absenteeism a constant problem. For example, twelve men deserted in May 1867 and thirty-seven the following month; six previous deserters were also recovered. Of the twenty-seven who left in April 1868, four were from Company E; three were prisoners in the guardhouse serving general court-martial sentences, and the fourth the sentinel assigned to guard them. Pursuit, recapture, and punishment were not the only hazards which a defector faced. In April 1867, while attempting to get away, Private James Byrnes was fatally wounded by Indians. Isolation and monotonous duty, compounded by personal problems, sometimes induced even more desperate measures than desertion. During the summer of 1868 two enlisted men took their own lives.[20]

As the Union Pacific Railroad approached completion, the reconstruction of the South was also proceeding. Readmission into the Union of former Confederate states permitted a decrease in the number of troops occupying the defeated Confederacy. Consequently, in 1869 Congress reduced the number of infantry regiments from forty-five to twenty-five. Gibbon had barely had enough time to become thoroughly acquainted with his command and duties when the 36th Infantry was disbanded, its personnel reassigned to the 7th and 13th Regiments. The authorized strength of the Army fell to 37,000-odd. Gibbon's Rocky Mountain District vanished from the Army organizational structure in December 1868 and on the 2nd of that month its commander left for thirty days' léave. Soon he had to apply for a five-month extension because of the death of his father. In 1868 John Heysham Gibbons had combined a trip to Chicago with a visit to Fort Sanders, by then John Gibbon's headquarters, and this was the last time Gibbon saw his father. On 4 January 1869 he died. Making his way to Charlotte, Gibbon enjoyed a reunion with his mother and several of his sisters and brothers.[21]

During his eastern leave Gibbon for the first time fell into the kind of controversy with superiors that was to stud the record of his remaining Army career. Deep antagonism toward Irwin McDowell clearly appears to have underlain Gibbon's actions at this time, despite the fact that McDowell had done him a tremendous favor in sponsoring him for his first star. It is a tragedy of Gibbon's life that his post–Civil War years were marred by petty battles against two men, McDowell and Hancock, with whom he had once been on warm and friendly terms.

The explanation of Gibbon's hostility to McDowell almost certainly lies in the debacle of Second Bull Run. In the aftermath of that battle Gibbon's close friend Fitz John Porter, who has been called "an American Dreyfus," was stripped of his corps command, court-martialed on charges brought by John Pope, convicted, and dismissed from the Army. At Porter's trial McDowell was the prosecution's star witness. Since his own actions at Second Bull Run were also under investigation, McDowell was hardly unbiased. During the trial Porter told his wife, "McDowell has worked up his evidence to do me the most injury and has sworn to several things which are deliberately false." McDowell's role in the case was sufficient to make John Gibbon his enemy for life. Gibbon's actions toward McDowell in 1869 and again in 1873 can only be explained as deliberate attempts to flout that general's authority with impunity. Both times he failed.[22]

In February 1869, while spending his leave in Philadelphia, Gibbon was summoned to appear as a witness before the Retirement Board, which was meeting in New York City and was presided over by McDowell, now a permanent brigadier general. The summons, which called for his testimony before the board to be given on the 6th, reached him on the 4th or 5th. He did not appear on schedule, but sent the board a note in explanation: complying with the summons would have interfered with other engagements which he had already made; however, he would be in Brooklyn on the 9th for the wedding of an officer in his regiment, and would appear before the board at noon on the 10th. The note crossed in transmission with another summons from the board, delivered to him by the hand of the bridegroom; it called for him to report to the board at 11:00 A.M. on the 9th. Gibbon ignored the second summons, which would have caused him to miss the wedding. On the 10th he appeared at the board room precisely (by his reckoning) at 12:00 noon. Understandably, McDowell was also watching the time precisely, and adjourned the board a few seconds before Gibbon's arrival. The board called on him for a written explanation, found it "Not satisfactory," and referred the whole matter to Washington. In due course Gibbon received a written admonition from the new Commanding General of the Army, William Tecumseh Sherman.[23]

Back in Philadelphia he received orders on 15 March 1869 assigning him to the 7th Infantry as its colonel. He and his family joined the regiment at Omaha on 1 June and from there moved to the regiment's headquarters at Camp Douglas, Utah, arriving there on 15 June. The golden spike signifying the linkup of the Union Pacific and Central Pacific Railroads had been driven at Promontory on 10 May. Gibbon thus missed by a month the historic ceremony that he and his 36th Infantry had done much to bring about.[24]

The 7th Infantry, reinforced by part of the disbanded 36th, was dispersed throughout the territories of Utah and Wyoming. Companies E, H, and K were at Fort Bridger; A, C, G, and headquarters at Camp Douglas; B, D, F, and I at Fort Frederick Steele, Wyoming Territory. Their duties included protection of the Union Pacific line, of various Indian reservation agencies, and of the small settlement of "Miners' Delight." The troops also had to haul logs and lumber for construction of barracks and storehouses. Not all the casualties were caused by Indians. The 7th lost 1st Lieutenant Louis M. Hughes during action in a saloon at Miners' Delight, when the saloon bar fell on him.[25]

In the spring of 1870 the regiment was transferred to Montana Territory. The move was made largely on foot, over a distance of approximately 600 miles. One detachment of three companies, bound for Fort Buford at the confluence of the Yellowstone and Missouri Rivers, was more fortunate. It traveled by rail to Sioux City and thence by paddlewheel steamer to its destination, a total distance of 2,317 miles. During the move of this battalion, an incident occurred that brought Gibbon into one of his many postwar conflicts with Winfield Scott Hancock; it also gives some insight into the mores of the closed community that comprised the Indian-fighting army, Army internal politics, and the personnel procedures used to prune the officer strength of the Army in its post-Reconstruction reduction.[26]

On the night of 14–15 May, as the steamer "Emilie LaBarge" lay moored to the bank of the Missouri River, the mate of the vessel discovered 1st Lieutenant George Bomford and the wife of 1st Lieutenant Constant Williams in a compromising position on the sofa of the pilot house. The ensuing scandal rocked the entire detachment; court-martial charges were preferred against Lieutenant Bomford, while Lieutenant Williams hurriedly obtained leave to take his wife back East to her parents' home in Saratoga Springs, New York.

In order to escape a most unpleasant situation, Lieutenant Bomford applied to be detached from the regiment and placed in the status of "waiting orders." This action placed his whole Army career at risk. The Army was in the process of selecting officers for involuntary elimination from the service, an action necessitated by the reduction in the overall size of the Army which Congress had enacted the preceding year. Officers on the "unassigned" list were particularly vulnerable. Bomford was a member of an old Army family; his father was colonel of the 8th Infantry and his grandfather had been Chief of Ordnance. Colonel Bomford intervened with the Adjutant General of the Army to delay transferring his son, and drew a reply from Commanding General William Tecumseh Sherman that Lieutenant Bomford's only escape from the scandal would require leaving his present regiment.

Meanwhile, George Bomford had been sent to Fort Sully, Dakota, to await further orders. After several weeks of reflection, he decided to take his chances with the 7th Infantry, and withdrew his request for the unassigned list. This request was promptly granted by the Adjutant General. Accompanying the special order that returned him to his regiment was a highly unusual authorization from the General of the Army enabling the department commander, Hancock, to transfer Bomford from Fort Buford to another post within the 7th Infantry.

Under existing Army regulations, the position of an officer within the organizational structure was strictly controlled by fixed rules. When a second lieutenant was commissioned initially, he was assigned to a specific company in a specific regiment. He remained attached to that company until he reached the top of the second lieutenants' seniority list in his regiment; when a vacancy for first lieutenant occurred in the regiment, he went to the company in which the vacancy had occurred. The process was the same when, in the fullness of time, he became a captain. Normally, only the Adjutant General of the Army could change this process. Transfers between regiments could be made only by exchanging officers of the same rank, with the consent of the officers involved and their superiors in the chain of command, and with the provision that neither could gain an advantage on the regimental promotion list by the process.

At the first lieutenant level, a regimental commander had some influence through his power to appoint the regimental adjutant and regimental quartermaster, positions that were exchangeable with that of first lieutenant of a company. Granting to a department commander the authority to transfer a first lieutenant from one company to another, even within the same regiment, was a highly unusual step to take; it evidences the concern that Army brass evidently felt for the interests of the son of a senior Army officer.

It was this authorization that led to Gibbon's clash with Hancock. Hancock's adjutant general directed Gibbon, now at Fort Shaw, to nominate a first lieutenant for exchange with Bomford. Gibbon, not knowing of Sherman's authorization, promptly challenged Hancock's order as a violation of an Army general order. At the same time he expressed his view that "neither the services of [brevet] Major Bomford nor his conduct in the Regiment" entitled Bomford to a transfer, which would occasion "some meritorious officer great expense and inconvenience." Upon reiteration of Hancock's directive, Gibbon proposed a three-way exchange involving officers at Camp Baker and Fort Shaw, which would send Bomford to Camp Baker (a smaller and presumably less desirable post than Fort Shaw). Hancock overruled him and ordered a direct swap that took Bomford to Fort Shaw. Gibbon protested, and drew a reply from Hancock's adjutant general chiding him for lack of respect and subordination to the department commander. This was the first of what were to be many such exchanges between Gibbon and Hancock.

Court-martial charges alleging conduct unbecoming an officer and a gentleman and conduct to the prejudice of good order and discipline had been preferred against Bomford by 1st Lieutenant William Logan, the detachment adjutant, whom the detachment commander, Lieutenant Colonel Charles C. Gilbert, had assigned to investigate the matter. Over Logan's protest, they were quashed first by Hancock and then by the Adjutant General of the Army.

The injured husband received rather different treatment. When Williams learned that the charges against Bomford were not to be pressed, he asked that they be destroyed rather than be preserved in the records of the matter; his wishes were ignored. While returning from his leave in the East, he sent a request to Hancock for transfer. "I am in no condition to bear what I know awaits me if I join the command at Fort Buford," he wrote. Hancock's response was to order him to Buford "without delay." To his credit, however, Hancock also wrote to the Adjutant General: ". . . if this officer (Lieutenant Williams) is to remain in service, I think it would be only a matter of charity to him, to transfer him to another Regiment."

The arrival of Williams at Fort Buford triggered a series of events that Lieutenant General Philip H. Sheridan, commanding the Military Division of the Missouri, characterized a year later in restrained language as a serious garrison quarrel at "the most isolated post in the service." According to Williams, Logan instigated a conspiracy among the officers to "cut" Williams socially and also to "cut" anyone who visited or entertained him. (Williams' offenses, in Logan's eyes, seem to have been that he did not press charges against Bomford and that he did not divorce his wife.) Williams promptly began feuding with Lieutenant Colonel Gilbert, now the post commander, over the question of whether an enlisted man of the 7th who had been identified as a deserter from a previous enlistment had been properly reported and treated as such. Williams prepared court-martial charges against Gilbert that charged falsification of records and improper handling of the deserter's case; quite in violation of Army procedures, he forwarded them to Department of Dakota headquarters at St. Paul directly, rather than through Post Commander Gilbert. Gilbert in his turn charged Williams with conspiring with two enlisted men to produce his charges, and with transmitting them in violation of Army Regulations. Williams now turned his attention to Logan. That worthy's offense was that, while serving as Post Commissary and entrusted with public funds, he had violated Army Regulations on five occasions by playing "draw poker, at ten cents ante, with a dollar limit."

Second Lieutenant William L. English, the judge advocate of the courts martial, emerged as the peacemaker. The principal evidence against Williams was the papers that he had forwarded to St. Paul outside channels. English sent to headquarters for the papers to be returned to Buford; then he arranged for the court to convene at Buford before the papers had been received there. When he attempted to introduce copies of the correspondence as evidence, Williams entered successful objections to their admission. With no evidence to consider, the court had no option other than to acquit the defendant. Its finding, and the action of the judge advocate in proceeding to trial rather than asking for a continuance, were justly castigated by General Hancock in his review of the case; nonetheless, he had no choice but to confirm the court's finding.

The case of Logan was disposed of in different fashion. A quorum of the court was not available at Fort Buford in August 1871, when the trial was to be held. In addition, several of the witnesses were at distant posts. In his letter to Hancock's headquarters, requesting that they be ordered to Buford in order to testify, English openly disparaged the significance of the charges. The court met twice without action and then adjourned for the winter. The papers were sent to department headquarters; it does not appear that the matter was ever reopened.[27]

The charges against Gilbert likewise were never tried. After they had been bucked from Hancock, Department of Dakota, to Sheridan, Military Division of the Missouri, to the Adjutant General in Washington, the latter found "it doubtful that the trial of Lieutenant Colonel Gilbert would not result in more inconvenience than advantage to the public service." Again, the record went into the dead files.

Gibbon's involvement in this matter was peripheral, but his sympathy for Williams, and lack of sympathy for Bomford, is evident—not only in his opposition to transferring Bomford, but also in his relative evaluation of the two. In the process of selecting those who were to be separated from the service, he was asked to rank the officers of his regiment in order of merit. Of the ten first lieutenants on whom he reported, Constant Williams ("not personally known to me") was ranked second; George Bomford was eighth. (Despite the geographical dispersion of the 7th Infantry at this time, and the fact that Gibbon had been with it only a year, it seems likely that he had some personal knowledge of Bomford. Although the latter had not been in the 36th Infantry with Gibbon, he had been lieutenant colonel of the 42nd New York in Gibbon's 2nd Division, II Corps; his brevet rank of major was awarded him for Gettysburg.)

Gibbon recommended that the eighth, ninth, and tenth officer of each rank be replaced from the unassigned list; this recommendation placed Bomford's career in the army at risk. Again Hancock came to Bomford's rescue. In his endorsement, while staying neutral with regard to the other officers proposed for separation, he recommended that Bomford not be placed on the awaiting order list.[28]

Understandably, Charles Gilbert did not take the same view of Williams. At the same time that he and Williams were exchanging charges, Gilbert wrote to Hancock's adjutant general: ". . . in my judgment 1st Lieutenant Constant Williams, 7th U.S. Infantry, can be advantageously replaced from the list of unassigned officers. . . . I am satisfied that Lieutenant Williams's presence with any part of the Regiment will imperil its harmony to a serious degree." In support of his position he enclosed statements from Captains Richard Comba and Charles C. Rawn, the next two senior officers at Buford. Comba cited "reasons that are now well known in the Regt. and which must always stand to the prejudice of the social standing of Lieutenant Williams in the 7th Infantry." Hancock's endorsement was a recommendation that Williams be placed on the Awaiting Orders list.[29]

When General Order No. 1 of 1871 listed the officers to be separated, both George Bomford and Constant Williams were retained in the Army. Later in the year, with John Gibbon's blessing, Bomford arranged an exchange of places with 1st Lieutenant James H. Bradley of the 18th Infantry.[30] Constant Williams served in the 7th Infantry until 1897.

Upon the regiment's arrival in Montana Gibbon became commander of the Military District of Montana, with his headquarters at Fort Shaw, eighty miles north of Helena. Once again he had much territory to patrol and few men for the task. Despite an aggregate strength of thirty-four officers and 610 men, the 7th had only thirteen officers and 315 enlisted men fit for duty in January 1871. Twenty-nine men were too ill, fifty-eight were absent on detached service, and other causes, such as special duties, guardhouse confinement, and absence without leave, drained away manpower. A shortage of officers compelled those present to perform extra duty and wear several hats at the same time. For example, Captain Robert Chandler, the commander of Company E, was on detached service as an acting assistant adjutant general on the staff of General Hancock, the department commander, at Fort Snelling, Minnesota. Luckless 2nd Lieutenant Levi Burnett of Company E, back at Fort Benton, found himself serving as acting company commander, commissary officer, quartermaster, post adjutant, and acting signal officer. Divided among five posts, the 7th Infantry had minimal prospects of operating as a unit.[31]

Chandler's absence led to another paper quarrel between Gibbon and Hancock. A week after arriving at Fort Shaw on 8 June 1870, Gibbon wrote via Hancock to the Adjutant General of the Army, asking that Chandler be ordered to join his company at Fort Shaw, or that another captain be assigned to the regiment in his place. Hancock objected. Phil Sheridan, commander of the Military Division of the Missouri and the next higher in the chain of command, sided with Gibbon, and so did the Army's commanding general, Sherman. Hancock did not give up easily; he wrote an eight-page letter to Sherman offering reasons for his keeping Chandler at St. Paul, and for not giving Gibbon a replacement for him. If another officer were sent to the 7th Infantry in his place, Chandler would be transferred to the unassigned list, and, said Hancock, this is "now considered equivalent to being mustered out of service" [in the prospective reduction of 1 January 1871]. In the end, Hancock won. Sherman reversed himself and Chandler stayed on Hancock's staff.[32]

Neither Gibbon nor his wife had much fondness for their frontier duty or the isolation. Their main concern seems to have been the lack of educational facilities for the two daughters. On 14 August 1870 Gibbon wrote to Sherman, asking for transfer to a colonelcy of artillery so that he could return East and educate the children; to this message Fannie added a written endorsement. But nothing happened; five years later Gibbon was still trying for Eastern duty, this time by seeking to pull strings with Sheridan for the assignment of superintendent at West Point.[33]

Isolation, rather than its physical environment, kept Fort Shaw from being a desirable post. Located on the north bank of the Sun River, a few miles upstream from its confluence with the Missouri, the fort had quarters for 400 men, and the usual post structures: guardhouse, prison, storehouses, stables, and a sawmill. The nearest settlement was Helena, 83 miles to the south. Although the railroad had only come within 500 miles of the post, both the telegraph and the mail serviced Fort Shaw. All supplies came via the railroad to Corinne, Utah, thence by wagon train, or by steamboat up the Missouri to the head of navigation at Fort Benton and thence overland.

The valley of the Sun River, which the fort dominated, runs for fifty miles east and west. The land, a high, treeless plateau, was not wet enough for large-scale farming, but through irrigation the fort's garrison successfully maintained a large garden. Although winters produced little snow, the climate could be severe. A sudden wind and snow squall in November 1871 pushed the temperature down twenty degrees in an hour. Ten soldiers required amputations for frostbite.[34]

The principal Indian tribe near the fort was the Piegans. With them Gibbon maintained a stern but correct relationship. In August 1871 a haying party of civilians had two horses stolen from them one night. When the leader of the civilians complained to Gibbon, he had Grey Eagle, whose band was in the area, brought in and promised supplies if the horses were returned, with the thieves. Grey Eagle denied any knowledge of the matter, but eleven days later the horses appeared before the fort. No one ever claimed the reward, and no thieves were ever punished.[35]

For the next six years Gibbon and the 7th Infantry performed useful, if monotonous, duties as police and garrison for the District of Montana. Gibbon found that a main problem was intercepting the illegal liquor trade with the Indians from across the Canadian border. A major shipment fell into the garrison's hands in November 1871, when patrols from Companies E and H captured a group of Canadians who were trading liquor and ammunition to the Sioux in return for stolen property. Gibbon had some of the contraband liquor stores seized and the remainder burned; then the troops escorted the traders back to the border and ordered them not to return. About $4,000 in captured goods was turned over to the federal commissioner.[36]

The quality of the whiskey available on the Montana frontier in the 1870s was graphically described by the Fort Shaw post surgeon in a letter to Post Commander Gibbon in February 1871; the report was occasioned by the death of Private John Brown of Company B of the Seventh "from exposure while under the influence of poisonous liquors." Surgeon Town went on to describe

the dangerous qualities of the intoxicating fluid obtained by enlisted men at haunts in the vicinity of the Fort Shaw reservation . . . the greater proportion of deaths at the post since it was established in 1867 are attributable to their use. . . . It is the practice to concoct the liquors, notably a fluid denominated whiskey, at the place of sale. Rectified spirit, 95 per cent alcohol, the highest proof commonly sold . . . is largely shipped into the country for this purpose . . . as a matter of economy in freight. The pure spirit is greatly diluted by many volumes of water and to this is subsequently added, I am informed, an Infusion of Tobacco, also an Infusion or Tincture of Nux Vomica, a fixed proportion of sulphuric acid (oil of vitriol) and probably Tincture of Opium (Laudanum), besides other noxious drugs. . . . Men after partaking of it often get violent and wildly delirious. One man ran five miles to the post in a maniacal condition the past fall without any clothing whatever on his person except a pair of stockings—the temperature at the time being chilling and raw; he recovered his reason during the subsequent day. . . . This rank poison is I am told made in accordance with a recipe long in use throughout this country, modified somewhat perhaps by individual ideas and circumstances, and was devised especially for the manufacture of a cheap and lively whiskey for illegal trading to Indians, and which by common report is traded to, and drunk by them at the present time to a greater extent than at any previous period—and with corresponding disastrous results.[37]

Gibbon's efforts to counter the effects of the whiskey trade included encouragement of a temperance society, the Good Templars. Crown Butte Lodge No. 36 of the organization was established at Fort Shaw in December 1872. Among its activities was a series of lectures by officers assigned to the post, including three by Gibbon on astronomy under the title "Other Worlds Than Ours." As a lecturer on the same topic, Gibbon also appeared before the "social elite" of the town of Fort Benton, under the aegis of Fort Benton's Masonic lodge.[38]

The tedium of routine peacekeeping was relieved in the summer of 1871 by a typical Gibbon dispute with higher command. Survey parties for the Northern Pacific Railroad were exploring the Yellowstone Valley in search of possible routes for the road, and Dakota Department headquarters in St. Paul sent down orders to provide escorts for their protection. In transmitting the orders, the staff of department commander Major General Hancock forwarded them directly to the various posts concerned, bypassing headquarters of the Military District of Montana at Fort Shaw and its prickly commander.

The year was one of various alarms over Indian activity, although no large-scale hostilities occurred, and the number of soldiers made available for escort duty was below the expectations of both railroad people and department commander. When Gibbon, as district commander, was called upon for an explanation, he returned a tart reply in which he alluded to his having been given no responsibility for the matter. After an acerbic exchange of correspondence, he found himself suspended from command, placed in arrest, and facing court-martial charges for disrespect to General Hancock. General Phil Sheridan, commander of the Military Division of the Missouri and Hancock's immediate superior in the command chain, was the authority on whom rested the responsibility for ordering trial. He declined to do so. Quite possibly he knew of the strained personal relationship between the two, regarded it as a mitigating circumstance, and considered that the humiliation of the arrest was sufficient. In any event, he limited the punishment to a written reproof and restored Gibbon to duty.[39]

As district commander Gibbon was responsible for a broad expanse of territory over which military operations might be required. He also had command over the troops of the district—his own regiment and a battalion of cavalry—which comprised the Montana garrison. They were distributed among four posts, Fort Shaw, Fort Benton, Camp Baker, and Fort Ellis; the battalion of the 7th at Fort Buford was relieved by the 6th Infantry in 1872. These responsibilities gave him occasion for travel throughout the district, travel that provided opportunity for his favorite diversions of hunting and fishing and for exploring the wonders of Yellowstone National Park.[40]

Although Gibbon had been unable to gain the support of General-in-Chief Sherman for a permanent transfer out of the frontier army, Sheridan did push for a relief for Gibbon from duty in Montana. On 17 August 1872 he wrote to the Adjutant General recommending Gibbon for the soon to be vacated position of Superintendent of the General Recruiting Service in New York City. Sheridan felt that Gibbon's past services entitled him to the post.[41]

The appointment moved through the bureaucracy with no apparent difficulty, and Gibbon returned to the East on 1 February 1873 to relieve Colonel Jefferson C. Davis at New York, anticipating a year and a half's duty there. This was a choice assignment. The location gave Gibbon access to his family in Philadelphia and Baltimore, enabled him to see more of his daughters (now students at Eden Hall, a Catholic school near Philadelphia), and ended the monotony of a frontier post's limited social life. Unfortunately, Gibbon's penchant for involving himself in squabbles with his superiors resulted in his remaining in the post only a short six months.[42]

In June Gibbon again fell afoul of Irvin McDowell, now a major general and commander of the Department of the South. Having acted with less than full respect to McDowell as president of the Retirement Board, he now undertook to challenge the general's command authority.[43] As commander of the Department of the South, McDowell exercised control over a geographical area bounded on the north by the Ohio River; it included the post of Newport Barracks, Kentucky, across the river from Cincinnati. Cincinnati (technically just outside McDowell's jurisdiction) was the location of a recruiting station that fell under the command of the General Recruiting Service. Colonel Davis, Gibbon's immediate predecessor as Superintendent of the Service, had made an informal agreement with McDowell that permitted the latter to utilize the recruiting officer at Cincinnati as a member of courts-martial ordered by McDowell to try cases at Newport Barracks; since Newport Barracks served as a recruit depot, which was under the jurisdiction of the recruiting service, and court-martial cases arising there might involve recruits, it was logical and appropriate that the recruiting service contribute to staffing of the courts.

Whether Davis apprised Gibbon of this arrangement is not of record. In any event, when Gibbon discovered that the recruiting officer at Cincinnati was absent from his post for the purpose of serving on a court martial at Newport Barracks, he sent peremptory orders requiring the recruiter's immediate return to Cincinnati. His departure from the barracks reduced the court below the minimum number of members required by law and therefore abruptly interrupted its proceedings. Paradoxically, the defendants in the trial were recruits for whose discipline Gibbon had responsibility; not being a general, he could not himself convene a general court martial, but had to turn to the geographical commander for this service. McDowell, in effect, was assisting Gibbon in issuing the orders for the court.

Gibbon's rationalization for his actions appears to have been that McDowell had exceeded his authority by issuing orders to an officer not technically within his command without first obtaining the permission of the captain's regular superior, Gibbon. Despite this line of reasoning, Gibbon's peremptory actions could well be perceived as an affront to a senior, and McDowell, a general well aware of his prerogatives, immediately took the matter up with Sherman, now the commanding general of the Army.

It helped Gibbon little that at the same time he had become embroiled in a virtually identical quarrel with his other major antagonist, Winfield Scott Hancock, now commanding the Division of the Atlantic and Department of the East from headquarters at Governors Island, New York City. Although the Adjutant General had already written to Gibbon about the matter, Sherman compounded the situation by carrying the whole affair directly to the Secretary of War. He also told McDowell that Gibbon had to offer a formal apology or face relief from his New York post. To the Secretary, Sherman wrote: "I must add that General Gibbon has profited so little from his large experience, in learning what is due to his superiors in high and important commands—that he should be made to realize the consequences of his own act—and that he be relieved of his present duty."

Apology was far from Gibbon's mind. Detached from the Recruiting Service post on 7 August 1873, he wrote directly to President Grant on 20 September, asking for a court of inquiry on the matter. The court sat from 20 October to 1 November, hearing numerous witnesses, examining much correspondence, and taking hours of tedious testimony. Finally it arrived at the following conclusions:

1. Gibbon had shown no direct intention to disregard the competent authority of McDowell;

2. He did, however, exhibit "a lack of deference to superior authority;"

3. No further action was necessary in the case.

So Gibbon lost his assignment in New York. He managed to remain in the East on leave throughout the winter and on a brief assignment to the Naval Academy's Board of Visitors in the spring. Then he returned to Fort Shaw, resuming command on 24 July 1874.[44]

Tensions were rising in the District of Montana and throughout the Dakotas, generated by the issue of confining the powerful tribes of the Sioux nation to permanent reservations. After abandoning the Bozeman Trail to Red Cloud in late 1868, the federal government had come under increasing pressure to restrict the Indians and open their lands for exploitation and settlement. Not only was the government feeling the influence of various interest groups; so were the Indians. The Northern Pacific Railroad had reached central North Dakota, and its surveying parties were already marking out the roadbed toward Montana. Nothing so alarmed the Sioux as the railroad. To them it was "thoroughly obnoxious and sure to arouse every opposition." With it would come the elimination of the buffalo, and once that went, so would their independent existence.[45]

One of the Army's concerns of the period was the question of controlling the supply of arms to the Indians. As nomads who relied on the hunt for a principal source of food, they could show a justifiable need for firearms; the same weapons made them a deadly threat to the whites. One proposal advanced was to limit them to muzzle loaders, with ammunition to be made available to them in the form of bulk powder, caps, and lead. Breechloaders and fixed cartridges were to be forbidden. Philip Sheridan, for one, thought little of the suggestion. The Indians, he said, were just as adept as the whites in reloading cartridge cases, and the bulk ammunition would be used for this purpose. In any event, the continuing illegal trade of rifles to the tribes seems never to have been brought under effective control by the Army for any great length of time.[46]

The Government precipitated a crisis when a White House conference in November 1875 decided to open the Black Hills to miners. All troops guarding the entrances into the area were to be withdrawn. Once the troops were freed from police duties, they could be formed into field forces that would drive the Sioux and their allies onto the reservations. Runners went out to all Black Hills Indians on 6 December 1875, ordering them to move to reservations by 31 January 1876. When no discernible response to this ultimatum occurred, the problem was turned over to the War Department for solution.[47]

Sheridan decided to fight a winter campaign, since this was the most effective strategy against the mobile Indian tribes. With snow hampering their smaller ponies, and with food scarce, a major defeat would oblige them to obey the reservation order or starve. Early in February 1876, orders for the 1876 operations were issued to Sheridan's two principal field commanders, Brigadier Generals Alfred H. Terry, of the Department of Dakota, and George Crook, Department of the Platte.

The events of the next six months may be said to occupy the same position in frontier history that Fredericksburg and Chancellorsville do in that of the Civil War. Momentarily disastrous for the Army though they were, Reynolds's failure at Powder River and Custer's defeat on the Little Big Horn did not slow the settlement of the West. Nevertheless, the campaign of 1876 showed the Indian leadership and assessment of the situation to be superior to those of the trained professional. In their determination to fight for the only way of life they knew, they proved themselves to be as unyielding as the rugged frontier regulars. The next two years brought John Gibbon's only experience with large-scale Indian fighting, and they were not very pleasant ones.[48]

Despite Sheridan's desire for a winter campaign against the Sioux, the army did not manage to move until February. Atrocious weather and determined Indian resistance hampered Crook's column, operating from Fort Fetterman, Wyoming Territory. On 17 March his forces were frustrated at Powder River, largely because of command errors by Colonel J. J. Reynolds of the 3rd Cavalry. More heavy snow delayed the concentration of the 7th Cavalry and kept Terry at Fort Abraham Lincoln until early spring. These developments assured that the 1876 operations against the Sioux and their allies would be a summer war.

Sheridan used his wrecked winter plans as a basis for his summer strategy. Crook was to advance toward the Yellowstone from the south. Terry's column, basically Custer's 7th Cavalry, would move westward from Fort Abraham Lincoln at Bismarck, following the line of the river. Gibbon had orders to move eastward down the Yellowstone, patrolling the north bank and intercepting any Indians who tried to flee north. The three forces would converge somewhere in the area where the nontreaty Indians were expected to be found.

The first activities of the Yellowstone campaign occurred in late February and early March. In the summer of 1875 a group of traders and wolf trappers from Bozeman had established a trading post called "Fort Pease" (it was never a military post) on the left bank of the Yellowstone River, a few miles below the mouth of the Big Horn. From its inception Fort Pease was harassed by the Sioux, and eventually an appeal for a relief column to rescue its occupants was sent to General Terry, who assented. On 22 February 1876 Major James S. Brisbin, 2nd Cavalry, post commander of Fort Ellis, led his battalion of cavalry and a small detachment of the 7th Infantry. The force reached Pease on 4 March without having made contact with Indians, and found nineteen surviving occupants (six had been killed, eight wounded, and a number had fled the fort and returned to Bozeman on their own through Sioux-infested country). The survivors were escorted back to Bozeman, some returning with reluctance. The column reached Ellis on 17 March.[49]

Meanwhile, on 27 February 1876, Terry ordered Gibbon to strip his district garrisons of all available troops and prepare to march from Fort Ellis. On St. Patrick's day he moved out of Fort Shaw with five companies of infantry. The troops and supply train had to slog through heavy snow drifts and temperatures that reached forty degrees below zero.

A major danger during such a winter march was snow blindness. This occurred when the weather produced alternating periods of sunshine and shadow, with the glare off the snowfields becoming severe. In one company the captain was forced to turn over his command to a subordinate and return to Fort Shaw. Some of the company commanders had provided blue or green veils to their men as protection, but these were not adequate. Lieutenant James Bradley, who suffered from snow blindness, described it as being accompanied by intense pain, the eyeballs seeming to roll in liquid fire with a grating feeling as though filled with sand. Bradley advocated blackening the face close to the eyes to cut down the glare, using wet gunpowder, lampblack, or a similar greasy black substance. On 19 March he noted many cases of frostbite of more or less severity. His journal leaves the reader to ponder for himself the significance of the following entry: "Lieut. Kendrick and Dr. Hart were among the unfortunate victims of the frost, whose icy fingers, judged by the singular experience of these gentlemen, were unrestrained by any considerations of delicacy." Whatever the missing details of this experience may have been, on the 22nd Bradley recorded that Dr. Hart fell out of the ranks sick, and did not rejoin the expedition. Thereafter, until the column reached Fort Ellis, Lieutenant Charles A. Coolidge, who made the study of medicine a hobby, served as doctor.[50]

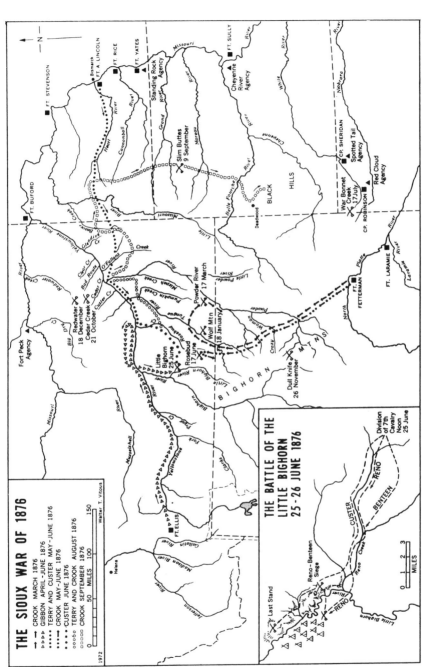

The Sioux War of 1876. Courtesy Robert Utley, *Frontier Regulars: The United States Army and the Indian, 1866–1891.*

Gibbon stayed behind to attend to last-minute matters, but joined his command near Helena on 22 March. He rested the column there, gave some men leave to visit the town, and augmented his supplies. By now another company from Camp Baker had joined the Fort Shaw group.[51]

From Helena, Gibbon led his men toward Fort Ellis on the 23rd. With moderating weather, the snow turned to water and converted the horrible roads into a chowder of mud and slush. Gibbon had seen in Virginia road conditions just as bad, and he pressed on, sighting Fort Ellis at midday on 28 March.[52] There a battalion of four companies of the 2nd Cavalry raised the column's rifle strength to about 400 men. While at Fort Ellis, the news of Crook's Powder River fight of the 17th reached them.

With the addition of the cavalry the column also gained a professional medical officer, Assistant Surgeon Holmes O. Paulding, who had been post surgeon at Ellis since October 1875. Dr. Paulding, not quite twenty-four years old, had served in the Army for a year and a half prior to the start of the campaign. His field experience during that time consisted of a few weeks with a battalion of the 1st Infantry on the White River, Dakota Territory, in the preceding autumn, and Major Brisbin's expedition to Fort Pease. Neither service had exposed him to combat. An indefatigable diarist and letter-writer, he embarked on the campaign with a grudge against Gibbon for not using his authority to employ a civilian contract surgeon. As the column left Ellis, he noted in his journal, "An air of impenetrable mystery overhangs the affair & none but God (Gibbon) knows what we are to do."[53]

The cavalry needed more time to prepare for the campaign, but because Terry and the other commanders feared the escape of the Indians, Gibbon sent the infantry forward on 30 March, while he remained behind with Major Brisbin, who commanded the cavalry element of Gibbon's Montana column. By the time they left, on 1 April, the weather had deteriorated. A steep and rock-strewn road led east toward the Yellowstone, and at many places streams intersected the trail, creating marshy swamps where the wagons sank to the hub. Wind and drifting snow also delayed the column, and not until the 6th did the scouts sight the Yellowstone. On 8 April the infantry and cavalry joined forces above the mouth of the Stillwater.[54]

The weather hampered operations, as did lack of expert knowledge about the area. With the exact location of the Sioux unknown, and with maps inaccurate and communications uncertain, the army remained dependent for intelligence on Indian scouts recruited from tribes hostile to the Sioux. The most implacable enemies of the Sioux were the Crows, and for his scouts Gibbon now sent to this tribe.

While the Montana column remained in camp, Gibbon and "Mitch" Bouyer, a famous guide and interpreter, traveled to the Crow Agency, eighteen miles away. The meeting was not without humor. Gibbon, in his stiff, regular army way, explained what he wanted and asked for twenty-five young warriors to serve as scouts. For three months they would receive soldiers' clothing, rations, and pay. After listening to Bouyer mangle—as he thought—his eloquence, Gibbon discovered that the chiefs, Iron Bull and Blackfoot, were utterly indifferent to his problem. They were at peace and wished to remain so. They would not force their young men to join; the choice was up to them. Fortunately, the next morning about twenty-five of what Gibbon called "Young America" came forward and were sworn into temporary service. To allay their fears that the soldiers might kill them in battle through misidentification, Gibbon gave each of them a six-inch-wide red band, to be worn on the left arm above the elbow.[55]

On 11 April Gibbon made his preparations to shift base to the south bank of the Yellowstone. Although a blizzard had covered the ground with two feet of snow, he decided not to risk staying where he was any longer, and moved the column out. With him were the Crows under the command of Bradley; the infantry battalion of thirteen officers and 220 men; and the cavalry, ten officers and 186 men. The swift current carried away two mules; otherwise the river crossing was without incident. Gibbon then dropped all supplies and extra baggage that the wagons could not move, with an infantry company to guard them, and resumed the march east.

On 15 April the column bivouacked on the site of an 1872 battle between the Sioux and a mixed force of 2nd Cavalry and 7th Infantry troops, under the command of Major E. M. Baker of the cavalry; the troops were serving as escort to a Northern Pacific Railroad survey party. Baker was alleged to have been drunk when the predawn attack fell on his camp at 3:00 A.M., and to have taken few if any precautions against surprise, but skillful troop dispositions by Captain C. C. Rawn and Lieutenant William Logan of the infantry enabled the force to rout the Indians with heavy casualties. When the Indians struck, some of the officers were engaged in an all-night poker party, a circumstance that led the engagement to be known as "the Battle of Poker Flat."

By 17 April the troops had reached Pompey's Pillar, a spectacular column of irregular sandstone. When Gibbon climbed to the top, he found the inscription:

Wm. Clark

July 25th 1806

On that date Lewis and Clark's journal recorded their ascent to the summit.[56]

The march was brought up short on 21 April, when a message from

Terry arrived, forwarded via the supply camp. Warning Gibbon that Crook would not be able to start before mid-May, and that the Dakota column likewise could not leave for some time, Terry ordered him to proceed no farther than the mouth of the Little Big Horn unless he was "sure of striking a successful blow."

For the next three weeks the Montana column marked time, enjoying the excellent trout fishing in the Yellowstone. The remaining supplies and troops rejoined the command, and it was not until 1 May that anything occurred to break the boredom. On that day the Crows set off a false alarm when they reported two companies of cavalry as a Sioux war party. This false alarm presaged a real raid: on the night of 2 May a group of Sioux crept in near enough to the picket line to run off thirty-four horses, including all the mounts of the Crow scouts.[57] This development was ominous, since it evidenced that the Indians were now fully aware of the location and size of Gibbon's isolated command. Diarist Paulding reported another false alarm on the following day:

In the afternoon some Infantry men saw [Cavalry captain] Ball driving in the herd a mile or so off through the misty snow & yelled out "The Herds gone" giving rise to a stampede. All the companies turned out under arms & several of them started out on a run for the herd. Gibbon & Staff appeared too much rattled to know what they were doing. The old man lit out with a rifle without giving any intelligible orders taking as conclusive evidence that the herd was being run off the fact that a man came riding in & leading a horse. When everyone had cooled down he began to blow around & try to raise the devil succeeding tolerably well.

On 4 May two messengers were fired on, leading Gibbon to believe that the camp was nearly surrounded. Although Bradley led out a group of scouts, he found nothing but a deserted Indian encampment.[58]

Bradley finally brought his superior some hard news. On 15 May he and twenty-seven scouts crossed the Yellowstone and combed the area toward the Rosebud River and the Wolf Mountains. Sighting a plume of smoke on the afternoon of the 16th, the scouting party traced it to an Indian village in the Tongue River valley. Bradley estimated its number at 300 tepees and 800–1,000 warriors. When he brought Gibbon the news, the always-aggressive colonel decided to cross the river and attack. Melting snow had turned the Yellowstone into a torrent, but Gibbon still tried to drive the horses over. After four drowned, he gave up the attempt.[59]

If James Bradley had found the Sioux, they had found Gibbon. During the forenoon, while the column was struggling to cross the river, a party of at least seventy-five braves appeared on the south bank. Gibbon's camp now became a target. The deaths of three men confirmed Gibbon's fears. When two cavalrymen and a teamster went beyond the sentry lines without permission, their bodies were found, stripped and mutilated. A knife belonging to one of them was later recovered on the Custer battlefield. Until he left the area Gibbon turned out the troops at 2:00 A.M. each morning and stood to until sunrise.

The march was not without occasional diversions. On the 24th a Bozeman merchant, Colonel Chesnut, arrived with a boatload of delicacies, including butter, eggs, vegetables, and tobacco. He found a ready market; perhaps the most appreciated among his wares was a keg of beer, reserved for the officers. It was the centerpiece for a convivial evening at the tent of Lieutenants Hamilton and Schofield, marked by "polemical contests of racy sort," and "put the voices of our singers once more in splendid tune. . . . [T]he occasion will long be remembered as one of the greenest of the green spots in the campaign."

Continued signs of increased Indian activity and aggressiveness, as well as of a major concentration, soon became evident. On 27 May Bradley and the scouts made yet another sighting. After crossing the river, his party stumbled across a trail of freshly killed buffalo and the tracks of hundreds of ponies. Upon reaching a vantage point in the mountains that he had previously discovered and that gave a view of the Rosebud valley for thirty miles, he sighted at a distance of eight or ten miles heavy smoke, some lodges, and a vast pony herd. This was the same group of Indians that he had found on the Tongue. Now only eighteen miles from Gibbon's command, the Indians were both aware of and utterly contemptuous of it. To the disappointment of at least some of his officers, Gibbon decided against attack but remained on guard. Bradley recorded the odds that they would have faced—about 350 men against 800 to 1,000—but noted that a majority of the officers would have favored an attack, and at least some were confident that the troops "would have gained a rousing victory, dispersed the village, and prevented that tremendous aggregation of force a month later that made the massacre of Custer's force possible. On the other hand," he reflected, "we might ourselves have been massacred." [60]

Gibbon has come under serious criticism for the report that he wrote to Terry following Bradley's return from this scout. Evidently he discounted the accuracy of Bradley's observations; Bradley had decided not to bring up to his lookout the men accompanying him, who could have vouched for the accuracy of his report. Fellow officers had expressed skepticism at his previous sightings; at a distance, was he seeing vast pony herds, or buffalo? In any event, Gibbon's letter of that day to Terry says ". . . no camps have been seen, but war parties of from twenty to fifty have been seen to the south of the river and a few on the north side." He qualifies this in his closing: "P. S. A camp some distance up the Rosebud was reported this morning by our scouts. If this proves true, I may not start down the Yellowstone so soon." [61]

It appears that Gibbon did not conclude that Bradley's report was correct, for on the following day, in compliance with Terry's orders, he moved out down the Yellowstone.[62] The Dakota column had finally left Fort Abraham Lincoln, and Terry now believed the Sioux to be concentrated somewhere between the Little Missouri and Powder rivers. On 9 June, from a high hill, Gibbon, Bouyer, and a cavalry company gained a view of the Yellowstone and Powder River areas. Up the stream came the steamer Far West, carrying supplies and General Terry's party. Gibbon soon went on board and received orders to countermarch his command toward the mouth of the Rosebud.[63] Terry agreed with Gibbon that the findings of the scouts made it fairly certain that no Sioux would be discovered east of the Rosebud. But he wanted to make sure.

Terry thereupon ordered Major Marcus Reno of the 7th Cavalry to take six troops of horse, a mule train, and Mitch Bouyer to comb the Powder and Tongue valleys. He told Reno to proceed to the mouth of the Little Powder River, cross to the headwaters of Mizpah Creek, and then go down that stream to its confluence with the Powder. From there he was to cross to Pumpkin Creek, follow it to the Tongue, and descend to the Yellowstone. Under no circumstances was he to go as far as the Rosebud.[64]

Reno did not comply with these orders. He struck out across country to the Rosebud, where he discovered the broad trail of a large Indian village, presumably the one that Bradley had sighted previously. After following it south up the Rosebud for a few miles, he returned to the Yellowstone. Although he brought with him intelligence of the fresh trail, he had failed to scout the area assigned to him, and in that respect left Terry in the dark. While he was gone, and unknown at the time to Terry, Gibbon, and Custer, Crook's column on 17 June collided on the Rosebud with Indians led by Crazy Horse and was forced to retreat.[65]

Upon Reno's return Terry moved to concentrate his cavalry and inform his subordinate commanders on his new strategy. On 21 June he summoned Gibbon, Custer, and Brisbin to the cabin of the Far West for a council. Still foremost in their minds was the fear that the Indians would refuse to fight and just slip away. As Gibbon later wrote, the problem was "to prevent the escape of the Indians, which was the idea pervading the minds of all of us." Since the Crow scouts had seen camp fires in the valley of the Little Big Horn, Terry decided to concentrate there. Custer was to start the next day with his regiment and a mule train, march up the Rosebud until he found the trail that Reno had discovered, and then, keeping to the south of the trail, cross to the Little Big Horn. Terry and Gibbon would move to the mouth of the Big Horn, cross the Yellowstone via the Far West, and move up the Big Horn and Little Big Horn to cooperate with Custer's force. Terry's plan envisioned that the two commands would then have the Indian encampment between them, and that they would be in position for joint operations on the evening of the 26th.[66]

Although Terry made a general provision for cooperation, he failed to take into account the ambitious nature of Custer and the danger of dividing his force in the face of an enemy that might outnumber his separate columns. His orders to Custer were a strange mixture of "the explicit and the permissive." Terry, an able man, widely liked and respected throughout the Army, was not a West Pointer. He had entered active duty in 1861 as a volunteer officer with no prior service, and may have felt a little unsure of himself in the presence of more experienced men. The question of why he did not go with Custer instead of the steady, methodical Gibbon remains unanswered to this day.

On 22 June Custer, decked out in his buckskin garb, led his troops in a review for Terry and Gibbon, and prepared to ascend the Rosebud. He refused a reinforcement from Brisbin's cavalry, wanting to keep his operation exclusively a 7th Cavalry show. Custer was in excellent spirits at the prospect of action and an independent command. Gibbon chaffed with him. There would be plenty of Indians, Gibbon remarked, and there was no need for Custer to be greedy. To this the flamboyant trooper replied, somewhat equivocally, "No, I think not."[67]

Gibbon and Terry went back to the Montana column on the steamboat, and by 4 P.M. the command was on the south bank with Bradley leading the march up the Big Horn. Unfortunately, Gibbon fell seriously ill, possibly with dysentery, and had to remain on the steamer. With Terry in command, Brisbin led the way over the divide between the Big Horn and Tullock's Creek, marching south through a choking cloud of alkaline dust. Soon the cavalrymen resembled snowmen, and the infantry, recipients of most of the dust, became too exhausted to continue. Terry pushed ahead with the horsemen. This was yet another indication that fear of missing the Indians had become the main tactical consideration. However, Gibbon moved upstream on the steamer and learned that his troops were only a few miles away. Although still very sick, he mounted his horse and overtook the 7th Infantry.

On 26 June the infantry rejoined the cavalry, and soon the column encountered several Crow scouts, men lent to Custer by Gibbon. The three commanders then heard news that stunned them. According to Gibbon's later recollection:

Our best interpreter had been left sick at the mouth of the river, and from what we could make out from the indifferent one with us, who appeared very much excited and demoralized by the news, Custer's command had been entirely cut to pieces by the Sioux who . . . were chasing our soldiers all over the hills and killing them like buffalo.[68]

Bradley carried this ominous story back to Terry and Gibbon, and was met with expressions of doubt and incredulity. Terry only bit his lip and said nothing.

About 5:00 P.M. Bradley found several Indian ponies on his front; then a report came in of the presence further ahead of a large body of Indians. Terry at once put the column into fighting order. He and Gibbon led them forward. Lieutenant Charles F. Roe of the 2nd Cavalry, after mounting to the bluffs, sighted an enormous Indian encampment, with about 300 warriors mounting guard between it and the troops.[69] Bradley estimated that about 1,000 braves were covering the withdrawal of the Sioux village, now in full retreat toward the Big Horn Mountains. The column halted and bivouacked in a defensive square; no fires were allowed.

The night halt became for a time a matter of criticism of Gibbon. In his journal entry of 13 July, Freeman noted: "Major B[risbin] told me Reno had in his report of his operations reflected somewhat severely upon the movements of the Montana Column." Paulding on 8 July wrote to his mother more specifically and at greater length:

I understood that Col. Reno has made a report of the affair in which he reflects strongly on us [Col. Gibbon who was in command of our column] for having gone into Camp on the evening of the 26th in the face of the enemy & without attempting to satisfy ourselves as to the character of a large body of men who crossed his front, or something to that effect, referring to the Indians Roe's co. [Company F, 2nd Cavalry] saw while scouting or flanking the column on the march up to which I referred in my last letter. [Paulding had written to his mother on 2 July 1876.]

The references to Reno's report seem to have been based on a first draft. The quoted items do not appear in Reno's report as carried in the annual report of the Secretary of War.[70]

Reno had ample basis for second thoughts in the matter. When it camped for the night at 9:00 P.M., the cavalry of the Montana column had marched eighteen miles that day; the infantry had covered thirty, after doing twenty-three the day before. It was facing an enemy of unknown but considerable strength. It had ample evidence that Custer's force—numerically about equal to the Montana column—had run into serious trouble, not yet clearly defined. Bradley (with of course the benefit of hindsight) expressed the view that the whole command would have experienced "a desperate fight had we advanced that evening another mile." The decision to camp in a defensive square and await daylight was sound. Finally, of course, at the moment Gibbon was not in command; that decision was for Terry to make.[71]

At 7:00 A.M., 27 June, the troops turned out, marched to the right, and climbed the low sandstone bluffs above the river. They came across evidence of disaster: soldiers' clothes; a bloody buckskin shirt; and some white men's heads, mutilated. Gibbon accepted the fact of calamitous defeat.[72]

Bradley brought back final confirmation. He reported to Terry and Gibbon that the bodies of 197 troopers lay in the hills above the river. Eventually, Reno and Benteen's force was located, and soon all knew the extent of the disaster. When the two groups met, the first question asked was, "Is General Custer with you?" No one of the party that went with Custer could be located, and "our inference was, that they were all, or nearly all, lying up in the hills where our scouting party had found the dead bodies."[73]

Near the river a soldier located the corpse of Mitch Bouyer. Many times the Sioux had claimed credit for his death, and now it was a fact. Gibbon had thought him to be "the best guide in his section of the country, and the only half-breed I ever met who could give the distance to be passed over with any accuracy in miles."[74]

Terry, Gibbon, and the United States Army had clashed with the largest concentration of Indian power ever seen on the northern plains. Facing a united enemy, led by brave and determined men, willing to fight for their land, the army, for all its plans and experience, had met crushing defeat. Although Gibbon had no part of the blame and was no admirer of Custer, on that June evening he doubtless shared the sorrow that swept over the camps along the Little Big Horn.[75]

NOTES

1. General Orders, No. 6, 30 January 1866, RG 94, WD AGO, NA.

2. House Miscellaneous Documents, 45th Congress, 2nd Session, No. 56, p. 270. The arrangement of buttons on officers' uniforms varied according to rank groups. Company-grade officers (second lieutenant to captain) wore single-breasted coats. Field-grade officers (major to colonel) wore double-breasted coats with the buttons uniformly spaced. Brigadier generals' coats were double-breasted, with the buttons spaced in pairs. Major generals' buttons were worn in groups of three. Thus, a captain who was a brevet colonel (e.g., Frederick W. Benteen of the 7th Cavalry) would wear two bars on his shoulder, but a double-breasted coat.

Frances M. A. Roe, *Army Letters from an Officer's Wife, 1871–1888*, 5 (New York, 1909).

3. John Gibbon to Winfield S. Hancock, 28 August 1864, Letters Received File G 560 CB 1864, RG 94, WD, AGO, NA. A proposal had been made to extend brevet promotions to a number of staff commissary officers for the sole purpose of giving them rank nominally equivalent to their counterparts in the quartermaster corps.

4. JG to Assistant Adjutant General, 19 December 1865, Letters Received File G 237 CB 1865, RG 94, WD, AGO, NA.

5. Letters Received File B 282 CB 1866, RG 94, WD, AGO, NA (Report of the St. Louis Brevet Board).

6. JG to E. D. Townsend, 19 December 1866, Letters Received File G 560 CB 1866, RG 94, WD, AGO, NA.

7. Ulysses S. Grant to E. M. Stanton, 7 August 1866, Letters Received File 815 G CB 66, RG 94, WD, AGO, NA.

8. Family tradition, related to Mark H. Jordan by the late Mrs. Bancroft Hill; JG to Adjutant General, 7 October 1866; Christopher C. Augur to Adjutant General, 3 November 1866, Letters Received File, RG 94, WD, AGO, NA.

9. U.S. War Department, Secretary of War, Annual Report, 1867, House Executive Document No. 1, 40th Congress 2nd Session, Vol. 2, Parts 1 and 2, p. 416.

10. 14 Stat. 223 (25 July 1866).

11. An Act to Increase and Fix the Military Peace Establishment of the United States, Statutes at Large, LXXII (16 June 1874.) An outstanding discussion of the promotion situation in the post–Civil War army is found in Paul Hutton, *Phil Sheridan and His Army* (Lincoln, Neb., 1985), 134–142.

12. For army life among the common soldiers, see Don Rickey, *Forty Miles a Day on Beans and Hay: The Enlisted Soldier Fighting the Indian Wars* (Norman, Okla., 1963).

13. House Committee on Military Affairs, 2 March 1876, House Reports, 44th Congress, 1st Session, No. 354, p. 210.

14. An Act to Fix the Size of the United States Army, Statutes at Large, XVI (15 July 1870); Hutton, *Phil Sheridan's Army,* 134–142.

15. For example, see Marvin E. Kroeker, *Great Plains Command: William B. Hazen in the Frontier West* (Norman, Okla., 1976).

16. John Gibbon to Catharine Lardner Gibbons, 27 November 1866, GP, HSP; Monthly Return, 36th Infantry, December 1866, WD, AGO, NA.

17. Special Orders No. 49, Department of the Platte, 26 March 1868, AGO, WD, NA.

18. Monthly return, 36th Infantry, May 1867, WD, AGO, NA. Among the officers of the 36th Infantry were Lieutenant Colonel Henry A. Morrow, formerly colonel of the 24th Michigan of the Iron Brigade; Captain Arthur MacArthur (father of Douglas MacArthur), later a lieutenant general; and 2nd Lieutenant Adolphus W. Greely, later a noted Arctic explorer and eventually a major general.

19. For a description of an army unit on the move between posts, accompanied by wives and children, see Oliver Knight, *Life and Manners in the Frontier Army* (Norman, Okla., 1978), 43–47.

20. The foregoing account of activities of the 36th Infantry is drawn from the regiment's monthly returns for 1867 and 1868, WD, AGO, NA. The intervention at Julesburg appears in J. R. Perkins, "Building the Union Pacific Railroad," *Engineering*, Samuel Rapport and Helen Wright, eds. (New York, 1964), 241.

21. General Orders No. 42, HQ, Department of the Platte, 3 December 1868; Special Order No. 127, HQ, Military Division of the Missouri, 16 November 1868; Special Order No. 294, Adjutant General's Office, 10 December 1868; Margaret Gibbon to Catharine Gibbons, 4 January 1869, GP, HSP; CLG to Jennie Gibbon Humbert, 7 April 1869, GP, HSP.

22. Otto Eisenschiml, *The Celebrated Case of Fitz John Porter: An American Dreyfus* (Indianapolis and New York, 1950), 96, 102.

23. Files 66 R 69, 270 M 69, WD, AGO, NA.

24. Monthly returns, June–July 1869, February 1870, 7th Infantry, WD, AGO, NA.

25. Monthly returns, 7th Infantry.

26. Letters Received file, Adjutant General's Office, 352 B AGO 1870, NA, RG 94, and attached correspondence.

27. Letters Received file 338, Military Division of the Missouri, 1872, NA, RG 94.

28. Letters Received file AGO, G 145 CB 1870, NA, RG 94.

29. Letters Received file AGO, G 181 CB 1870, NA, RG 94.

30. Special Order 457, 28 November 1871, Adjutant General's Office, NA, RG 94.

31. Monthly return, January 1871, 7th Infantry, WD, AGO, NA. The five posts were Forts Shaw, Benton, Ellis, and Buford and Camp Baker. After 1872 Fort Buford was garrisoned by another regiment. Organizationally it was not part of the Military District of Montana.

32. Letters Received file, Adjutant General's Office, 918 M 70, 1870, NA, RG 94.

33. John Gibbon to William T. Sherman, 14 August 1870, WD, AGO, NA; Philip H. Sheridan to John Gibbon, 24 May 1875, GP, MHS.

34. Outline Description of the Posts in the Military Division of the Missouri, Headquarters, Military Division of the Missouri, Chicago, 1876, WD, AGO, NA.

35. Robert Vaughn, *Then and Now; or, Thirty Six Years in the Rockies* (Minneapolis, 1900), 106.

36. Monthly return, 7th Infantry, November 1871, WD, AGO, NA.

37. Letters Received File 1009 AGO 1871, WD, AGO, NA.

38. Fort Benton [Montana] Record, 1 February 1875, Vol. 1, No. 1, carries a letter from M. J. McCabe, Fort Shaw, 10 January 1875 (Montana Historical Society, Helena). Paul F. Sharp, *Whoop-Up Country: The Canadian-American West, 1865–1885.* (Norman, Okla., 1978).

39. The correspondence on this matter is found in Letters Received, Military Division of the Missouri, Files 873- and 1096-1871, AGO, RG 94, NA.

40. John Gibbon, "Rambles in the Rocky Mountains," *American Catholic Quarterly Review*, April 1876, 312 ff, July 1876, 455 ff; John Gibbon, "An Autumn in the Rocky Mountains," *American Catholic Quarterly Review*, January 1879, 81 ff.

41. Sheridan to Adjutant General, 17 August 1872, 3322 AGO 72, WD, AGO, NA.

42. Monthly return, February 1873, 7th Infantry, WD, AGO, NA; Mother M. E. Tobin, R.S.C.J., letter of 7 July 1958 to Mark H. Jordan.

43. The correspondence and subsequent court of inquiry proceedings may be found in file 2533 AGO 73, WD, AGO, NA.

44. Special Orders, No. 161, Paragraph 3, Adjutant General's Office, 7 August 1873, WD, AGO, NA; monthly return, 7th Infantry, July 1874, WD, AGO, NA.

45. Robert Utley, *Frontier Regulars: The United States Army and the Indian, 1866–1890* (New York, 1973), 242.

46. Letters Received File 4408 AGO 76, WD, AGO, NA. In the fall of 1876 Gibbon deemed it necessary to warn T. C. Power and Brother Company, one of the leading trading firms in Montana, concerning a large shipment of munitions which it had received: ". . . should any portion of these arms and ammunition find its way into the hands of the Indians, you will be held responsible by an outraged community." Sharp, *Whoop-Up Country*, 216.

47. There is much literature on the Sioux War of 1876. The best accounts are

Robert Utley, *Custer and the Great Controversy* (Baton Rouge, 1962); W. A. Graham, *The Story of the Little Big Horn* (New York, 1945); John S. Gray, *Centennial Campaign: The Sioux War of 1876* (Norman, Okla., 1988); Edgar I. Stewart, *Custer's Luck* (Norman, Okla., 1955).

48. U.S. Department of War, Secretary of War, Annual Report, 1876; Report of Alfred H. Terry, 44th Congress, 2nd Session, House Executive Documents No. 1, Part 2, p. 459.

49. Edgar I Stewart, "Major Brisbin's Relief of Fort Pease," in *The Great Sioux War, 1876–1877*, Paul L. Hedren, ed. (Helena, Mont., 1991), 115–121.

50. James H. Bradley, *The March of the Montana Column* (Norman, Okla., 1961), 13.

51. John Gibbon, *Gibbon on the Sioux Campaign of 1876* (Bellevue, Neb., 1970), 4; James H. Bradley, "Journal of the Sioux Campaign of 1876 under the command of General John Gibbon," *Contributions to the Historical Society of Montana*, II (1896), 141.

52. Bradley, *Montana Column*, 23.

53. Information on Dr. Paulding and his views are drawn from W. Boyes, ed., *Surgeon's Diary with the Custer Relief Column* (Washington, D.C., 1974), and Thomas R. Buecker, ed., "A Surgeon at the Little Big Horn: The Letters of Dr. Holmes O. Paulding," in *The Great Sioux War 1876–1877*, 123–151. The quotation appears on page 2 of the diary. Editor Boyes remarks that the diary displays "a contemptuous dislike for insipid military martinets." To the writers of this book, it also seems to evidence a self-assumed expertise on military matters that may not be supported by Dr. Paulding's experience.

Gray notes that Gibbon had appointed Lieutenant Coolidge as "Acting Surgeon," which evidently added to Paulding's unhappiness. (Gray, *Centennial Campaign*, 276.)

54. Gibbon, *Sioux Campaign*, 6–7.

55. Gibbon, *Sioux Campaign*, 9; Bradley, *Montana Column*, 39–48.

56. Gibbon, *Sioux Campaign*, 12; Bradley, *Montana Column*, 55–66; Paulding, *Diary*, 5.

57. Bradley, *Journal*, 184; Stewart, *Custer's Luck*, 141–143; Gibbon, *Sioux Campaign*, 12–14.

58. Bradley, *Montana Column*, 87–88.

59. Gibbon, *Sioux Campaign*, 16–17; Bradley, *Montana Column*, 102–105. The lesson was not lost on Gibbon; he later wrote that cavalry should have horses trained to cross rivers. "Arms to Fight Indians," *The United Service: A Quarterly Review of Military and Naval Affairs*, Vol. I, April 1879, 237–244.

60. Bradley, *Montana Column*, 123–126.

61. Gray, *Centennial Campaign*, 83–85.

62. Terry, *Report*, 461.

63. Robert P. Hughes, "The Campaign against the Sioux in 1876," *Journal of the Military Service Institution of the United States*, Vol. XVIII, No. LXXIX (January 1896), reprinted in Graham, *Little Big Horn*, 103.

64. Gibbon, *Sioux Campaign*, 21–22: Terry, *Report*, 460–462; Utley, *Frontier Regulars*, 256.

65. Gibbon, *Sioux Campaign*, 21–22; Graham, *Little Big Horn*, 11–12.

66. Gibbon, *Sioux Campaign*, 22; Graham, *Little Big Horn*, 110–111, 114.

67. Gibbon, *Sioux Campaign,* 23.

68. Gibbon, ibid., 25.

69. Bradley, *Journal,* 221.

70. George A. Schneider, editor, *The Freeman Journal: The Infantry in the Sioux Campaign of 1876,* 68 and n; Buecker, "A Surgeon at the Little Big Horn," 146.

71. Bradley, *Montana Column,* 160–161; Gregory J. W. Urwin, " 'Custar Had Not Waited for Us': One of Gibbon's Doughboys on the Custer Battle," in Gregory J. W. Urwin, *Custer and His Times: Book Three* [([no place of publication], 1987), n35, 199–200.

72. Gibbon, *Sioux Campaign,* 30–31.

73. Gibbon, ibid., 30.

74. Gibbon, ibid., 41.

75. Gibbon later criticized Custer's tactics for "dividing his force in the presence of so numerous an enemy" (Gibbon, *Sioux Campaign,* 41). It is ironic that Gibbon himself could be criticized for doing the same thing a year later at Big Hole.

9 Last Battle, General's Star

In the face of this serious setback to the summer campaign against the Sioux, Terry and Gibbon turned their attention to the immediate problem of burying the dead and transporting the wounded to where they could receive adequate medical care. With no litters or stretchers available, Gibbon had Indian tent poles collected, blankets draped across them, and the wounded carried down the bluffs to the 7th Infantry camp. From there they had to be taken to the mouth of the Little Big Horn, from whence the Far West would move them to Fort Abraham Lincoln.[1]

After some experimentation with horse and mule litters, and utilizing the troops as stretcher bearers, Gibbon managed to get the wretched men about four miles down the river valley. Fortunately, a lieutenant suggested using the Indian travois—a one-horse litter, flexible and generally comfortable. Using the most docile animals from the pack train, the wounded were carried to the steamer's mooring. On 30 June they were loaded aboard and made as comfortable as possible. Captain Grant Marsh began his epic run down the Yellowstone and Missouri on 3 July, carrying news of the disaster that would go out from Fort Abraham Lincoln to the nation.[2]

In the turmoil of clearing the battlefield Gibbon found time to think of his own and the other 7th Regiment wives, and of the worries which news of the Custer defeat would engender. During his absence on the campaign Fannie had gone East to visit their daughters, still in school in Philadelphia, and other relatives. On 28 June he scribbled a message on sheets torn from a notebook and sent it off to Captain D. W. Benham of the 7th Infantry, commanding at Fort Ellis, the post nearest the battlefield. After reporting that "my command is intact and in fine order," he requested Benham to wire this intelligence to Fort Shaw and Camp Baker, in order to allay anxieties there. Having thus looked to the concerns of his subordinates' families, he added, "You might wire Mr. Henry Moale, 18 Commerce Street, Baltimore. 'Tell Fannie myself and command are well. J. G.' Date it Camp on the Little Big Horn, June 28."[3]

Terry began concentrating all available troops to pursue and catch the Sioux and Cheyenne before they dispersed to the Big Horn and Wolf Mountains, and went into camp at the mouth of the Big Horn to await reinforcements. On 1 August six companies of the 22nd Infantry joined, and the next day six companies of the 5th Infantry debarked under Colonel Nelson A. Miles. With the infantry organized into a four-battalion brigade under Gibbon, and the troops of the 2nd and 7th Cavalry under Brisbin, Terry and his 1,700 men ascended the Rosebud. On 10 August he met Crook and his column. The combined force combed the area to the east for a week, but they could not find Sitting Bull.[4]

Cold rains, mud, and supply problems kept the pursuit from being anything but an exercise in futility. Eventually hopes of finding the Sioux died out, and Crook took his men away from the Montana column. By September the evidence was in: the tribes had scattered. Terry disbanded the command and ordered Gibbon back to western Montana. On 6 October the last companies of the 7th Infantry passed through the gates of Fort Shaw. Not since the bloody and frustrating summer of 1864 had Gibbon expended so much effort for so little result. The campaign had consumed six weary months. Temperatures had ranged from the forty below zero in which they departed on St. Patrick's Day to 111 degrees in the shade on the banks of the Rosebud in August. A general had washed his underclothes in the Yellowstone and sat on the bank, "wrapped in meditation," while they dried. Onlookers could discern the brand of flour from which the 7th baked its bread by reading the seats of the officers' trousers that the sacks had been used to patch. The regiment had slogged over 1,600 miles; it had taken casualties, though not many; in the aftermath, it had witnessed the grisly slaughter of hundreds of its fellow soldiers; and ironically, most of its members had not fired a shot in battle.[5]

Late in the fall a band of Nez Perces under the leadership of Chief Looking Glass gave the 7th Infantry a glimpse of things to come. En route to their home in Oregon and Idaho from buffalo hunting on the Montana plains, they paused at Fort Shaw, where they received gifts of food and an invitation to put on a sham battle. The Indians first marched around the garrison to display their gay trappings and garishly painted faces, then assembled for the fight on the prairie outside the fort. During a pause in the battle the Nez Perces' half-breed interpreter asked Gibbon for rags to make a fire. Gibbon suggested that a handful of hay be used. With this kindling the Indians fired the prairie grass; a favorable wind carried the smoke on their "enemy," and under its cover the victorious party charged and routed their opponents. The onlookers were not impressed by the performance, remarking that if the Nez Perces did not do better in a real battle, they would not cause their enemies much harm. Many of the spectators found cause to reconsider the following year.[6]

Gibbon passed the winter of 1876–77 in routine administrative duties. The trial of Colonel J. J. Reynolds, in which he served as a member of the general court martial, took Gibbon to Cheyenne for several weeks of temporary duty. (As the third-ranking member of the court, Gibbon would have been seated immediately to the left of the court's president, Brigadier General John Pope. It takes little imagination to picture the atmosphere of frost that must have pervaded the court's proceedings.) Reynolds, commander of the 3rd Cavalry, was convicted of several charges arising from his retreat after the debacle of Powder River in the preceding March. Although in light of Reynolds' long service President Grant remitted the sentence, Reynolds shortly thereafter retired in disgrace.

The winter also led Gibbon to resume writing for publication. The *American Catholic Quarterly Review* had previously carried articles on his travels in the wilds of the Rocky Mountains. Now he turned to describing his Indian campaigns and to reflecting on the government's Indian policy.[7]

John Gibbon's first exposure to large-scale plains campaigning led him to serious soul searching. Generally, any officer who gave some thought to his duties and was not totally insensitive remained frustrated by an almost schizophrenic attitude on the part of the American public. By applying a policy guaranteed to instigate hostilities, the Washington officials seemed determined on provoking a series of these small, vicious wars. But they never tried to provide an army large enough either to force a quick battlefield decision or to enforce peace by an overwhelming show of military strength. The public seemed annoyed when conflict broke out but never once wondered if their government's Indian policy was the cause.[8]

Gibbon took advantage of several opportunities to express his views in print. In an article written in the aftermath of the 1876 war, the veteran officer asked the question, "How do you avoid war?" He asserted that this could be done by exercising "a spirit of concession and justice," something directly the reverse of the characteristic American Indian policy. With increasing eloquence, he went on to say

The Indian, although a savage, is still a man with . . . quite as much instinctive sense of right and wrong as a white man. . . . He argues this way: the white man has come into my country and taken away everything which formerly belonged to me. He even drives off and . . . destroys the game which the Great Spirit gave me to subsist on. He owes me something for this, but refuses to pay.[9]

When the Indian, driven to the edge of starvation and frustration by misconduct and fraud on the part of the Indian agents, turned to war, the

Army had to bring into subjugation "a people forced into war by the very agents of the government which makes war upon them." Strange, Gibbon thought, that the American people insisted on pretending both to support the Indian and to attempt his eradication.[10]

In an essay that won the 1880 prize offered by the *Journal of the Military Service Institution,* Gibbon repeated these points and developed them. As did many of his fellow officers, he wanted the management of Indian affairs transferred to the War Department. This would eliminate, or severely reduce, any chance of fraud. By turning the Indians to cattle raising, and by providing good breeding stock, the government could solve many existing problems.[11]

John Gibbon was no twentieth-century man in his attitudes. He viewed the Indian as a savage, but also as a skilled opponent; a belligerent but also a man. As an Army officer, John Gibbon performed his duty; as a sensitive human being, he sympathized with the plight of the Indians and hoped to see their lot improved. Clearly, Gibbon saw a future time when America's strength and advanced technology would roll over the frontier and obliterate the Indian way of life. People of the twentieth century have tried to find a third alternative between this destruction and total submission. Gibbon in his time argued for such an alternative: justice and fair dealing toward a hardy and worthy opponent. Caught in a crossfire between humanitarians, who characterized the soldiers as butchers, and settlers, who argued that the soldiers did not do enough, the Army thoroughly disliked its task of Indian fighting. In 1877 Gibbon participated in a campaign that came to symbolize all the elements of the end of the Plains Indian: the Nez Perce War.[12]

The lands of the powerful Nez Perce tribe lay in Oregon and Idaho, adjacent to the western boundary of the Department of Dakota. Although a large reservation had been set aside for them in 1866, it was shortly reduced in size because of the discovery of gold and an influx of white settlers. Adding to the ambiguity of the situation was the fact that several Nez Perce bands had refused to accept reservation life. With the tribe divided between "treaty" and "nontreaty" Indians, the natives were scattered between the reservation along Idaho's Clearwater River and the Salmon, Snake, and Grande Ronde Rivers. The latter group had acquired an eloquent and effective spokesman when Young Joseph followed his father as leader of the Grande Ronde band.[13]

Government conduct toward the non-treaty bands prior to 1876 was largely characterized by repeated breaches of faith. When Brigadier General O. O. Howard became Department of the Columbia commander in September 1874, he determined on a course that would eventually force them onto the reservation. After the failure of a conference with the non-treaty Indians in November 1876, the Interior Department on 7 March 1877 requested help from the army in the removal of the Nez Perces to

The Nez Perce War, 1877. Courtesy Robert Utley, *Frontier Regulars: The United States Army and the Indian, 1866–1891.*

their reservation. Although the Indians did agree to move, the situation grew tense. It was complicated by anger and grief on the part of the Indians, the murder of four whites, and a crushing defeat inflicted on a detachment of the 1st Cavalry on 17 June at White Bird Canyon by Chief Joseph's band. As a result a large group of the nontreaty Indians began to move toward the east, out of Howard's department.[14]

Conditions deteriorated further when Howard failed to defeat and capture the Nez Perce group at the battle of the Clearwater on 11–12 July. On 15 July the chiefs made the decision to cross the Bitterroot Mountains and gain the buffalo plains of Montana. Here they could hope to find sanctuary, either with the Sioux or by entering Canada. This decision drew Gibbon's command into the war.

Terry had already warned Gibbon on 1 July that Howard's Indian difficulties might spill over into the District of Montana. The field force available to Gibbon for countering such a threat was meager. The 2nd Cavalry battalion from Fort Ellis had been ordered to join Nelson Miles and his 5th Infantry in their operations against the Sioux, leaving only the 7th Infantry for Gibbon's use against Joseph. The four posts could not be completely stripped of troops for a campaign; an understrength company had to be left as a minimum garrison at each fort. On 9 June Gibbon had dispatched Company I from Fort Shaw to Missoula, with the mission of building a fort there. Including Company I, Gibbon would be able to field six companies against Joseph.

Thus matters stood when on 22 July Sheridan, acting directly in Terry's absence from his headquarters, ordered Gibbon to concentrate all his infantry at Missoula.[15] Upon receipt of the order Gibbon put the 7th in motion. By 28 July the troops available from Forts Benton and Camp Baker had been concentrated at Shaw; a company from Fort Ellis was en route directly to Missoula in wagons. Gibbon moved out with three companies, considerably understrength; altogether he had only eight officers and seventy-six enlisted men. After covering 150 miles in seven days, over extremely rough and difficult country, the small battalion sighted Missoula and its fort on 3 August. Here Gibbon obtained recent information on the Indian situation. The troops already at Missoula had been ordered to block the Lolo Trail leading into Missoula from the west, and in compliance had built a temporary defensive work, derisively named "Fort Fizzle." Joseph had simply outflanked it without fighting and started south up the Bitterroot Valley. During the march, through trade and intimidation, the Nez Perces managed to obtain arms, ammunition, and food.

Gibbon immediately notified Howard that he was going in pursuit of Joseph. On 4 August, as the Indians crossed the Continental Divide, Gibbon, having assembled a six-company force, put his fifteen officers and 146 men in wagons and set off up the valley for Stevensville. Using the vehicles increased the infantry's mobility, and over the next two days the command covered almost fifty-five miles. During this part of his march Gibbon received his only reinforcements; a number of civilians of the valley offered to go along as volunteers. Although he held a low opinion of their discipline and fighting qualities, Gibbon accepted. One of them, Joe Blodgett, led the wagons far beyond the point where Gibbon thought they would have to be abandoned.[16]

By adding the thirty-four civilians to Lieutenant Bradley's scout company, Gibbon managed to make the best use of the settlers. He also increased his firepower with a small mountain howitzer found at Fort Owen. Until the column started to climb the divide separating the force from Ross's Hole, it made good time. Then the ascent became so steep and rugged that Gibbon decided to halt his men and not risk a night march. On 7 August the going became more difficult, and progress for the day dropped to thirteen miles.[17]

The Nez Perces, totally unaware of the Montana column's approach, made no effort to disguise their trace. Gibbon's scouts continually found and followed a trail marked by abandoned brush shelters and camp debris. The Indians would soon be overtaken, since their pace was only twelve to fourteen miles per day. Gibbon still had no idea of the strength of his opponents. The best estimate obtained from civilians was about 260 warriors, all well-armed and with plenty of ammunition. Any fight promised to be a very risky affair.[18]

When the force camped for the night on 7 August, the energetic Lieutenant Bradley volunteered to take his mounted scouts and a party of the volunteers, make a night march, and attempt to overtake the Indians. He might be able to stampede their pony herd and reduce their chance of escape. Gibbon told him to go ahead, and he departed with sixty men.[19]

At 5:00 A.M. on the 8th Gibbon led the main body out, and immediately ran into obstacles. A steep ascent and much fallen timber compelled the lightening of the wagons and the use of double teams and drag ropes to get the transport over the divide. Without Blodgett's services, Gibbon later remarked, "we could not have made the time we did."[20]

While the field force toiled and sweated over the Bitterroot ridges, a courier from Bradley arrived. Although the distance which he had had to cover was too great to permit a night attack, he had found the Indian camp and was watching it from concealment. Gibbon immediately dropped Company A to guard the train and assist its progress. With the rest of the troops and the howitzer he pushed ahead to overtake Bradley. The two forces united around sunset, with the enemy about four or five miles away. When the train came up, Gibbon ordered it parked and hidden, the animals turned out to graze, and rations distributed. He then ordered his men to rest until 10:00 P.M., when the approach march would start. By then, Gibbon hoped, the Indians would be asleep.[21]

The bivouac was an uncomfortable one. The order "no fires" meant cold food, hardtack and raw salt pork. Silence was to be strictly maintained, and the men were not even permitted to smoke. The prospect of action raised the level of tension. Gibbon fully intended to attack the Indians at first light, and prepared accordingly. Each man received ninety rounds of ammunition, and a pack mule was loaded with an additional 2,000 rounds.[22]

With Bradley and the scouts leading, the infantry set out toward the Indian encampment at Big Hole Basin. As the mountains opened into a valley, the trail turned to the left. Soon Gibbon discerned the Nez Perce campfires. Large groups of ponies could be seen grazing on the hillsides. As the troops passed through the herds, outlines of tepees could be made out in the flat country below.[23]

A detachment of fourteen soldiers remained behind to bring up the wagons and howitzer. The men with Gibbon lay down in the woods to await the dawn. Gibbon had done very well to achieve complete tactical surprise. His approach march had not alarmed the Nez Perces, who were completely unaware of their danger. Not even the camp dogs were alerted by the proximity of a large body of troops. Joe Blodgett and the Fort Shaw post guide, H. O. Bostwick, warned Gibbon that he should attack in force, since the Nez Perces would prove to be much more tenacious opponents than the Sioux. Bostwick also told Gibbon that if the Indian women came out during the night to build up the fires, this would be a sure sign that the troops remained undiscovered. About an hour later women appeared to throw wood on the flames.[24]

The still night and clear mountain air carried the sounds of the slumbering encampment up the western slopes to the men of the 7th. For two hours they listened to the intermittent barking of the ubiquitous camp dogs and the occasional cry of a baby. As the sky grew lighter Gibbon could make out the disposition of the village. He ordered Companies D and E to deploy as skirmishers and proceed down into the valley.[25]

The Big Hole Basin, 6,800 feet above sea level, is almost sixty miles long, fairly wide, and well watered by many streams; the waters form the north and south forks of the Big Hole River. Although the white man had used the valley for cattle grazing, vegetation—sagebrush, grasses, and flowers—still covered the ground. In 1877 it was a beautiful and attractive campsite. When the Nez Perces laid out their village of about eighty-nine lodges, the camp took the form of a V. The apex now pointed toward Gibbon's lines, with a large stream between the lodges and the slope. Gibbon estimated the camp's length to be from 200 to 300 feet. Any advance toward the village would be hindered by the pony herd, thick brush, and waist-deep water on both sides of the stream.[26]

The colonel divided his small force into three wings. The two infantry companies assigned as skirmishers led the way. Bradley's scouts and the volunteers under John B. Catlin made up the left wing, and Captain William Logan's Company A the right. The other three companies—F, G and I—constituted the center. The colonel and Bradley mounted their horses; all other officers remained on foot. Gibbon took position on the extreme right, and at 3:30 A.M. signaled the line forward.[27]

Although the troops maintained silence as they advanced, the element of surprise vanished when a lone Indian warrior went out to the pony herd, mounted, and inadvertently rode his horse into the middle of the skirmish line. The volunteers shot and killed him. At this the whole line pushed forward, and the skirmishers ran toward the village. On the right the infantry actually broke into the encampment. The troops poured heavy fire into the startled Nez Perces, who at first did not respond. Many of them sought cover.

Confusion and near panic at first stalled the Indian defense; then the admirable Nez Perce leadership asserted itself. Rallied by Joseph, Looking Glass, and White Bird, the warriors recovered and began to pour a deadly fire into Gibbon's thin formation. On the right the soldiers tried to set the camp ablaze, and thus illuminated they presented static targets for Indian marksmen. Gibbon's troops in their turn became badly disorganized, and almost every crack of an Indian rifle brought down a soldier.[28]

The fighting became a melee, and casualties spread to the women and children. The deaths of their loved ones reinforced the Indians' combative spirit. Chiefs Joseph and Ollokot both saw their wives killed, and the braves could hear White Bird shouting, "Fight for women and children! . . . Now is our time. Fight! It is better we should be killed fighting. . . ."[29] Gibbon found the battle comparable to that along the Hagerstown pike between the East and West Woods at Antietam. His efforts to make some sense out of a combat that had no organized form were hampered by the loss of key officers. Logan killed an Indian and in turn was shot through the head and killed by his sister, who seized a revolver from her dead brother's hand.[30] The able Bradley also fell to the deadly fire. Four other officers were wounded, one mortally. Gibbon, still mounted, toppled into the stream when a rifle bullet inflicted a painful wound in his left thigh and killed his horse. Limping, he continued to command.[31]

Fearing panic due to the heavy loss in officers, Gibbon ordered a withdrawal back to the wooded hill that had been his predawn camp. The retreat was orderly. As the men recrossed the stream, at about 8:00 A.M., an Indian sharpshooter killed several of them. Upon reaching the woods the troops quickly began to pile up logs and construct primitive fortifications. Catlin, who did not think much of the position, demanded: "Who in hell called a halt here?" When someone told him that Gibbon had, he retorted, "I don't give a damn, it's a hell of a place to camp!" Gibbon was too busy to rebuke the civilian volunteers' leader.[32]

The Nez Perce fire into the new position remained accurate and deadly.

The howitzer managed to get off only two shots before it and the ammunition pack mule were captured. Immobilized by the enemy fire, the 7th remained where it was for twelve hours, its only food being the raw flesh of a horse killed within the lines. The Indians left about thirty warriors to keep Gibbon's men pinned down while the rest returned to their camp. When they discovered the bodies of their families, a cry arose that carried to the ears of the 7th Infantry. Years later Gibbon wrote, "Few of us will soon forget the wail of mingled grief, rage, and horror which came from the camp when the Indians . . . recognized their slaughtered warriors, women, and children."[33]

The Nez Perces tried to dislodge their foes by igniting the grass, but it was too green to burn. All that night Indian riflemen kept up a sporadic fire into Gibbon's lines, gradually withdrawing as the tribe left the Big Hole. After 11:00 P.M., 10 August, when all firing had stopped, Gibbon sent out parties to bury the dead and count the Indian bodies. He had already dispatched a runner to Howard, who was still pursuing the Nez Perces, having followed them all the way from Idaho. Another runner carried a message for transmission to the governor of Montana Territory, asking for medical assistance.[34]

Attended by a small escort, Howard rode ahead of his main body, reaching the Big Hole at about 10:00 A.M. on 11 August. Gibbon greeted him with "Oh, I'm not much hurt; a flesh wound in the thigh." The next day Howard departed to continue the pursuit, his force bolstered by fifty men from the 7th. Gibbon accompanied the other wounded to Deer Lodge, arriving there on 15 August.[35]

In his report to Terry on the action, Gibbon declined to single out any individual for special mention, stating that the entire command had promptly obeyed orders and were "active, zealous, and courageous." For such a small battle, the losses were severe. Of 191 engaged, twenty-nine were killed and forty wounded; three officers were among the dead. The Indians had suffered more; Gibbon's burial detail counted eighty-nine bodies, including women and children. In his surprise attack Gibbon had deprived the Nez Perces of many of their best men. He made no error in deciding to fight; his problem was that he did not have enough infantry. Terry believed that if Gibbon's six companies had been up to strength, the Nez Perces would have been halted at the Big Hole. He was probably right.[36]

On 5 October Chief Joseph surrendered himself and his band to Howard and Miles at Bear Paw Mountain, Montana. Thus ended the campaign, and Gibbon's last battle faded into history. But controversy over several of his actions at Big Hole did not evaporate. Perhaps the most heated discussion was generated by the casualties suffered by the Nez Perce women and children. A real problem for any army unit engaged in Indian fighting was the difficulty in distinguishing noncombatants from belligerents. During the attack on the Big Hole camp, distinction between the two groups would have been impossible. As has been noted, Logan was slain by a woman. Gibbon reported that one young officer was nearly killed by another woman who fired a pistol at him as he tore open the door of a tepee; understandably, he shot her dead. Gibbon had to assault without warning; with his understrength companies, no other tactic would have had any prospect of success. Once the fighting reached its peak of intensity, as the formal lines dissolved in confusion, and as the camp became the arena of battle, losses among the nonwarrior elements were inevitable. When Indian women took up arms the soldiers were certain to retaliate.[37]

Another serious issue is the story that Gibbon ordered no prisoners to be taken. None of the official documents include this detail. The tale has its origins with a civilian volunteer named Thomas Sherrill, who reported that when the volunteers asked Catlin about prisoners, Catlin queried Gibbon, who answered, "We don't want any prisoners." Sherrill told his story to Alva J. Noyes, who recorded it in a manuscript history of the Big Hole battle. Sherrill also passed it on to Will Cave, who quoted the order in an article carried by the *Wallace Press Times* of Wallace, Idaho.[38] Some historians have accepted the story; Beal, Josephy, and Mark Brown repeated it without discussion. Dee Brown, in *Bury My Heart at Wounded Knee*, adds a detail to the effect that several soldiers were drunk before the attack. On the other hand, Robert Utley does not mention the "no prisoners" tale.[39]

To Gibbon's biographers, the story remains suspect. Recorded long after the event, and passed down through several sources, its origins are dubious. Gibbon and the volunteers did not think much of each other, and this reciprocal disdain may have had something to do with its genesis. Why would Gibbon have given such an order? Gibbon's objective was the defeat of the Indians; this could have been accomplished without wholesale massacre. With a command one-half the size of the Nez Perce band, such a slaughter would have been hard to engineer. Gibbon knew he would have a tough fight on his hands. Why should he have expended energy on needless terror that might stiffen resistance?

More importantly, the remark was completely out of character.[40] Gibbon was not a ruthless man; he did not enjoy or advocate total war; he evidenced considerable empathy for the Indian plight, and characterized American Indian policy as disgusting and hypocritical. It is hard to conceive that a man who had stated in print a sympathetic view of the Indian, who would later go on to befriend Chief Joseph, could or would have given such an unnecessary and barbarous order.

In the aftermath of the Bear Paw surrender, the general opinion in the Army was that Gibbon had done all he could. Sherman wrote to the Secretary of War that "If General Gibbon could have had one hundred more men, there would be few hostile Nez Perce left . . . he did all that a man could possibly do." Sheridan commended his courage in attacking, and considered that he had inflicted "a severe if not a disastrous punishment."[41]

The 7th Infantry, its temporary concentration over, dispersed to its various posts during October. The end of the 1877 war and the subsequent collapse of Sioux resistance in the Dakotas by 1881 left the Montana army without much of a mission. Very little more of Gibbon's service was in western Montana. In March 1878, he left for Washington, ordered there to testify before the House Committee on Military Affairs. His return west in June was followed by the temporary command of the Department of Dakota at St. Paul from July to November 1878, and from there he shuttled between the capital and various posts in the Dakota Department.[42]

While in Washington during this period to serve on the court of inquiry into Stanton's removal in January 1864 of Dr. William Hammond, the Army's Surgeon General, Gibbon entangled himself in the continuing controversy over the Fitz John Porter case. As has already been noted, John Pope had managed to make Porter the scapegoat for the Union defeat at Second Bull Run. After many years of effort to obtain a rehearing, in 1878 Porter's adherents succeeded in persuading President Hayes to appoint a board of senior officers to review the entire matter. Gibbon had long been a friend of Porter and of Porter's principal protagonist, George McClellan, and believed that Porter had been dealt with most unjustly. On that account he seems to have hated John Pope.

While the altercation does not reflect much credit on anyone concerned, it does reveal how seriously these veterans regarded their Civil War reputations, and how vigorously they defended them, often to the edge of absurdity. Gibbon started his involvement in 1874, when he challenged John Pope on the question of the correct dating of portions of Stonewall Jackson's report on Second Bull Run. Quotations from the report were incorporated into a circular that Pope periodically broadcast to support his position in the continuing Porter dispute. As quoted by Pope, the bulk of Jackson's report appeared to vindicate Pope's criticism of Porter's conduct on 30 August 1862. Gibbon maintained, correctly, that a part of the Jackson report cited by Pope referred to the events, not of 30 August, but rather of the 29th. Pope and Gibbon then began a correspondence which disputed the date and whether the Adjutant General of the Army (the official custodian of captured Confederate documents) agreed with the chronology in which Pope used the Jackson account.[43]

Townsend, the Adjutant General, had no intention of becoming involved in this thorny question. He tried to end the matter by telling Gibbon that the Secretary of War wished him to know that the official records would soon be published, and that whoever was interested could then make his own evaluation. Gibbon let the matter go into abeyance early in 1875, telling the War Department that "the facts will be on file for future reference."[44]

When the Porter case surfaced in 1878, Gibbon trundled out his dispute with Pope over Pope's circular. Gibbon thought that Pope was trying to use what Gibbon described as a "deliberate act of forgery" to vindicate the conduct of an officer "not noted for the accuracy of his assertions" (Pope). Then he proceeded to bring charges against Pope. The specifications were that Pope

1. has wilfully, maliciously, and falsely contrived to adhere to the assertion, the falsity of which he well knew, and has continued to permit the circulation of copies . . . and has continued to circulate copies . . . to the great scandal and disgrace of the military service.
2. In that Pope . . . has continued to stick to such false assertion . . .[45]

By this time the Army's high command had had quite enough of Porter, Pope, and the colonel who seemed to thrive on controversy. Sherman managed to stall Gibbon's charges on a technicality until March 1879, when Gibbon wrote to Townsend from Fort Snelling, Minnesota. Now that the Porter court had reported, he wanted to know what had happened to his charges? Upon the forwarding of the matter to the Secretary of War, the latter agreed with Sherman that "no action will be taken on his charges. . . . There should be an end to this controversy." Gibbon protested in a letter to Sherman, on which the latter wrote a note: "Show it to the Secretary and then file it."[46]

Wary of being accused of disrespect to his superiors, Gibbon wrote back on 4 June, disclaiming any such intention. The Commanding General's reply, in full, gives an insight into the old army:

Washington, D.C. June 15, 1879

Dear Gibbon,

Yours of June 4 is rec'd and I am glad you disclaim any want of personal respect to the President and myself—for trying to discourage—the bad habit of preferring charges against prominent officers, for perjury and falsehood growing out of transactions in the Civil War. I don [sic] want to admonish you or any officer of your age and rank with as much knowledge and experience as I profess to possess, but I do claim to be in a better position to judge of what will prejudice, or damage the general interests of the Army than you can possibly be, and I do think it hard when I am doing my best to advance the interest of all on the Frontier against the persistent and insidious influences of hangers about Washington that you should accuse me of being negligent of the honor of our profession.

I have always regarded you as one of our best duty officers always to be relied on in an emergency, and will ever be glad to hear from you especially in a pleasant strain instead of one of complaint.

Truly your friend,

W. T. Sherman[47]

When Gibbon's challenge to Pope foundered on Sherman's adamant refusal to let it continue, Gibbon was Acting Assistant Inspector General for the Department of Dakota. He had already served for a second time as acting department commander. But on 1 November 1879, he returned to his command of the 7th Infantry, with its headquarters now at Fort Snelling, Minnesota. What followed was a six-year period generally consisting of garrison duty, interspersed by some railroad guard mounting and reservation supervision. The interlude at Snelling was enlivened by new disputes with authority, this time over the question of succession to command in the absence of the regular department commander. During Terry's 1878 service at West Point on President Hayes' board to review the Porter case, Gibbon had received orders to assume command of the department. He served as a brevet major general, with powers to convene general courts martial. This assignment terminated upon Terry's return to St. Paul. When Terry left again, a few weeks later, the question arose as to whether Gibbon was temporarily in command as the senior colonel in the department, or whether his previous assignment to command as a brevet major general was again effective. Gibbon, adhering to the latter interpretation, triggered off a spate of correspondence; he was overruled by Washington, but little of substance was at issue.

A more serious dispute arose in 1882, when Terry again left the department. This time no temporary replacement for him was named, on the basis that Terry could communicate with his headquarters by telegraph, and his staff would issue orders under a delegation of authority. Gibbon took violent exception to this arrangement. In his view, the department was being commanded by a staff major. He announced that, as senior officer, he was assuming command. Sheridan immediately ordered him out of the department to temporary duty in Texas. Shortly thereafter a shift of the 7th Infantry to Fort Laramie, Wyoming, in the Department of the Platte, ended Gibbon's claims to command the Department of Dakota.[48]

On a happier note, the time at Fort Snelling brought Gibbon the reestablishment of old ties with the Iron Brigade. Hearing of a brigade reunion at Boscobel, Wisconsin, Gibbon traveled there and appeared at the meeting unannounced. He went unrecognized until, in answer to a question, he stated his purpose for being there as "looking for the man who put the leggings on my horse when we were opposite Fredericksburg," whereupon he was greeted resoundingly as "Johnny the War Horse." From the trip to Boscobel grew a strong relationship with his old troops that lasted until his death. They elected him permanent president of the Iron Brigade Association, and in tangible token of their esteem presented to him a shotgun bearing on the stock an engraved gold plate.[49]

Gibbon also found time to pursue an avocation as a writer, a rather surprising occupation for one who, as a cadet, had had such problems with the study of English. His articles on the Indian campaigns in which he had participated, travels in the Western wilderness, and his views on professional matters appeared in the *American Catholic Quarterly Review, United Service,* and the *Journal of the Military Service Institute.* His essay on "Our Indian Question" won the prize medal in the Institute's essay competition of 1880.[50]

In the winter of 1883 Gibbon learned that Private Daniel Coffee, on his deathbed some months earlier, had named the colonel as executor of his will. The estate, consisting of some $144 in Army back pay, fell under the jurisdiction of the Minnesota courts. Gibbon applied to Army headquarters for official orders to cover his travel between Fort Laramie and St. Paul, in connection with his filing the will for probate. Understandably, he was told that the matter did not qualify as official Army business, and that therefore no Army funds could be used to pay his travel costs. The official reply went on to point out that the executor's expenses were a legitimate charge against the estate itself. Shortly thereafter Gibbon went East on three months' leave. He arranged to travel via St. Paul, the will was duly probated, and the proceeds paid to Coffee's heir, his sister. Court fees amounting to $5.25 were taken from the estate. Gibbon's own expenses presumably came from his own pocket.[51]

During the Fort Laramie tour Gibbon found an outlet for his combative urges in a new battle with his old antagonist Hancock. With publication of the Official Records of the Civil War well under way, Hancock's report on the Wilderness battle was about to come into print, and during a visit to Washington on his 1883 leave, Gibbon saw it for the first time. Indirect accounts of it had previously reached him through Swinton's history of the Army of the Potomac. The old charge—that he had failed on 6 May 1864 to carry out Hancock's order for a crucial attack—still rankled, and on the day that he read Hancock's report Gibbon fired off a letter to his old commander, demanding the name of the officer who had delivered the alleged order. It helped not at all to have Hancock reply that the messenger had been his late aide Mitchell, who had recently died.

Exchanges of correspondence followed, not only with Hancock but also with Gibbon's fellow division commander Francis Barlow and a former member of Hancock's staff, Captain W. D. W. Miller; although he included them in his memoirs, the replies that he received could hardly have given Gibbon much satisfaction. The incident did motivate Hancock to forward to the War Department, for inclusion in the Official Records, additional evidence to bolster his side of the case, in the form of a notebook written by Mitchell in 1864. The notebook, however, had been prepared in the Fall of 1864 by copying various memoranda previously made by Mitchell during the course of the campaign. Hancock did not submit and probably no longer had the original memoranda themselves; the value of the notebook as evidence on events of May 1864 is open to question.[52]

While Gibbon continued to serve on the Great Plains, the logjam of promotion at the top of the Army eventually broke. In 1882 Congress finally passed a mandatory retirement act, setting the age of sixty-four as the maximum limit of service.[53] This legislation had a beneficial effect on the lethargic promotion process. The advancement situation in the post–Civil War Army was characterized by stagnation. In the 1866 expansion the ranks of the new regiments and the few general officer spaces created were filled by relatively young and vigorous men; positions from second lieutenant to colonel were packed with officers who had many years of active service ahead. This condition was compounded by the 1870 Army reduction, in which older officers were forced into retirement. Since seniority governed promotion through colonel, officers in the company and field grades could do little but wait.

For appointment to general the story was different. Seniority was not the criterion for advancement to star rank, selections for which were made by the President on whatever basis he chose. Political support was a key element in attaining rank above colonel. Family connections helped Nelson Miles, a relative by marriage to William Tecumseh Sherman and his brother, the powerful Senator John Sherman of Ohio. George Crook, William B. Hazen, and David Stanley, advanced to brigadier general in the promotion doldrums of the 1870s and early 1880s, were all from Ohio, a state that dominated the Republican party and provided three successive presidents, Grant, Hayes, and Garfield. Clearly identified as a Democrat in a series of Republican administrations, John Gibbon could do little but watch as every man promoted to brigadier general after 1869 was jumped over his head.

In 1885 Brigadier General Christopher C. Augur's impending retirement finally opened a prospect for Gibbon. His case for promotion was strong. Long frontier service, a notable Civil War record, wide acquaintance throughout the Army, and a distinctive personality were among the factors that favored his advancement. By 1884 he had become the senior colonel of the line and the second-ranking colonel in the Army at large.[54] Equally as important were his credentials as a Democrat. After a long period of Republican ascendancy, Grover Cleveland had broken the pattern and gained the White House. The vacancy would be created on Augur's sixty-fourth birthday, 10 July; as early as April 1885 rumors were circulating that Cleveland would give Gibbon the appointment. The *Washington Sunday Herald* mentioned Gibbon, along with Edward Hatch, Wesley Merritt, and O. B. Willcox as potential nominees, stating that among Army officers the majority favored Gibbon. The *Army and Navy Journal* also put forward Gibbon's name and published a story that McClellan had made a special effort to secure Gibbon's promotion.[55]

Momentum began building in the Army on Gibbon's behalf. O. O. Howard started applying pressure two days before Cleveland's inauguration, when he wrote to the President-elect, praising Gibbon's record, his loyalty to the Union, and his character. One month later Cleveland heard from George L. Miller, a prominent Nebraska Democrat and a strong Tilden man. Gibbon, wrote Miller, had been passed over because of his political sympathies. From Oregon the President received a joint letter from Colonel James K. Kelly, former Senator H. W. Corbett, and former Governor L. F. Grover. Abram S. Hewitt, reform Democrat, congressman, later to be mayor of New York, was among the others whose voices were raised in Gibbon's cause.[56]

Far more persuasive than these missives were two sent by Edward S. Bragg, Gibbon's old Iron Brigade subordinate, now chairman of the House Military Affairs Committee and a highly influential Democrat. Bragg, who had seconded Cleveland's nomination at the Democratic convention of 1884, marshalled an impressive array of facts on his wartime comrade's claim. Effectively laying his arguments along the lines of service record and seniority of rank, Bragg included a memorandum he had drawn up emphasizing the latter factor as the best argument for promoting his old commander. This action would restore seniority to its proper place as a criterion for advancement, avoiding the scandal caused when Brigadier General Edward O. C. Ord had been forced into retirement in order to advance the relatively junior Nelson A. Miles to a star. Gibbon's selection would also meet the general approbation of the officer corps.[57]

Bragg followed up this letter on 5 July, restating and reinforcing his points. He also forwarded letters from Howard, Major General John M. Schofield, and Terry, advocating Gibbon's promotion. In the meantime, Bragg kept his candidate fully informed of all developments. He sent Gibbon copies of the Cleveland correspondence, saying "my whole heart is in this thing." Beyond providing certain materials that his sponsor had requested, Gibbon did nothing and kept a low profile.[58]

No one can know which of the various arguments had the most influence on Cleveland, but on 10 July 1885, John Gibbon received word from the Adjutant General of his promotion to brigadier general and immediately sent in his acceptance. Since he was already fifty-eight, this was the highest peacetime rank he would be likely to reach. For a transplanted North Carolinian who had started out with a meager educational background forty-three years before, the brigadier's star was no small achievement. With Bragg's support, Gibbon's long-ago understanding of the volunteer soldier had finally paid off.[59]

NOTES

1. John Gibbon, *Gibbon on the Sioux Campaign of 1876* (Bellevue, Neb., 1970), 35.

2. Gibbon, *Sioux Campaign*, 43–44; Robert Utley, *Frontier Regulars: The United States Army and the Indian, 1866–1890* (New York, 1973), 267.

3. *Contributions to the Historical Society of Montana*, IV, 284 (reprinted from *Billings Times* of July 22, 1902).

4. Gibbon, *Sioux Campaign*, 52–54.

5. Charles A. Woodruff, "Woodruff on the '76 Campaign," *Contributions to the Historical Society of Montana*, Vol. VII, 97 ff.

6. John Gibbon, "The Pursuit of Joseph," *American Catholic Quarterly Review* (hereafter *ACQR*), April 1879, 317 ff.

7. Monthly Returns, 7th Infantry, December 1876, January, February 1877, WD, AGO, NA; J. W. Vaughn, *The Reynolds Campaign on Powder River* (Norman, Okla., 1961), 172 ff; John Gibbon, "Last Summer's Expedition Against the Sioux and Its Great Catastrophe," *ACQR*, April 1877, 271 ff; John Gibbon, "Hunting Sitting Bull," *ACQR*, October 1877, 665 ff.

8. Gibbon, *Sioux Campaign*, 60.

9. Gibbon, ibid., 61.

10. Gibbon, ibid., 62.

11. John Gibbon, "Our Indian Question," *Journal of the Military Service Institution of the United States*, Vol. XI, No. 6 (1881).

12. A good treatment of the Army's ambiguous position is in Utley, *Frontier Regulars*, 44–46. A most eloquent visual depiction of the Army's attitude is in John Ford's film, *She Wore a Yellow Ribbon* (1950).

13. Studies of the Nez Perce War and its origins include: Alvin H. Josephy Jr., *The Nez Perce Indians and the Opening of the Northwest* (New Haven, 1963); Merrill D. Beal, *"I Will Fight No More Forever," Chief Joseph and the Nez Perce War* (Seattle, 1964); Mark H. Brown, *The Flight of the Nez Perce: A History of the Nez Perce War* (New York, 1967); and David Lavender, *Let Me Be Free: The Nez Perce Tragedy* (New York, 1992.).

14. Utley, *Frontier Regulars*, 296–302; Beal, *Fight No More*, 1–65.

15. U.S. Secretary of War, *Annual Report 1877*, House Executive Document No. 1, Part 2, 45th Congress, 2nd session, Vol. 2 (Washington, D.C., 1877). As a consequence of successive reductions in the authorized size of the Army, a full-strength infantry company now numbered thirty-seven men.

16. SecWar, *Annual Report 1877*, 67–68.

17. SecWar, ibid., 67–68.

18. SecWar, ibid., 69.

19. SecWar, ibid., 70.

20. SecWar, ibid.

21. SecWar, ibid., 71.

22. SecWar, ibid.

23. SecWar, ibid.

24. SecWar, ibid.

25. SecWar, ibid.

26. U.S. Department of the Interior, *Big Hole Battlefield National Monument* (Washington, D.C., 1962), 4–5.

27. John Gibbon, "The Battle of the Big Hole," *Harper's Weekly*, April 1895, 1235–36; Charles A. Woodruff, "Woodruff on the '76 Campaign," *Contributions to the Historical Society of Montana*, VII, 97ff.

28. Gibbon was much impressed with Indian marksmanship. He later wrote that an Indian who could not hit a man-sized target at 400 to 500 yards "would be ridiculed by his comrades and laughed at as a squaw." In advocating more target practice for infantry, he saw the Indians' superiority in battle as attributable to their better marksmanship, rather than to any rapidity of fire that could be achieved with their repeating rifles. John Gibbon, "Arms to Fight Indians," *The United Service: A Quarterly Review of Military and Naval Affairs*, Vol. I, April 1879, 237–244.

29. Beal, *Fight No More*, 131.

30. G. O. Shields ("Coquina"), *The Battle of the Big Hole* (Chicago and New York, 1889), 53.

31. Josephy, *Nez Perce*, 582–583.

32. Beal, *Fight No More*, 136.

33. Gibbon, *Big Hole*, 1236.

34. O. O. Howard, *Nez Perce Joseph* (Boston, 1881), 203.

35. Gibbon, *Big Hole*, 1236.

36. SecWar, *Annual Report, 1877*, 72.

37. For a discussion of this point, see Lavender, *Let Me Be Free*, 282.

38. Beal, *Fight No More*, 126, 350, n. 1.

39. Beal, *Fight No More*, 126; Josephy, *Nez Perce*, 581, gives no source; Mark Brown, *Flight of Nez Perce*, 253. Dee Brown, in *Bury My Heart at Wounded Knee* (New York, 1970), 324, offers no source. Given Gibbon's iron insistence on discipline, it is inconceivable that he would have allowed the regulars to drink to excess. On the other hand, the extent to which he was able to exercise control over the civilian volunteers in such matters is open to question.

40. Simply to note Gibbon's expressed opinions on Indian policy is enough to cast doubt on the entire story.

41. W. T. Sherman to G. W. McCrary, 19 August 1877, in Robert Vaughn, *Then and Now; or, Thirty Six Years in the Rockies* (Minneapolis, 1900), 342; P. H. Sheridan to Adjutant General, 13 August 1877, 3464 AGO 77, WD, AGO, NA.

42. Adjutant General to Commander, Department of Dakota, 14 March 1878, 1208 AGO 78, WD, AGO, NA.

43. John Gibbon to Adjutant General E. D. Townsend, 15 November 1874, Letters Received File, AGO, WD, NA; Adjutant General to JG, 5 December 1874, Letters Sent File; JG to Adjutant General, 1 February 1875, 953 AGO 75, WD, AGO, NA. A part of the circular was written by Irwin McDowell. Otto Eisenschiml, *The Celebrated Case of Fitz John Porter* (Indianapolis and New York, 1950), 231.

44. JG to Adjutant General, 15 November 1874.

45. JG to Adjutant General, 30 September 1878, 7123 AGO 78, AGO, WD, NA.

46. JG to AG, 24 March 1879, 1845 AGO 79; Sherman to Secretary of War, 1845

AGO 1879; JG to AG, 19 April 1879, 2530 AGO 79; Sherman to AG, 28 April 1879, 2530 AGO 79, AGO, WD, NA.

47. William T. Sherman to JG, 15 June 1879, GP, MHS.

48. Monthly Returns, 7th Infantry; the material on the command controversy is in 4415 AGO 1878, AGO, WD, NA. In the long run Gibbon may have won his point; in 1884, when Brigadier General O. O. Howard, then commanding the Department of the Platte, went on leave, Gibbon was ordered from Fort Laramie to Omaha to assume command temporarily in Howard's place. Monthly Returns, 7th Infantry, March through November 1884.

49. Military Order of the Loyal Legion of the United States, Minnesota Commandery, Vol. 4 (St. Paul, 1898), 557. Quoted by Paul C. Smith, Rhinelander, Wisconsin, letter to Mark H. Jordan, 2 July 1961; W. Roy Stephenson, "Hunting with General Gibbon," *Confederate Veteran*, November 1913 (Vol. XXI, No. 11), 535.

50. John Gibbon, "Arms to Fight Indians," *The United Service: A Quarterly Review of Military and Naval Affairs*, Vol. I, April 1879, 237–244; John Gibbon, "Tents for Armies," *United Service*, Vol. I, October 1879, 517–519; John Gibbon, "Law in the Army" (in which he sets forth his position on the succession to command issue), *Journal of the Military Service Institute*, Vol. I, No. 4, 1880, 438; John Gibbon, "Our Indian Question," *Journal of the MSI*, Vol. II, No. 6, 1881. See also notes 6 and 7, supra, and footnotes to Chapter 8.

51. John Gibbon to Colonel Robert Williams, AAG, Military Division of the Missouri, 1 March 1883, and endorsements thereto, WD, AGO, NA, RG 94; Rose Fosseen, Clerk of Probate Court, Hennepin County, Minnesota, letter to Mark H. Jordan, 30 December 1957.

52. Gibbon, *Personal Recollections*, 387–411. The published volumes of the Official Records do not indicate the manner in which the Mitchell notebook became incorporated thereinto, and might lead to the impression that it was submitted in February 1865 with the Hancock report itself. The correspondence with which Hancock forwarded the notebook to the War Department for copying in 1884 is in the National Archives (Winfield S. Hancock to Colonel R. N. Scott, USA, 21 October 1884, number 295, enclosed in Box 8, Entry 710, RG 94, NA), along with a typewritten copy of the notes. At his request the original notebook was returned to Hancock in November 1884 and has apparently vanished. Similarly, during the same period Hancock submitted a modification to his Wilderness report (Winfield S. Hancock to Adjutant General, 22 May 1882, 2283 AGO 82, Letters Received, RG 94, NA), changing the date on which he says that George W. Getty was wounded. In the printed record this correction of 1882 appears only by showing the correct date in brackets [ ] after the incorrect date given in Hancock's original report.

By way of contrast, Gibbon's letter of 30 November 1862, to Burnside, submitting his campaign proposal for a move against Petersburg, carries a notation in the printed records indicating that it was found among Burnside's personal papers after his death and only then sent to the War Department.

It seems a fair inference that Hancock was stimulated to make this correction and addition by the surfacing of the long-simmering controversy with Gibbon. It also seems a fair inference that in 1882–84 the editors of the Official Records felt that some deference was due to the (then) second-senior general in the Army, and that it was not necessary to highlight the fact that he was augmenting and correcting his wartime reports nearly twenty years after the fact.

53. The passage of the law obliged Gibbon to correct the Army records as to his age. Upon his admission to the Military Academy in 1842 he was represented as being sixteen years and four months old; actually he was a year younger. His brother Robert came to his assistance by certifying to the date of John's birth as recorded in the family Bible. (Letters Received File 6953 ACP 82, WD, AGO, NA, RG 94.)

54. William B. Hazen to Secretary of War, 9 February 1884, Letters Received File, WD, AGO, NA.

55. *Washington Sunday Herald*, 5, 19 April 1885; "Vacancies in the Army," *The Army and Navy Journal*, 11, 16 July 1885. An excellent discussion of factors influencing post–Civil War promotions to general is contained in Paul A. Hutton, *Phil Sheridan and His Army* (Lincoln, Neb., 1985), 135ff.

56. All references are letters to Grover Cleveland: O. O. Howard, 2 March 1885; George L. Miller, 28 April 1885; James K. Kelly, L. F. Grover, H. W. Corbett, 30 June 1885; Abram S. Hewitt, 2 May 1885, Letters Received File, WD, AGO, NA.

57. E. S. Bragg to Grover Cleveland, 27 June 1885, Bragg papers, SHSW; Utley, *Frontier Regulars*, 356.

58. E. S. Bragg to JG, 27 June 1885, Bragg papers, SHSW.

59. JG to Secretary of War, 10 July 1885; JG to AG, 10 July 1885, WD, AGO, NA.

10 "A Mind Girt Up for Action"

As a brigadier general Gibbon received command of the Department of the Columbia, encompassing Washington, Oregon, and Idaho. On 29 July 1885 he took up his new post at Vancouver Barracks, Washington, replacing Nelson Miles.[1] Situated in some of the most beautiful country in America, this Pacific Northwest military area was a fairly substantial one. Besides Vancouver Barracks and the department Ordnance Bureau, Gibbon controlled seven additional posts and barracks. The garrison of 139 officers and 1,661 enlisted men was provided by two infantry regiments (2nd and 14th), nine companies of the 2nd Cavalry, and three companies of the 1st Artillery.[2]

An ugly situation with heavily racial overtones soon drew Gibbon into the domestic troubles of Washington Territory. The lack of efficient police forces in the population centers and of a reliable territorial militia made the federal troops the only potentially effective constabulary in the area, a role for which soldiers were ill-prepared. The surface peace vanished soon after Gibbon arrived. Starting that fall and continuing into 1886, anti-Chinese agitation swept California and carried over into the Pacific Northwest. The targets of exclusion legislation because of their failure to become assimilated, the Chinese immigrants aroused the hatred of white workers by their diligent work habits and antipathy toward labor organizations. As one historian has remarked, "the pressure of these unorganized laborers on the Pacific coast was an abomination to American workers."[3]

Eventually, the agitation took a violent turn. Although in 1882 Congress had prohibited immigration for ten years, this did little to quell unrest, or stop outrages that often ended in murder. Perhaps the worst was at Rock Springs, Wyoming, in the summer of 1885, when Chinese coal miners were attacked by whites. Twenty-eight Orientals were murdered, another fifteen wounded, and the remainder driven from the town. Additional disturbances took place at Squaw Valley, Wyoming, with three Chinese slain, and at Tacoma, Washington Territory.[4]

The trouble at Tacoma turned out to be only the first act of rioting in Gibbon's department. He was on an inspection tour of installations on 6 November 1885, when he received a telegram from the territorial governor, asking that troops be dispatched to Seattle as protection for the Chinese residents. Army action involving intervention in civilian matters had to have the approval of the War Department, so from Fort Canby he immediately telegraphed a request for orders. A heavy storm tore down the lines and cut him off from Washington; on his own initiative he left for Seattle. There on 8 November he found a message from Secretary of War Endicott authorizing him to use troops. Gibbon's department adjutant, Captain C. A. Woodruff, also informed him that ten companies of the 14th Infantry were in the city, but were not deployed. Before taking any drastic action, Gibbon toured the community and held a conference with the authorities. By now he was convinced that the danger had been vastly overrated. Understandably hesitant over using his men for police duty, he urged the mayor to establish an effective force of peace officers. The troops, still unused, left for Vancouver Barracks on 18 November.[5]

That was not the end of the trouble. A more serious outbreak ripped apart the fragile truce in February 1886, and drew Gibbon and the 14th Infantry back to Seattle. When a mob of workers tried to evict the Chinese forcibly by placing them on a steamer, territorial governor Squire asked the federal authorities for permission to declare martial law. By the time this came through on 8 February, two rioters were dead, a number wounded, and the militia involved.[6]

When the city went under martial law on 9 February, the governor asked Gibbon for troops. He at once ordered Lieutenant Colonel Isaac DeRussey to take eight companies of his 14th Infantry (313 men) to Seattle, where Gibbon joined the soldiers on 10 February. He found the Chinese terrified and desirous of leaving, the police chief allied with the rioters, and the civilian authorities generally ineffective.[7]

The general brought with him a reputation as a man who would brook no nonsense. A Seattle newspaper characterized him as "a very strict disciplinarian, and [one who] would deal very severely with all offenders who might be arrested."[8] Such publicity probably helped keep order as much as the presence of regular infantry. Gibbon operated under no illusions as to the touchiness of this assignment. He was thoroughly disgusted with the disdain that most of Seattle's residents displayed toward the law and the rights of the Chinese. Any attempt to try the rioters would merely result in the harassment of witnesses and acquittals.

In the territorial governor Gibbon leaned on a pillar of sand. The man failed to act on his own initiative, and turned to Gibbon at the slightest show of trouble. At any other time the imposition of martial law, the appearance of troops in the streets, and the enforcement of curfews would have been seen as a symbol of civic decay. Here in Seattle men received it with an "expression of satisfaction."[9]

Gibbon knew, and told the governor and municipal officials, that his troops could not remain forever. Domestic order, he warned, was ultimately their responsibility, not his. He then proceeded to restore tranquility. Not wanting to overexpose his troops, he restricted them to the area around the Pacific House Hotel, his headquarters. This kept them out of the public eye, but present as a veiled threat. Then Gibbon laid down curfew regulations, established a system of passes, and closed all the saloons. A general roundup of agitators began.[10]

By 14 February the city had grown quiet. Fourteen of the mob's leaders were under arrest, 110 Chinese had left the community, and a start was underway toward recruiting a reliable police force. Tension had dropped so much that Gibbon responded to the petitions of the bar owners and permitted them to open from 5:00 A.M. to 7:00 P.M.[11] Martial law ended on 23 February and all but two infantry companies left for Vancouver Barracks. Although these two stayed in Seattle until August, the trouble was over. Through restrained action, and by refraining from excessive force, Gibbon restored order, ensured the maintenance of civil authority, and discouraged the territorial officials from calling on the military too frequently. In an unfamiliar situation, he had acted with commendable judgment.[12]

The restoration of civic peace to Seattle was the last major act of John Gibbon's career. With the end of the Indian fighting and the closing of the frontier, Army post life became a routine of administrative duties and occasional events that brought memories of an older, more violent, more interesting past. Gibbon gave the address when the statue of his friend George Gordon Meade was unveiled in Philadelphia. He also had the honor of addressing the graduating class of 1886 at West Point—a class in which the highest cadet military rank, "first captain" of the Corps of Cadets, was held by a tall, lean Nebraskan named John J. Pershing. Returning to the starting point of his military career, the veteran gave a speech that was filled with nostalgia for his five years there as a cadet. He blended stories of his conflicts with the demerit system with a statement of approval regarding the present system of officer education.[13]

Eighteen eighty six brought a fleeting chance for promotion to major general. John Pope reached the age limit for retirement and Winfield Scott Hancock died suddenly, creating two two-star vacancies for President Cleveland to fill. A year before, Edward Bragg had argued successfully for Gibbon's first star on the basis of his position at the top of the colonels' list. Although Gibbon was now the junior in current seniority of the six brigadier generals, he had served as an officer for far longer than any of the other five. In an adroit shift of stance, Bragg now advocated a new approach, that of seniority in total service.

Bragg's effort failed. Very likely he had cashed in all his political credits in effecting Gibbon's previous promotion. Moreover, the ghost of the Wilderness dispute appeared again. Someone asked Theodore Lyman, the Boston Brahmin who had served on Meade's staff, to write a letter supporting Nelson Miles. Instead, Lyman penned an appraisal of all the brigadier generals. He spoke favorably of Gibbon, but alluded to Hancock's criticism. Cleveland decided to stick to the seniority principle. The two men at the head of the brigadier generals' list, Terry and Howard, had worn their single stars since 1865; they got the nod.[14]

Gibbon's former associates were passing away. In addition to Hancock, Grant was gone and Sherman had retired. Gibbon's parents were dead, and on 17 February 1888, his daughter Katherine succumbed to pneumonia. She was followed shortly by her husband, leaving John and Fannie Gibbon with the custody of two grandchildren.[15]

Gibbon's tenure as commander of the Department of the Columbia brought him into intermittent contact with his old adversary, Chief Joseph. The lands now allocated to the Nez Perces fell within Gibbon's geographical area of jurisdiction, although not his responsibility. Gibbon met with Chief Joseph from time to time, and at what was probably their last conference, assured the eloquent Indian leader that he would do all he could to obtain money due Joseph for animals and farm equipment sold earlier. No animosity remained between the two men, despite the slow tragedy of the Nez Perce reservation life. As the Indian patriot and statesman told Gibbon, "We fought before, and are good friends now. I say this because we fought a long time ago. . . . I am glad the fighting is over and now I am glad to see you."[16]

One final clash with authority enlivened Gibbon's last years in uniform. Although the 112th Article of War authorized department commanders to grant pardons to prisoners sentenced by Army courts martial, Secretary of War Endicott had promulgated orders forbidding the exercise of this power. John Gibbon nonetheless issued a pardon; his rationale probably was that since the Articles of War were acts of Congress, his authority derived from the law itself and the Secretary was without power to deprive him of it. Publicly reprimanded by the Secretary for disobedience to orders, Gibbon took an appeal to President Cleveland. It failed.[17]

In August 1890 Gibbon was ordered to command the Military Division of the Pacific, headquartered in San Francisco; this was to be the last step in his career. With the act of 30 June 1882, setting mandatory retirement at age sixty-four, his time on active duty had about eight months left to run. Promotion was unlikely. Although other vacancies had opened with the retirement of Terry and the death of Crook, promoted on Terry's retirement, the seniority principle continued to prevail. Terry, Howard,

Crook, and then Miles advanced in turn to the major generalcies. David Stanley, a year younger than Gibbon, was still senior to him on the list of brigadiers. Gibbon's age negated the prospect of further promotion.

At San Francisco, on 20 April 1891, the staff of the Division of the Pacific donned their dress uniforms and assembled in the commanding general's office. There John Gibbon announced that, in accordance with Special Orders No. 89, Headquarters, U.S. Army, he was retiring that day from the active list and that General Thomas Ruger would follow him in the post. With him was his brother-in-law, Edward Moale, now a major. Gibbon did not even wait for Ruger's arrival, but left at once for a hunting and fishing trip to Idaho.[18] For Gibbon it was not a happy moment, and he did not wish to prolong it.

Gibbon soon returned to the East. With no permanent home, he tried to secure appointment as governor of the Washington, D.C., Soldiers' Home. Although Grenville M. Dodge and Major General John M. Schofield, now Commanding General of the Army, supported his application, the post went to Brigadier General John C. Kelton. Gibbon eventually settled at 239 West Biddle Street, Baltimore. A final honor came in 1895 when, at its eleventh annual meeting, he won election as Commander-in-Chief of the Military Order of the Loyal Legion, the veterans' organization of former Union Army officers. Coincidentally, the retiring Commander-in-Chief was Lucius Fairchild, once colonel of the 2nd Wisconsin. With Major General Nelson A. Miles, still an active Army officer, as his chief rival, Gibbon was elected on the second ballot—a victory that surely must have been especially pleasing to him. Among those present were Charles A. Woodruff, Gibbon's former adjutant and subordinate in the 7th Infantry, and John W. Turner, once a division commander in XXIV Corps. The next day Gibbon led a delegation to call upon President Cleveland.[19]

Although he now had time for his family, his grandchildren, and his friends, his retirement period was not prolonged. What Confederate guns and a Nez Perce sharpshooter could not accomplish, disease did. For once John Gibbon's iron constitution failed him, and in February 1896 he contracted pneumonia. Surrounded by his wife and family, he died at 3:40 P.M., 6 February, in Baltimore.[20]

The army that John Gibbon served, fought for and with, did not long survive him. The changes that swept away the old army had their origins in the events of the 1880s. Once the frontier began to close, the United States began to look outward, first becoming involved in Latin America and then in the western Pacific. Inadequacies emphasized by the Spanish-American War spurred reforms. The evolution of modern staff structure, the introduction of advanced weaponry, and the appearance of mass armies created an organization that Gibbon would have had trouble recognizing.

The world of John Gibbon's army was far smaller and less complicated, but no less interesting, than that of a century later. The officer corps was so small that its members were almost a fraternity, one where personalities often counted more than policy. Its generation saw in the Civil War the towering event of their lives, as did many of the hundreds of thousands of civilians who wore the uniform with them for those four unforgettable years. After 1865 the Army and America drifted apart, and Gibbon's world became the Army. Although he came close several times to leaving it, he always drew back from such a precipitous step. Even after his retirement, Gibbon sought to maintain his ties with men of his own background. Doubtless he felt more comfortable in their company.

Gibbon has faded from public memory, and that is too bad, for he was an interesting man—honest, sturdy, individualistic. Courageous, combative, and in battle apparently nerveless, he stands as one of the best Civil War combat leaders, an excellent example of the sort of officer on whom other men could build victories. His comrades tried to keep his memory bright. In 1911 the Iron Brigade Association, the men who once put leggings on their general's horse, contributed funds to erect a monument over his grave. A granite marker of some size, with the insignia of the five illustrious regiments and Battery B engraved upon its side, the stone stands in Arlington Cemetery, passed daily by dozens of people who, sadly, have no idea who John Gibbon was. At the end he had his oft-expressed wish: to be with Wisconsin soldiers.[21]

NOTES

1. General Orders No. 19, 29 July 1885, Department of the Columbia, AGO, WD, NA.

2. Monthly Returns, July 1885, Department of the Columbia, WD, AGO, NA.

3. Charles S. Campbell, *The Transformation of American Foreign Relations, 1865–1900* (New York, 1976), 113.

4. Campbell, *Foreign Relations*, 117; J. A. Karlin, "The Anti-Chinese Outbreak at Tacoma, 1885," *Pacific Historical Quarterly*, XXIII (1954), 271–283.

5. Robert C. Nesbitt, *"He Built Seattle": A Biography of Judge Thomas Burke* (Seattle, 1961), 192–193; John Gibbon, "Chinese Troubles," (unpublished manuscript, Gibbon Papers, HSP), 336–342.

6. Nesbitt, *"He Built Seattle,"* 200–204; JG to Adjutant General, 16 February 1886, WD, AGO, NA; Gibbon, "Chinese Troubles," 349–350; *Seattle Pacific Intelligencier*, 11 February 1886.

7. JG to Adjutant General, 16 February 1886; Monthly returns, February, 1886, Department of the Columbia, WD, AGO, NA.

8. *Seattle Pacific Intelligencier*, 18 February 1886.

9. JG to Adjutant General, 16 February 1886.

10. Gibbon, "Chinese Troubles," 350–352.

11. *Seattle Pacific Intelligencier*, 17 February 1886.

12. Gibbon, "Chinese Troubles," 352–364; see also J. A. Karlin, "Anti-Chinese

Outbreaks in Seattle, 1885–1886," *Pacific Northwest Quarterly,* XXXIX (1948), 103–130; Nesbitt, *"He Built Seattle,"* 205.

13. John Gibbon, Address to the Graduating Class at West Point, 12 June 1886 (Vancouver Barracks, Headquarters, Department of the Columbia, 1886.)

14. Letters Received File 549 ACP 1886, WD, AGO, NA, RG 94.

15. John Gibbon to Edward S. Bragg, 28 July 1888, Bragg Papers, SHSW.

16. Undated memorandum of conversation between Chief Joseph and John Gibbon, n. p., GP, HSP.

17. G. O. Shields ("Coquina"), *The Battle of the Big Hole* (Chicago and New York, 1889), 110–111; John Gibbon to E. S. Bragg, 28 July 1888, Bragg Papers, SHSW.

18. *San Francisco Chronicle,* 21 April 1891.

19. Grenville M. Dodge to Benjamin Harrison, 16 March 1892; John M. Schofield to Redfield Proctor, 1 November 1891, WD, AGO, NA; *Washington Star,* 16 February 1895.

20. *Washington Star,* 10 February 1896.

21. "John Gibbon," *Dictionary of American Biography,* Volume 7, 237.

Selected Bibliography

MANUSCRIPT COLLECTIONS

Bragg, Edward S. Papers. State Historical Society of Wisconsin, Madison, Wisconsin (hereafter "SHSW").

Fairchild, Lucius. Papers. SHSW.

Fairfield, George. Papers. SHSW.

Gibbon Family Papers. Maryland Historical Society, Baltimore, Maryland.

Gibbon, John. Papers. Historical Society of Pennsylvania, Philadelphia, Pennsylvania.

Gibbon, John. Papers. United States Military Academy, West Point, New York.

Haskell, Frank A. Papers. SHSW.

Mead, Sydney B. Papers. SHSW.

Perry, James M. Papers. SHSW.

Record Group 94. Records of the Office of the Adjutant General, National Archives, Washington, D.C.

Records of Cadets. United States Military Academy, West Point, New York.

Roberts, Jesse. Papers. SHSW.

Young, Henry F. Papers. SHSW.

PUBLIC DOCUMENTS

U.S. Congress. House of Representatives, Committee on Military Affairs, *House Reports*, 44th Congress, 1st Session, 1876.

———. *Report of the Joint Committee on the Conduct of the War at the Second Session, Thirty-Eighth Congress, Vol. I.* Washington, D.C.: Government Printing Office, 1865.

United States Department of War. *Annual Report of the Secretary of War to the Congress, 1867*, House Executive Document No. 1, 40th Congress, 2nd session, Vol. II, Parts 1 and 2.

———. *Annual Report of the Secretary of War to the Congress, 1876*, House

Executive Document No. 1, Part 2, 44th Congress, 1st session, Vol. 2, Part 1.

———. *Annual Report of the Secretary of War to the Congress, 1877*, House Executive Document No. 1, Part 2, 45th Congress, 2nd session.

U.S. Department of War. *The War of the Rebellion: A Compilation of the Official Records of the Union and Confederate Armies*. Washington, D.C.: Government Printing Office, 1887.

ARTICLES

Bradley, James H. "Journal of the Sioux Campaign of 1876 under the command of General John Gibbon," *Contributions to the Historical Society of Montana*, II (1896), 149–228.

Carroll, Matthew. "Diary of Matthew Carroll, Master in Charge of Transportation for Gibbon's '76 Expedition," *Contributions to the Historical Society of Montana*, Vol. II (1896), 229.

Gibbon, John. "Rambles in the Rocky Mountains," *American Catholic Quarterly Review* (hereafter *ACQR*), April 1876, 312.

———. "Last Summer's Expedition Against the Sioux and Its Great Catastrophe," *ACQR*, April 1877, 271.

———. "Hunting Sitting Bull," *ACQR*, October 1877, 665.

———. "An Autumn in the Rocky Mountains," *ACQR*, January 1879.

———. "The Pursuit of Joseph," *ACQR*, April 1879, 317.

———. "Arms to Fight Indians," *The United Service: A Quarterly Review of Military and Naval Affairs*, Vol. I, April 1879, 237–244.

———. "Life Among the Mormons," *ACQR*, October 1879, 664.

———. "Tents for Armies," *United Service*, Vol. I, October 1879, 517–519.

———. "Law in the Army," *Journal of the Military Services Institution of the United States* (hereafter *MSI*), Vol. I, No. 4 (1880), 438.

———. "Our Indian Question," *MSI*, XI (1881), 81–95.

———. "Reading Signs," *MSI*, December 1884, 22.

———. "The Transfer of the Indian Bureau to the War Department," *ACQR*, April 1894, 244.

———. "The Battle of the Big Hole," *Harper's Weekly*, 26 November 1895, 1212–1216, 1235–1236.

Jordan, Mark H., and Dennis Lavery. "Across the Plains," *Military Images* (hereafter *MI*), Vol. III, No. 2 (September–October 1981), 6–9.

Jordan, Mark H. "Gainesville," *MI*, Vol. VI, No. 5 (March–April 1985), 16–25.

Karlin, J. A. "The Anti-Chinese Outbreak at Tacoma, 1885," *Pacific Historical Quarterly*, XXIII (1954), 271–283.

———. "Anti-Chinese Outbreaks in Seattle, 1885–1886," *Pacific Northwest Quarterly*, XXXIX (1948), 103–110.

Porter, Charles H. "The Battle of Cold Harbor," *Military Historical Society of Massachusetts Papers*, IV (1905), 319–340.

Woodruff, Charles A. "Woodruff on the '76 Campaign," *Contributions to the Historical Society of Montana*, VII, 97.

NEWSPAPERS and PERIODICALS

Charleston Courier
Fort Benton (Montana) *Record*
Harper's Weekly
San Francisco Chronicle
Seattle Pacific Intelligencier
Washington Star
Washington Sunday Herald

BOOKS

Adams, J.G.B. *Reminiscences of the Nineteenth Massachusetts Regiment.* Boston: Wright & Potter Printing Co., 1899.

Agassiz, George A., editor. *Meade's Headquarters, 1863–1865. Letters of Colonel Theodore Lyman from The Wilderness to Appomattox.* Boston: The Atlantic Monthly Press, 1922.

Alexander, J. B. *History of Mecklenburg County.* Charlotte: Observer Print. House, 1902.

Ambrose, Stephen. *Duty, Honor, Country: A History of West Point.* Baltimore: Johns Hopkins Press, 1966.

Aubery, James M. *The Thirty-Sixth Wisconsin Volunteers.* [no publisher nor place of publication], 1900.

Bauer, K. Jack. *The Mexican War, 1846–1848.* New York: Macmillan, 1974.

Beal, Merrill D. *"I Will Fight No More Forever," Chief Joseph and the Nez Perce War.* Seattle: University of Washington Press, 1964.

Bigelow, John Jr. *The Campaign of Chancellorsville.* New Haven: Yale University Press, 1910.

Billings, John D. *History of the Tenth Massachusetts Battery of Light Artillery in the War of the Rebellion.* Boston: Hall & Whiting, 1881.

Boyes, W., editor. *Surgeon's Diary with the Custer Relief Column.* Washington, D.C.: South Capitol Press, 1974.

Bradley, James H. *The March of the Montana Column: A Prelude to the Custer Disaster.* Norman: University of Oklahoma Press, 1961.

Brown, Dee. *Bury My Heart at Wounded Knee.* New York: Holt, Rinehart Winston, 1970.

Brown, Mark H. *The Flight of the Nez Perce: A History of the Nez Perce War.* New York: Putnam, 1967.

Buell, Augustus. *The Cannoneer.* Washington, D.C.: The National Tribune, 1890.

Byrne, Frank L., and Andrew T. Weaver, editors. *Haskell of Gettysburg: His Life and Civil War Papers.* Madison: State Historical Society of Wisconsin, 1970.

Campbell, Charles S. *The Transformation of American Foreign Relations.* New York: Harper and Row, 1976.

Catton, Bruce. *Grant Moves South.* Boston: Little, Brown, 1960.

———. *Grant Takes Command.* Boston: Little, Brown, 1969.

———. *Mr. Lincoln's Army.* New York: Pocket Books, 1964.

———. *Glory Road.* New York: Pocket Books, 1964.

———. *A Stillness at Appomattox.* Garden City, N.Y.: Doubleday, 1954.

Cheek, Philip, and Mair Pointon. *History of the Sauk County Riflemen.* Marietta, Wis.: E. R. Alderman & Sons, 1909.

Coddington, Edwin B. *The Gettysburg Campaign: A Study in Command.* New York: Charles Scribner's Sons, 1968.

Coe, Charles F. *Red Patriots.* Cincinnati: The Editor Publishing Co., 1898.

Cook, Benjamin F. *History of the 12th Massachusetts Volunteers.* Boston: Twelfth (Webster) Regiment Association, 1882.

Curtis, O. B. *History of the 24th Michigan of the Iron Brigade.* Detroit: Win and Hammond, 1891.

Davis, Burke. *To Appomattox: Nine April Days, 1865.* New York and Toronto: Rinehart & Co., 1959.

Dawes, Rufus R. *Service with the Sixth Wisconsin Volunteers.* Madison: State Historical Society of Wisconsin, 1962.

Eisenschiml, Otto. *The Celebrated Case of Fitz John Porter: An American Dreyfus.* Indianapolis and New York: Bobbs-Merrill, 1950.

Foote, Shelby. *The Civil War: A Narrative.* New York: Random House, 1974.

Ford, Andrew A. *The Story of the Fifteenth Regiment Massachusetts Volunteer Infantry.* Clinton, Mass.: Press of W. J. Coulter, 1898.

Freeman, Douglas S. *Lee's Lieutenants.* Three volumes. New York: Charles Scribner's Sons, 1942–1944.

Gibbon, John. *An Address on the Unveiling of the Statue of Major-General George Gordon Meade* in Philadelphia, October 18, 1887. Philadelphia: Allen, Lane and Small's Printing House, 1887.

———. *Address to the Graduating Class at West Point, June 12, 1886.* Vancouver Barracks: Headquarters, Department of the Columbia, Assistant Adjutant General's Office, 1886.

———. *The Artillerist's Manual.* New York: D. Van Nostrand, 1859.

———. *Gibbon on the Sioux Campaign of 1876.* Bellevue, Neb.: The Old Army Press, 1970.

———. *Personal Recollections of the Civil War.* New York: G. P. Putnam's Sons, 1928.

Graham, W. A. *The Story of the Little Big Horn.* New York: Collier Books, 1962.

Grant, Ulysses S. *Personal Memoirs.* New York: Charles L. Webster and Company, 1885.

Gray, John S. *Centennial Campaign: The Sioux War of 1876.* Norman: University of Oklahoma Press, 1988.

Haskell, Frank A. *The Battle of Gettysburg.* Boston: Houghton Mifflin Company, 1958.

Hassler, Warren W., Jr. *General George B. McClellan: Shield of the Union.* Baton Rouge: Louisiana State University Press, 1957.

Hedren, Paul L., editor. *The Great Sioux War, 1876–1877.* Helena: Montana Historical Society Press, 1991.

History Committee. *History of the Nineteenth Regiment Massachusetts Volunteer Infantry 1861–1865.* Salem, Mass.: The Salem Press Co., 1906.

Howard, O. O. *Nez Perce Joseph.* Boston: Lee and Shepard, 1881.

Humphreys, Andrew A. *The Virginia Campaigns of 1864 and 1865.* New York: Charles Scribner's Sons, 1883.

Huntington, Samuel P. *The Soldier and the State: The Theory and Politics of Civil-Military Relations.* New York: Vantage Books, 1957.

Hutton, Paul Andrew. *Phil Sheridan and His Army.* Lincoln and London: University of Nebraska Press, 1985.

————, editor. *The Custer Reader.* Lincoln: University of Nebraska Press, 1992.

Indiana Antietam Monument Commission. *Indiana at Antietam.* Indianapolis: Indiana Antietam Monument Commission, 1911.

Johnson, R. U., and C. C. Buel, editors. *Battles and Leaders of the Civil War.* Four volumes. New York: Thomas Yoseloff, 1956.

Jordan, David. *Winfield Scott Hancock: A Soldier's Life.* Bloomington: Indiana University Press, 1988.

Josephy, Alvin H., Jr. *The Nez Perce Indians and the Opening of the Northwest.* New Haven: Yale University Press, 1963.

Keegan, John. *The Face of Battle.* New York: The Viking Press, 1976.

Knight, Oliver. *Life and Manners in the Frontier Army.* Norman: University of Oklahoma Press, 1978.

Kroeker, Marvin E. *Great Plains Command: William B. Hazen in the Frontier West.* Norman: University of Oklahoma Press, 1976.

Lavender, David. *Let Me Be Free: The Nez Perce Tragedy.* New York: HarperCollins Publishers, 1992.

Lavery, Dennis S. *John Gibbon and the Old Army: Portrait of an American Professional Soldier.* Ann Arbor: University Microfilms, 1975.

Long, E. B. *The Civil War Day by Day.* New York: Doubleday and Co., 1971.

Matter, William D. *If It Takes All Summer: The Battle of Spotsylvania.* Chapel Hill: University of North Carolina Press, 1988.

Meade, George G., Jr., editor. *The Life and Letters of George G. Meade, Major-General, United States Army.* Two volumes. New York: Charles Scribner's Sons, 1913.

Murfin, James V. *The Gleam of Bayonets: The Battle of Antietam and the Maryland Campaign of 1862.* New York: Thomas Yoseloff, 1965.

Nesbitt, Robert C. *"He Built Seattle": A Biography of Judge Thomas Burke.* Seattle: University of Washington Press, 1961.

Nichols, Edward J. *Toward Gettysburg.* University Park: Pennsylvania State University Press, 1958.

Nolan, Alan T. *Lee Considered.* Chapel Hill: University of North Carolina Press, 1991.

————. *The Iron Brigade: A Military History.* New York: Macmillan, 1961.

Pfanz, Harry W. *Gettysburg: The Second Day.* Chapel Hill: University of North Carolina Press, 1987.

Porter, Horace. *Campaigning with Grant.* New York: Century, 1907.

Rickey, Don. *Forty Miles a Day on Beans and Hay: The Enlisted Soldier Fighting the Indian Wars.* Norman: University of Oklahoma Press, 1963.

Roe, Frances M. A. *Army Letters from an Officer's Wife, 1871–1888.* New York: D. Appleton & Co., 1909.

Ropes, John C. *The Army Under Pope.* New York: Charles Scribner's Sons, 1882.

Ropp, Theodore. *War in the Modern World.* New York: Collier Books, 1962.

Schneider, George A., editor. *The Freeman Journal: The Infantry in the Sioux Campaign of 1876.* San Rafael, Calif.: Presidio Press, 1977.

Scott, Robert Garth, editor. *Fallen Leaves: The Civil War Letters of Major Henry Livermore Abbott.* Kent: The Kent University Press, 1991.

Sharp, Paul F. *Whoop-Up Country: The Canadian-American West, 1865–1885.* Norman: University of Oklahoma Press, 1978.

Shields, G. O. ("Coquina"). *The Battle of the Big Hole.* Chicago and New York: Rand McNally & Co., 1889.

Smith, J. D. *History of the Nineteenth Regiment of Maine Volunteer Infantry.* Minneapolis: A. H. Jenkins Company, 1909.

Stallard, Patricia Y. *Glittering Misery.* Fort Collins, Colo.: The Old Army Press, 1978.

Steere, Edward. *The Wilderness Campaign.* New York: Bonanza Books, 1965.

Stewart, Edgar I. *Custer's Luck.* Norman: University of Oklahoma Press, 1955.

Stewart, George R. *Pickett's Charge.* Boston: Houghton Mifflin, 1959.

Tompkins, D. A. *History of Mecklenburg County and the City of Charlotte.* Charlotte: A. H. Campbell and Sons, 1903.

Tucker, Glenn A. *Hancock the Superb.* New York: Bobbs-Merrill Company, 1960.

Urwin, Gregory J. W., editor. *Custer and His Times:* Book Three. (no place of publication) Little Big Horn Associates, Inc., 1987.

Utley, Robert M. *Custer and the Great Controversy.* Baton Rouge: Louisiana State University Press, 1962.

———. *Frontiersmen in Blue: The United States Army and the Indian, 1848–1866.* New York: Macmillan, 1967.

———. *Frontier Regulars: The United States Army and the Indian, 1866–1890.* New York: Macmillan, 1973.

Vaughn, J. W. *The Reynolds Campaign on Powder River.* Norman: University of Oklahoma Press, 1961.

Vaughn, Robert. *Then and Now; or, Thirty Six Years in the Rockies.* Minneapolis: Tribune Printing Company, 1900.

Walker, Francis A. *History of the Second Army Corps in the Army of the Potomac.* New York: Charles Scribner's Sons, 1886.

Ward, Joseph R. C. *History of the One Hundred and Sixth Regiment Pennsylvania Volunteers.* Philadelphia: Grant, Faires & Rogers, 1883.

Weigley, Russell F. *History of the United States Army.* New York: Macmillan, 1967.

Williams, Kenneth P. *Lincoln Finds a General,* Vols. I and II. New York: The Macmillan Company, 1949.

Index

About the Authors

DENNIS S. LAVERY is an administrative officer with the U.S. Army at Fort Belvoir, Virginia. He received his Ph.D. in American history from Pennsylvania State University and has served as a historian with the U.S. Army Corps of Engineers and the Bureau of Indian Affairs.

MARK H. JORDAN practices as a consulting engineer in Troy, New York. He has served as Professor of Civil Engineering and Dean of Continuing Studies at Rensselaer Polytechnic Institute and as a career officer in the Navy Engineer Corps ("Seabees"). He coauthored *Saga of the Sixth*, a history of the Sixth Naval Construction Battalion in World War II, and has written a number of articles on historical, military, engineering, and educational subjects.